ANIMAL DAYS

DESMOND MORRIS

ANIMAL DAYS

BOOK CLUB ASSOCIATES
LONDON

First published 1979
Copyright © 1979 by Desmond Morris

This edition published 1979 by
Book Club Associates
By arrangement with Jonathan Cape Ltd

Printed in Great Britain by The Anchor Press Ltd
and bound by Wm Brendon & Son Ltd
both of Tiptree, Essex

To Ramona

CONTENTS

ILLUSTRATIONS

The author thanks the following for permission to reproduce photographs: Stanley Hurwitz, Larry Schaffer, Photo Hallery, Granada Television, UPI/Popperfoto, Iain Stewart Macmillan and the Lutterworth Press, the *Sun*, the Zoological Society of London.

1

NAPOLEON STARTED IT ALL. If it weren't for him, I might not be sitting here now writing these words. I am not thinking of a belligerent golden hamster I once owned, who went by that name, but of the original Napoleon — Bonaparte himself — for it was one of his cannon-balls, fired in the Peninsular War, that shot off the arm of my great great grandfather, James Morris, and altered the whole course of my family history.

Although it sounds callous, I have to admit that I am grateful to that cannon-ball. Prior to its flight, my ancestors had been farmers, cultivating the rich sloping fields of the borderlands between England and Wales, but once it had whistled through the Spanish air and disarmed poor James, farming, for him, was out of the question. Invalided home, he decided to become a bookseller and opened a shop in the small market town of Swindon in Wiltshire. His son William, my great grandfather, grew up surrounded by books and with an increasing obsession for the printed word.

As a young man, in 1854, William started his own newspaper, acting as publisher, editor, printer and writer. It was the first penny paper ever published in Great Britain and heralded a revolution in British journalism. Previously news-sheets had been so expensive that only the elite could afford them, but William for some reason hated what he called 'the squirearchy' and was determined to make the news available to the general public.

The venture was an immediate success and, although he was constantly under attack from the town's conservative elements and was even burnt in effigy in the market square, the paper flourished and grew in size. William continued as editor for the remaining thirty-seven years of his life, during which time he also developed a passion for natural history. As a boy he had coveted the scientific books his father had sold to local naturalists and now he was able to amass a huge library of his own. It was a solitary remnant from that library that was to change my life. The bulk of his collection was sold shortly after his death, but my father had inherited a trunkful of the old man's belongings and in that trunk nestled one, glorious volume.

The trunk itself had been relegated to the farthest corner of the mountain of junk that clogged the family attic. My father, a writer of children's fiction, had the delightful weakness of never being able to throw anything away, which had gradually transformed the attic into a mysterious treasure-house for an inquisitive schoolboy like myself. I used to spend many hours up there, examining the strange trophies he had brought back from his travels abroad. Some of the trunks were too heavy for me to move and open, in amongst all that dense clutter, and I developed the childish fantasy that, in the darkest recesses, there must surely be something truly sinister and magical. One day I would find out.

The great moment came when I had eventually grown strong enough to heave several crates and boxes to one side and uncovered William's trunk. Prizing open the lid, I was rewarded by the sight of a magnificent old, brass microscope in a mahogany case. Next to it, wrapped in yellowed paper, were beautiful rocks and crystals – fluorite and malachite, glowing with colour, dark and sinister iron pyrites, and bright, glistening quartz. In a separate box I found a hoard of shells and fossils – huge ammonites and tiny gastropods, smooth bivalves and knobbly echinoderms, and an object that particularly fascinated me – a perfect piece of fossilized wood. Inside a rusty tin, carefully covered in tissue paper and cotton wool, were some dried seahorses and, in a glass case, a collection of velvety, tropical butterflies.

At the very bottom of the trunk lay a large, seventeenth-century book, a heavy folio volume, bound in decaying, blackened leather like the skin from an Egyptian mummy. Its title, which immediately appealed to me, was *The Comparative*

Anatomy of Stomachs and Guts Begun. It was the word 'Begun' that I found especially pleasing. As a beginner myself I was greatly encouraged to think that you could actually publish a book on a subject you had only 'begun'. The illustrations were curious, to say the least. Each set of guts that the author, a physiologist called Nehemiah Grew, had dissected, was shown looped up and down across the page in a compulsively neat manner, making it look like an old-fashioned central-heating radiator. There were elegant guts, obscene guts, gothic guts and rococo guts. My favourite was No. 28, the 'Crop, Gizard and Guts of a Dunghil Cock', which would have delighted the Surrealists who were busily painting in Paris at that time, had they only known about it. Disembodied, odour-free, and exquisitely engraved, the entrails of the animal world presented themselves to me as objects of great beauty.

There was another section to Grew's book, an illustrated catalogue of the 'Natural and Artificial Rarities' belonging to the Royal Society, of which he was the secretary. The catalogue was full of bizarre entries that made me feel that, after all, I was not alone in my fascination for strange objects. For instance: 'A Great Stone taken out of a dog's bladder, given by the most Reverend Seth Lord Bishop of Sarum.' The juxtaposition of a dog's bladder and a Lord Bishop had immediate appeal for me. Or: 'Two Hairy Balls, sphaerical, and incrustated. About two inches diametre, cover'd with a smooth and very thin crust, of the colour of Occidental Bezoar, having neither tast or smell, not stirring at all, upon the effusion of acids.' These were balls found in the stomach of an unidentified beast, and the idea of the learned Dr Grew actually tasting them struck me as the height of devotion to scientific duty.

Some of the entries were confusing, to put it mildly. I had no idea what to make of: 'A tooth taken out of the testicle or ovary of a woman, and given to Dr Edward Tyson. As hard and white as any tooth in the head.' There were clearly mysteries of the human body beyond my comprehension, but this only made the subject more intriguing than ever.

Above all I loved the names of animals listed in the book. They

included: The Blobber-lip'd Snail; The Tobaccopipe Fish; The
Spiked Punee; The Great Goggle-eyed Beetle; The Nocoonaca;
The Asse-foot Oyster; The Pearly Sailer; The Belly'd-long
Whirle; The Bunch-backed Venus-shell; The Whame; The
Humgum; The Black Gaping Cockle; The Egyptian Glob-fish;
and The Great Speckled Loon of Norway. It would be hard to
invent more outlandish names, as a joke, yet these were all listed
with great seriousness as Natural Rarities in the great collection
of the Royal Society. I was most impressed. Clearly natural
history was not only marvellously sinister (the collection, I
noticed, included 'The womb of a woman, blown up and dried',
and 'A monstrous Calf with two heads') but it was also great fun.
Nehemiah Grew and I became immediate soul-mates.

Clambering down the steep attic stairs, clutching the heavy
microscope, I felt a surge of excitement. All through my childhood I had been fascinated by animals and my pet-keeping
activities had become excessive. Fortunately, my mother's toler-
ance of my schoolboy eccentricities was boundless. So many other
parents would have tried to curb their sons' more wayward
enthusiasms, but I was lucky. The house, garden and garage, of
our Swindon home were already brimming over with a collection
of wildlife that would have driven most mothers to despair, but
mine viewed my animal obsessions with a calmly sympathetic
eye which, in retrospect, I find astonishing. She had suffered
lizards and snakes in the playroom, kittens in the kitchen, hedge-
hogs in the garage, voles and fieldmice in the loft, finches in the
conservatory, guinea-pigs and rabbits in the summer-house, perch
and roach in the fishpond, newts on the rockery, toads in the
garden, foxes in the aviary and a parrot in the dining room. Now,
armed with the ancestral microscope and with the friendly ghost
of Nehemiah Grew urging me on, I was about to plunge even
further into the private world of natural history that already
absorbed so much of my time.

At the base of the microscope case there was a shallow drawer
and in it I discovered some Victorian slides. I enjoyed looking at
these under the lens, but it was living things I really wanted to

study, so I set off on an urgent collecting trip. My grandmother owned a small lake and that was where I headed, jangling a suitable array of buckets, bottles and jars to hold the slime, sludge and weed that I needed. Once there, I squelched about in the shallows like a diminutive water buffalo, scooping up strands and globules of unspeakable filth until all my containers were full. Triumphantly I returned to the gleaming microscope and began my impatiently awaited exploration into the microscopic world.

I was shattered by what I saw. I felt I was entering a secret kingdom, where flagella undulated, cilia beat, cells divided, antennae twitched and tiny organs pulsated. I spent so much time with my head bowed over the eye-piece of this magical instrument, and became so engrossed with what I saw, that I would cheerfully have dived down the tube of the microscope, like Alice down her rabbit-hole.

It seemed amazing to me that people who raved about the Wiltshire countryside were unaware of this other, equally fascinating landscape of microscopic shapes and organisms. They were missing so much and it was all around them, in every drop of pond water, every blob of mud, every speck of mould. The most despised piece of dirt could be transformed into a teeming forest of strange and unbelievably complex life forms, beside which the monsters and robots of science fiction seemed crude and boringly simple-minded.

As I grew older my interest in pet-keeping declined slightly, to be replaced by a greater fascination for observing animals in their natural habitat. Imperceptibly I was changing from an animal-keeper to an animal-watcher. I spent more and more time at the family lake, alone except for my animal friends. Being an only child, whose father's health had been ruined in the trenches of the First World War, so that he was now increasingly bed-ridden, and whose mother was therefore doubly busy caring for him and running the small family business, I was on my own a great deal. But I was never lonely. I relished my solitude and retreated more and more into my biological domain.

I stopped trying to catch animals, even fish, and my fishing rod

was relegated to the garage where it soon became damaged and
unusable. In an old shed I found the skeleton of a canoe, its canvas
torn and battered, but the wooden framework still intact. I
bought pitch and melted it in a large pot over a fire. Cutting some
old canvas into squares I patched and patched the canoe until it
was whole again. With some help, I took it down to the lake and
launched it, gliding out for the first time over the surface. Lying
in the canoe with my face hanging low over the water, I was able
to watch the fish in their dark world below. I spent hours, day
after day, drifting over the smooth water, my face almost pressed
against the skin of the lake. The idea of catching a fish with a
sharp hook became horrific to me. I knew where the big tench
foraged, and where the largest of the sharp-nosed pike lay in wait
for unwary young roach. I saw the way the pike's jaws juddered
from side to side when it struck its prey with a snake-like dart,
and how this strange juddering slowly rotated the prey in the
pike's jaws, turning it until it could be swallowed head-first. I saw
the way the perch were much bolder than the other fish, because
they had sharp, spiny fins that would stick in the gullet of the pike
and render them impossible to swallow.

My urge to control and interfere with the animals I met, so
common in young boys, was being converted into an urge to
understand them. I was not able to express this change to my
friends. It would have been thought rather wet in a farming
county, so I kept quiet about it, and went on watching.

Waterfowl congregated at the lake in the spring and I was often
diverted from my fish studies by their strange courtship dances
and displays. I found it hard to understand these actions but I was
impressed by them none the less. Leaving the lake, I often
wandered through the dense undergrowth that surrounded it,
where many other, smaller birds nested in the trees and bushes. I
learned the value of sitting still and waiting quietly. It was amazing how busy with life the undergrowth became after a few
minutes of silence. My farming friends would only have appreci-
ated my actions if I had been crouching ready to blaze away with
an air rifle or a shotgun, but nothing was further from my mind,

I had become a hunter searching only for things to see, not to kill.

In a clearing there were several small ponds and in one of these a colony of toads was spawning. I returned to it daily to keep a check on the development of the tadpoles and was puzzled to see that they often swarmed together in one part of the water, ignoring the other stretches of the pond. I could see no reason for this and began to wonder what went on in the brain of a tadpole to make it cluster with others in this way. I started to speculate on whether, if a tadpole learned something, the toad it changed into would remember the learnt thing. Or would metamorphosis destroy the memory? Of course, I didn't know the word metamorphosis, and my ideas were not at all sharp or clearly worked out, but the vague thoughts were there. Somehow, without any specific instruction, I was beginning to develop a scientific curiosity. And I was shortly to meet a man who was going to nudge this curiosity a vital step further ...

2

NOBODY KNOWS WHY HE WAS CALLED BUTTERCUP, and I have never liked to ask him, but the name was so perversely unsuitable that it was irresistible. Most teachers ignore their nicknames, but not this one, and to this day he always signs his letters with this curious title, on the rare occasions when we correspond.

Buttercup was my boarding-school zoology teacher and in his fashion he was a minor genius. He taught like no other teacher I ever encountered and it was my great good fortune that zoology was both my passion and his subject. His unorthodox approach included an open disdain for the examination syllabus and a demand that, as sixth-formers, we should go far beyond it, undertaking research projects as if we were already university scientists. And it is surprising just how far a sixth-form schoolboy is capable of going, given half the chance. The other side of his coin was an anger with, and scornful disregard for, any boy who lacked interest in his subject. There was nothing fair or impartial about Buttercup, and that was part of his charm. He was a real person with strong feelings, eccentrically ignoring the usual schoolmasterly 'front'.

His first principle was that it is impossible to teach zoology. All he could do, he said, was to teach us to learn. To make us proficient at asking ourselves questions. Then it was up to us to find the answers. Other teachers, he said disparagingly, teach answers, which is useless because it clogs up the brain with undigested facts and inhibits real thinking. I was fascinated by this approach and worked harder to please him than I had ever done for anyone else before.

My earlier days at school, before I came under his influence,

had been less happy. In fact, it would not be exaggerating to say
that the 18th of September, 1941, my first day away at public
school, was the most miserable of my entire life. As an only child,
growing up in the depression years of the thirties, I had never
been away from my parents for a single night, and we had hardly
travelled at all in those lean, despondent times. My preoccupation
with my private world of animals had made me increasingly with-
drawn. I loathed the idea of going away to school, but my parents
were determined that I should have a better education than the
local Swindon institutions could offer, so I had no choice. My
father was sufficiently concerned about my attitude to this move
to write a special letter to the headmaster of my new school, in
which he said of me: 'If he has any characteristic that I need
mention, it is that in my opinion he is inclined to be somewhat
reserved.' And the headmaster of my old day school in Swindon
wrote of me: 'Desmond Morris is a quiet, rather retiring, un-
assuming boy ... When he possesses more confidence in his own
ability he will do better.' The truth was that I did not lack faith in
myself – my ego was well intact – but I had somehow become a
very private person. Whether I had sought out animals as my
companions because I was shy, or whether I had simply become
reserved because I enjoyed spending so much time alone with
them, was not clear to me. But certainly the idea of being jettisoned into a whole new social world of human strangers filled me
with dread and foreboding.

As a result, my first few days at boarding school, with all the
other boys so active and out-going, were a nightmare. Matters
were made worse for me by the fact that, at the time, my father
was slowly dying, and had entered the final year of his life. My
letters home had to be as cheerful as possible, not to worry him,
and I had a private arrangement with my mother, a secret code-
word to be added to each letter if I was still feeling miserable, to
let her know my true mood. The word was 'fooey', borrowed
from an old Burgess Meredith movie we had seen together in the
holidays, and it appeared regularly at the foot of each letter home
for many months.

Gradually I began to adapt. I was helped by the fact that the boarding school to which I had been sent—Dauntsey's School at West Lavington—was isolated deep in the Wiltshire countryside I loved so well. And the school encouraged its boys to explore this countryside at every opportunity. Before long I had discovered new animal friends. There were slow-worms on the railway embankment, hiding under the cinders at the side of the track. Sometimes called blind-worms, they were neither blind, nor slow, nor worms, but bright-eyed, shiny-bronze, legless lizards, beautiful to the touch. And there was the strange, bloody-nose beetle, a fat, clumsy, blue-black insect that was easy to catch but, once handled, had the disconcerting habit of appearing to pour blood from its mouth. I assumed the red fluid was somehow poisonous and compensated for the beetle's inability to escape, but I never had the courage to taste it, to put this theory to the test. I had once been squirted in the eye by a violet ground beetle I picked up in the garden at home, and the pain of the stinging fluid of that beetle had given me a healthy respect for the defensive reactions of all large beetles. The special appeal of the bloody-nose beetle for a schoolboy, of course, was that it enabled me to use the (then strictly taboo) word 'bloody' without apology.

I encountered many other animals during my countryside wanderings, but those are the two that I remember with particular affection. Before long I joined the school Natural History Society and was eventually put in charge of the school vivarium. Butter-cup had noticed my enthusiasm for toads, and when I mentioned that at home I had established a garden colony of about a hundred of them, he encouraged me to write about them for the Natural History Magazine. And so it was that I produced my first 'published' article, a long piece with the snappy title of 'Toad in the Hole', for which I won a prize of five shillings. In my mind, this already made me a professional writer, and I rushed off in great haste to spend my 'earnings' as quickly as possible in the nearby town—a reaction which I must confess has persisted throughout my entire writing career. With *The Naked Ape* it took me several years before I managed to spend all my earnings, but with 'Toad in the Hole' I achieved my goal in one glorious afternoon, by buying a copy of *British Shells* by F. Martin Duncan and a small booklet called *War Pictures by British Artists*. Modern art was a new interest for me, and one which was eventually to increase to the point where it rivalled my preoccupation with animals. It also helped me greatly with the business of drawing the animals I was studying.

Without my noticing, my shyness was dropping away. I knew enough about animals now to give a lecture to the Natural History Society on the subject of amphibia and reptiles and, later, on British bats. I was making friends more easily and, as my seniority in the school increased, the enforced independence of boarding-school life worked its magic. I was no longer the reserved, retiring boy of my early days at Dauntsey's, but my new extroversion was far from simple. For many others, an out-going attitude was automatic, but for me it was like a new discovery and I did not always handle it well. In fact, I think it is perhaps wrong to say that my shyness vanished – it remained but was overlaid, as it were, by my new self-confidence. As a result I often over-compensated and became almost painfully extrovert, as if determined to obliterate my inner relish for privacy. I became a joker, an entertainer. My talk on bats, for instance, was given standing on the lecture table, where I imitated the postures and movements of the various species of British bats. It must have made some kind of impact because, although I had completely forgotten the incident myself, Buttercup reminded me of it in a letter he wrote twenty-four years later. For some reason he never tried to tame these excesses of mine, perhaps recognizing that they were part of some strange, private struggle I was enduring. If I am honest, it is a struggle I have never fully resolved, the 'ham' and the academic in me still doing battle with one another, with first one, then the other, getting the upper hand. The private academic element keeps forcing me towards research and serious study, and then the ham element fights back and I swing over to the role of popularizer and public communicator and entertainer. I suppose, in a way, it is a struggle I never wish to resolve, the combination of the two elements over the years having proved very rewarding for me. Without the research element, you have nothing new and original to say, and without the ham element you never do anything about saying it in a way that people can understand.

The success of my 'Toad in the Hole' article led Buttercup to suggest that I should think about doing some original toad research. In the article I had written: 'In order to hibernate, the toad may dig itself a hole with its hind legs. In sandy soil it can dig to a depth of 18 inches. In clay soil to 8 inches. But this is not the only place in which the toad may hibernate. Any hole or cavity that suits its taste may be selected for its six months' snooze. In Spring it emerges and instinctively makes for the water where mating takes place.' Buttercup asked me how I thought the toad found its way to the water, after such a long period of time asleep. I said I thought that it simply wandered around until it happened across a suitable pond. He pointed out that I had quite distinctly said that it 'instinctively made for water', and should I not test this in some way? As always, he was not giving me an answer, but making me ask the right question.

Late in February I noticed that a large number of toads had been squashed flat on the road near the local village. The toads had obviously been trying to cross it in the night and had been run over by passing cars. Here was the chance I needed. If I could visit this stretch of road at night, with a torch, and map the positions, directions and movements of the toads, I could try to answer the question. The difficulty was that boys were not allowed out of the school after dark. Part of the reason for this was that there were some very attractive young girls in the village, a fact which had not escaped me in my eagerness to further the cause of science. With some misgiving, Buttercup obtained permission for myself and a friend, with the delightful name of Freddie Tweddle, to embark on our nocturnal sortie. Armed with torches and note-pads, we set off, with migrating toads and the image of a delicious young milkmaid called Jessica firmly in our minds.

The toads had to come first. Arriving at the spot where the dead ones had been seen, the beams of our torchlights picked out a veritable army of toads marching across the tarmac surface. Working section by section we began to construct a toad-map, showing the position, sex and direction of movement of each animal in turn. We became so engrossed in our task that the time sped past and other imagined delights were submerged in our work. Hours later, we returned triumphantly and next day set about producing a neat version of our map. To cut a long story short, it was clear that toads were migrating from fields to the north of the road, ignoring certain stretches of water on the north side, and crossing over to one big pond in a copse to the south. For their slow-moving bodies, this was a marathon journey, a true migration. There was no question of them simply emerging from the earth near the mating pond and wandering around until they blundered into it. They were not driven merely by an urge to move about, following their emergence from their winter sleep, they were driven by a *directional* urge. They were returning in a deliberate fashion to their ancestral pond and ignoring other water on the way.

This meant that somehow each toad knew which way it had to go, but how? The most obvious answer was that it remembered its journey of the previous year, when it had last left the mating pond, and managed to recall a series of landmarks. But the fields were farmed and details of the environment had changed. So landmarks could not be the explanation. Nor could the dampness of the pond area be the explanation. Not only did they ignore other water, but in February at night the whole land surface was damp. Something else had to be guiding them. We were stumped. Our study had revealed the possession by the common toad of a most uncommon faculty. We put the problem to Buttercup, expecting some simple answer that would be obvious once he had explained it to us. To our surprise, he replied that he had no idea how the toads managed it, and that for every phenomenon zoology could explain, there were hundreds more that it could not. Although, at first, this came as something of a disappointment, I eventually realized how exciting it was. Schoolboys tend to think that if they cannot answer a problem it is simply because they have not read the right books or been taught that particular lesson yet. The realization of the vast ignorance of scientists comes as a shock. Surely someone, somewhere, must know how toads manage to migrate? There must be whole books on the subject in some learned library.

In this case there certainly were not, and today, over thirty years later, the problem has still not been solved, as far as I know. In 1958 a Swiss zoologist by the name of H. Heusser published a much more professional study of the same problem. Our own juvenile paper covered only three pages of the school Natural History Magazine, while Heusser's paper was spread over twenty-four pages of the learned journal *Behaviour*, but despite this he was not able to go much further than we were in his explanation. He found his toads at some ponds near Zurich and, after marking a batch of them with small, numbered labels, he transported them 800 metres (about half a mile) from their home pond, to another equally suitable breeding pond. Although this new pond oozed toad-appeal, a large number of the displaced toads set off, across land they had never covered before, and made the long journey back to their original, ancestral pond. This proved conclusively that they do not need landmarks to guide them. Heusser also discovered that this ability to find their way to the ancestral pond only operates before they have actually reached the water. Once they are in the home pond, their mood changes. If they are taken out of the *water* and placed in another pond, then they stay in their new home quite happily and breed there. In other words, there is a mysterious homing ability that is switched on, so to speak, as soon as they emerge from their winter sleep, and then switched off again once they are successfully in the home water.

This presents the facts in a much more elegant way than we were able to do with our schoolboy report, but it still fails to answer the key question. How on earth do they do it? Heusser ends his paper with the rather lame remark that: 'It is suggested that adult toads return each year to the water where they hatched, and that a sense of direction enables them to do so without learning.' So, for anyone interested, the mystery remains. And it is an extraordinary mystery, elevating the humble toad even higher in my estimation. The distance of half a mile involves an epic journey for a toad, hopping slowly along – with *what* to guide it? To call it a sense of direction is no explanation at all. Does it navigate by the stars, by magnetic fields, or does it have an incredibly complex, directional memory? Late February is so often overcast that stars would be unreliable. Magnetic fields? But what fields and how on earth could they work? Memory? But how could the displaced toads recall the exact direction in which they were bundled off to the new pond? None of it makes sense. No wonder the toad was one of the witch's familiars, cared for, baptized, dressed in black velvet and adorned with tiny bells. Long live the toad.

This continuing obsession with animals of no economic importance was becoming a matter of concern for my family. As my schooldays began to draw to a close they were naturally worried about my future. The Second World War was still raging, and if it went on much longer, I was going to be called up and hauled off to fight. My grandmother's solution to this was to encourage me to follow a medical career. As a doctor I would at least be trying to repair people instead of damaging them. So she started a strange campaign of showering me with medical gifts. For my birthday there was a set of hypodermics. What does a schoolboy do with hypodermics? I wondered. Then for Christmas, there was a splendid stethoscope. I listened to the heartbeat of anyone who would stand still long enough, then put it away with the case of hypodermics, and contemplated what might come next. A set of bed-pans, perhaps? As the war got worse, the pressure grew. To be a doctor was such a laudable, respectable thing, so much nicer than messing about with bugs and newts and things. I was too polite to expose my true feelings. Most of my childhood had involved me in watching a sick father getting sicker and finally dying when I was just fourteen. I had seen enough illness to last me a lifetime, and I wanted no more of it. Even to visit a hospital was a horror for me. But I was a dutiful

son and allowed myself to be enrolled for a first medical course
examination, to get me into medical school at London University.
This was a reserved occupation and would delay my call-up until
I was a fully qualified doctor. But my heart was not in it, and I
managed to fail the exam. The war was going better now and
D-day was upon us. Although the school was in the thick of it,
with vast convoys of lorries and tanks passing hour by hour,
heading for the south coast, to a schoolboy it was all rather unreal.
In a letter home at about that time there was the memorable
sentence: 'I do hope that the invasion will not interfere with half-
term.' First things first. But even I was aware that, if the war was
soon over, there might be less urgency in the family campaign to
turn me away from my animals and towards doctoring. So I
began to take a more active interest in military affairs.

At last it was VE-day – Victory in Europe, and everyone set
about celebrating like mad, dancing in the streets and getting
wildly drunk. My own celebration took the form of a long
bicycle ride through the Wiltshire countryside, where I spent
several hours watching a colony of rooks, and contemplated that,
for them, it was just another day – rather hot and threatening to
thunder, but otherwise unremarkable. Even the most momentous
events in history dwindle into insignificance when one allows
oneself to float off into the dateless world of animals.

I was soon to be wrenched back to the human world by the
discovery that, war or no war, I was not going to be allowed to
escape a medical destiny. I had to spend another year working for
my Ist M.B. exam and was expected to make a special effort. But
the fact was that I was starting to move into a phase of minor
rebellion. In every sphere I had to be different. Not only were my
animal loves becoming more and more esoteric – my latest preoccupation was with a species of pink woodlouse – but my other
interests, on which I am not dwelling in this book, were also off-
beat and certainly against the tidal flow of my social environment.
While my friends listened to Mozart, I was taken up with
Muggsy Spanier and early jazz; while my friends read traditional
English novels, I was delving deep into James Joyce, Auden and

Isherwood, and my favourite poet, E. E. Cummings; while they enjoyed pastoral landscapes, I was discovering Klee and Brauner, Miro and Tanguy; and while they were out on the sportsfield, I was more likely to be in the long grass with a girl. Ever since my early encounters with Jessica the milkmaid, whose body pranced and swished as she walked and whose face was full of laughter, I had started thinking that perhaps girls should be elevated to the supreme status of 'animals' and included in my list of private biological pursuits. So, in the cause of science, I set about examining these fascinating new specimens. At home, I was writing reams of immature poetry and painting furiously in a small studio I had set up.

None of these activities was conducive to medical advancement and when examination time came round again I approached the ordeal with some trepidation. At the practical examination in London I was so nervous that I fumbled an experiment, with dramatic results. I was supposed to suck up a limited quantity of silver nitrate into a glass pipette, so that I could measure it before adding it to another chemical reagent. In my tense condition I failed to stop sucking at the appropriate moment and suddenly my mouth was full of burning chemical. It felt as though I was on fire. Spitting and dribbling silver nitrate all around me I gurgled and spluttered my way to the nearest exit. The skin inside my mouth seemed to be coming off and I was terrified because I knew I had swallowed some of the wretched liquid. I received precious little sympathy from the examiners, who seemed faintly amused by the spectacle that was relieving for them the boredom of what must have been just another dull examination routine. When I asked them what might happen to me and whether I would be poisoned, one of the stewards replied that there might be some change in the morning, and they started laughing. I was in no mood for medical jokes, and only later realized that he had been playing on the word 'change' in relation to the silver I had swallowed.

As it happened, I suffered little more than belly-ache and a sore mouth, but the incident was enough to wipe out my hope of passing the exam, and my medical career was over for good. In retrospect, it proved to be one of the luckiest accidents of my life, and I have often thought that many accidents are more constructive than most people imagine. There is frequently a secret advantage that does not emerge until much later in life. It certainly did not emerge for me immediately, because the result of this failure was army call-up for two years' national service. The war was over now, even in the Far East, but conscription was still in force, and what I looked upon as a two-year prison sentence with hard labour was horribly imminent. While I waited for my papers to arrive I passed the time by learning to ride, but my tuition had only reached as far as the canter when I was whisked away to a bleak, cold army camp at Tidworth.

The first day in the army was as bad as that first day at boarding school. We were given a short talk on venereal disease by an officer who, for some Freudian reason, had forgotten to do up his fly buttons, and then we were marched in for the compulsory army hair-cut. These two events were curiously degrading. The first implied that we were such pathetic young men that we would be driven to use street girls and the second implied that we had lice in our hair and needed to have it cropped. The hair-cropping also had the curious effect of taking away the friend in the mirror that one knew so well, and replacing him with a strange, alien head. I was angry and depressed. My anger boiled over when we were trundled into a classroom and given an intelligence test. In one of the first tasks, we were shown a picture of a river running into the sea with two boats, one floating in the river and one in the sea. The question was: which boat is higher, A or B? And there was a tiny box in which to write the answer. I refused to answer this because I claimed the question was badly conceived. This created a problem the army was not equipped to deal with. I had to answer A or B. I pointed out that, because water flows downhill, the boat in the river was, in one sense, higher than the boat in the sea. But, because sea water is more buoyant than fresh water, the boat in the sea, in another sense, was floating higher in the water than the one in the river. Which had they in mind, when they set the question? Stalemate. I was noted down as a trouble-maker and sent to an even bleaker army camp, where I did nothing but march up and down on a frozen parade ground, or crawl across icy earth on manoeuvres.

Life indoors was almost as bad as that outside. The barrack hut, which in my view should have been a haven of rest and security, emerged as yet another parade ground where we were repeatedly 'standing by our beds' instead of lying on them. A variety of god-kings disguised as senior ranks would then inspect our wretched possessions, which had to be ritually laid out for their scathing eyes to scan. For me, these kit inspections became a minor nightmare. I seemed to be constitutionally incapable of making an unlumpy bed, with the result that nothing would lie flat on it. And my locker was even more of a shambles. The god-kings were not amused, and I decided that a special strategy was called for, to escape their mounting wrath. The obvious solution was a distraction display, something to divert their attention. I noticed that one or two of my fellow-sufferers had small pin-ups stuck to their locker doors – usually pictures of their favourite film-stars, and that gave me an idea.

One of the girls I had known in Swindon had recently launched herself on a promising career as an actress. Her name was Diana Dors and she had already appeared in several films. I guessed that her studio must by now have a collection of promotional photos of her in suitably alluring poses, so I wrote off to her without delay, explaining my plight, and back came a batch of large, inscribed, glossy prints that put to shame the tatty adornments of the other lockers. I plastered them all over my locker door and awaited the next kit inspection with interest.

Spying my crumpled bed, the officer on duty had just raised his baton to the wrath position when he caught sight of the glistening array of Diana's exceptional anatomy. My bed-chaos forgotten, he homed in on the locker door, and the day was mine. After that, my locker became a regular stopping point and, thanks to Diana, my barrack-room status soared to heights that even the lumpiest of beds could not diminish.

On manoeuvres I was less successful. One day we were told to clamber along a wet rope that supposedly spanned a fast river which was under fire from enemy guns and grenades. The river was imaginary and the 'grenades' consisted of huge, explosive fireworks called thunderflashes, which were being lobbed at us by watching officers. When it came to my turn to cross the rope, I was horrified to see a thunderflash land right beneath me, where it lay fizzing venomously. It occurred to me that, if we were simulating combat conditions, the obvious action to be taken was to kick the 'grenade' away with my foot before it exploded and 'killed' me. I swung my leg down and struck at it with my boot as hard as I could. The thunderflash, fizzing even more ominously now, sailed through the air in an elegant trajectory, straight towards the enemy—in the form of a large, moustachioed major —and exploded right between his legs, at roughly the place where his left trouser joined his right. It was at this point in my army career that I discovered that, contrary to my expectations, the military authorities were less keen on eliciting initiative than on instilling obedience to a rigid hierarchical system of dominance.

Shortly after this incident I made another valuable discovery. Seeing a group of soldiers loafing about doing nothing, while I was cleaning latrines (the military award for the use of initiative above and beyond the call of duty), I asked how they managed to get away with such a soft solution to survival. I was told that they had applied for a transfer to another corps, and were waiting around for the posting to come through. This came as a revelation and I thereafter dedicated myself to applying for transfers from each camp to which I was sent, with the result that I remained for some time in a kind of khaki limbo.

After a relaxing interlude as a professional transferee, during which I developed 'lying low' to a fine art, I was accidentally placed on a list of men considered suitable as officer-material. I am not sure how this happened, but I suspect it had something to do with the fact that I had been helping the commandant's wife with her shopping. Occasionally they had to find *some* work for me to do, and I think she may have misguidedly put in a good word for me. At any rate, for some reason, the commandant decided that I should be shipped out of the camp for a while. To my alarm I was sent to an officer-selection establishment – an old country house where, clearly, it seemed to me, there was torture and interrogation in store. To my pleasant surprise, indeed shock, we were all greeted as human beings and gentlemen, and invited to give lectures to one another, while experts eavesdropped to note which were the true officer types among us.

The young men with me all seemed frantically keen, and gave talks on such subjects as 'How I would set about taking command of a camp where my predecessor was a popular hero', or 'How I would booby-trap a jeep and blow up an enemy ammunition dump'. When it came to my turn and I stood up in front of their eager, shiny-cheeked faces, I heard myself announce that the subject of my talk would be 'The revolutionary effect of the invention of the electric torch on bat-catching in caves'. I do not have the slightest recollection of what I said, but I managed to speak on this subject for the full time allocated. Never have I seen such a sea of glazed expressions.

The following day we were taken outside and confronted with an 18-foot high wall and a jumble of what appeared to be surplus telegraph poles and old rope. The object of the exercise, we were told, was to get our group over the wall in the shortest possible time. Go! Now I knew they were watching us to see who took charge of the situation. I also knew that no self-respecting officer would soil his hands on surplus telegraph poles full of splinters, so I stood to one side and made encouraging noises – well done that man, keep it up, keep it up, steady there, lift, now, lift, that's it, well done. This seemed to me to be a perfect replica of everything I had observed as officer behaviour in my brief military career, and I was sure that they would approve of the way I was handling matters. The rest of the rosy-cheeked, now rather red-faced, group were heaving and cursing and sweating and eventually managed to lever their roped pyramid of slippery poles up to the top of the wall and clamber over. As it was only a short, mock wall, I simply walked around one end of it and repeated my words of encouragement to them as they slid and fell down the other side, fracturing this and that as they did so. I was well pleased with my work, but detected a less than ecstatic response on the part of our pip-shouldered hosts. On the final day we were each interviewed individually and the first question they asked me was: Do you really *want* to be an officer? I said that really I didn't and that I was awaiting a transfer to the Education Corps, where I could do some teaching. This seemed to make them uncontrollably angry for some reason and they demanded to know what I was doing there at their establishment. I did not think they would appreciate it if I told them about the way I had helped the commandant's wife, so I simply said that I had been sent, and when you are sent somewhere in the army, well, you go.

I think they must have written something unfriendly on my report because I was promptly transferred to the Medical Corps. Venturing to ask why this had been done, when I had applied for the Education Corps, I was told it was because of my 'previous experience', namely that I had failed a medical exam. I was alarmed to think that this qualified me to tend to the military sick and wounded, and made an immediate resolution to keep in the healthiest possible condition during the rest of my stay in the Forces.

At the Medical Corps barracks we were marched in for our first lecture. The sergeant strode forward and announced loudly the single word: Symptoms.

'Nah then, there's a man lying 'ere, so wot dew yew look for?'

We suggested such things as breathing rate, pulse, condition of the eyes, and so on, but without wiping the scorn from the sergeant's face.

'No, no, no. I'll tell yew wot yew look for: colour, that's wot yew look for. Wot do yew look for?'

'Colour, sergeant.'

'C'rect. Colour. Nah then.' He paused dramatically, eyeing us. 'If ee's *red*, ee's bleedin'. If ee's blue, ee's cold. If ee's yeller, ee's Chinese. If ee's white, ee's dead. And if ee's green – if ee's green, ee's gawn orf.'

The next day I applied again for a transfer to the Education Corps. This meant that I was no longer in the medical 'stream' and was given the delightful job of camp librarian, with my own private bed tucked away in one of the library alcoves, behind shelves full of adventure fiction and war stories telling of the exciting lives of British soldiers. I celebrated this achievement by investigating the taste of rum in a local pub. It tasted good, and with some friends we made a night of it. Slumping into bed I fell into a deep sleep and, without the usual barrack room routine to wake me, overslept badly. Suffering from a terrible hangover, I staggered out of bed in my pyjamas and tried to remember where I was. Books, yes, the library. I tottered out from behind my alcove and surveyed the scene. What I saw froze me in horror for a split second, before I leapt back into hiding behind the war stories. Nobody had told me that in the mornings the library was occasionally used for court martial proceedings. There, on the other side of the book-stack, a full military court martial was in progress, with some wretched man being sentenced to 200 years of rock-breaking for failing to whitewash a piece of coal, or some such heinous crime. And there was I, hung-over, unshaved and pyjama'd, in mid-morning, with nothing between me and discovery except a few rows of books. My whole future was in jeopardy. It would be back to square-bashing, if not actual rock-breaking, if not a full-dress firing squad, should any one person from that crowded impromptu courtroom so much as move a few feet in my direction.

There was only one thing to do: get back into bed. I was dying, that was it. What had the sergeant said? 'If ee's white, ee's dead.' If only I could go white. I peered in the small hand-mirror beside my bed. I *was* white! I looked terrible. I felt sick from the night's rum-tasting and it showed. So I lay there, very still, with my eyes closed, as if in a coma. If they did discover me, I would be rushed to the camp hospital. That was a less comforting thought, but it was all I had to go on. The minutes ticked by, the barking and droning and foot-stamping of the court martial ritual went on and on, until eventually there were doors closing and silence. I lay there for a long while, still not daring to move. At last I crept into my clothes, took a book from a shelf over my bed and sauntered slowly out from my retreat, as if reading it avidly. Someone coughed, and I looked up, startled. It was a small bespectacled private with two grubby volumes held out towards me.

'Have you anything on poultry-breeding?' he asked, apologetically with a quick, thin smile. I nearly embraced him.

My transfer came through a few weeks later, and by luck I was posted to an Army College at Chisledon, only a few miles from my home in Swindon. I was at last in the Education Corps as a teacher, and because the college was over-crowded, I was asked if I minded sleeping at home, since I lived so near by. I was over-joyed. Life had suddenly become civilized again, and I spent the rest of my conscription time in the most un-military fashion imaginable.

The immediate problem was selecting the subject I was going to teach. The college operated on a monthly basis and offered a four-week demobilization course to wartime soldiers who were finally leaving the Forces and returning to civilian life. It was meant to rehabilitate them in some way, but in reality it was just a pleasant way of spending the last few weeks of army life. The atmosphere was somewhere between a 'Carry On' film and a bloodless M.A.S.H. The teachers were a motley collection of eccentrics and misfits like myself, and every day was a delight. I was asked what my subjects were and, since nobody ever seemed to want to be rehabilitated in woodlouse ecology or toad worship, I mentioned that I was also a painter. That struck an immediate chord, the previous lecturer in Fine Arts having recently departed under a cloud. I was given Fine Arts and became one of the few British soldiers ever to be employed as a full-time art teacher.

A certain amount of bluff was called for, when I realized that I was taking my first life-class and art history class the following week. I spent several frenzied days swotting up the subjects and braced myself for my first lesson. Entering the art room, I found it deserted except for a voluptuous blonde reclining on a padded

rostrum. She smiled, introduced herself, and disappeared behind
a screen, re-emerging a few minutes later stark naked.

'How do you want me?' was the question she asked. Although
I had now risen to the dizzy rank of sergeant, I was still only a
teenager and, faced with this sudden display of female anatomy,
found myself at a loss for words. I was aware there was to be a
model, but I had never attended a life-class, let alone taught one,
and I knew that this was the moment my bluff had to start. Trying
to sound as matter-of-fact as possible, I suggested a reclining pose
and the girl draped herself dutifully across the rostrum.

My students began to drift in and take up their positions at the
drawing boards and I was relieved to see that they, too, were
slightly disconcerted by the nakedness of the model. It occurred to
me that like myself they were probably inexperienced in life
drawing, and this was indeed the case. There was a charming old
colonel who wanted to improve his landscape water-colours, a
young corporal who wanted to learn how to draw pin-ups, an
apprentice architect, and a whole variety of novice artists with as
little knowledge as myself. Genuine, trained, art students were
thankfully in the minority, and I was able to get by without too
much difficulty.

As the weeks passed, my need to bluff decreased and I was soon
able to run a reasonable month's course, using Buttercup's old
dictum of 'you can't teach a subject—only how to learn it'. And
I was learning a great deal myself in the process. I painted more and
more and held my first exhibition. Art was coming to dominate
my thinking and animals were, for the time being, forgotten.
Forgotten, that is, except in my paintings, where I tried to create
a private world in which my own, invented organisms evolved
and developed, like a personal fauna and flora from my imagination. They looked quite unlike animals in the outside world, but
somehow they obeyed biological rules and grew and metamor-
phosed as if they were real. And to me they did become increasingly
real, so much so that I could almost study them and their natural
history as if I were still an exploring zoologist.

At about this time, my departmental head, an art critic called

Mervyn Levy, asked me if I would like to go with him to a party at a nearby mansion, where a famous art collector was holding court. I could hardly believe my eyes when I walked into the house and I was certainly not prepared for the way the visit was going to change my life. The walls were covered with paintings of a breath-taking quality and variety. Their owner, James Bomford, was an ex-stockbroker and ex-international motor-boat racing champion who had turned his back both on the city and the sea. Before the war, he had bought a 1,000-ton schooner that had become a millionaire's white elephant, refurbished it, and then sold it for ten times its cost, making himself rich over-night. With the money, he set out to acquire an art collection, guided by the advice of the French painter André Derain. In the 1930s modern paintings were comparatively inexpensive. They had yet to become the priceless collector's pieces of the post-war years. There, on his walls, were Gauguins and Utrillos, de' Chiricos and Renoirs, Bonnards and Klees. I was encouraged to explore and in further rooms I found works by Corot and Cézanne, Manet and Modigliani, Daumier and Degas, Poussin and Picasso, and my favourite British artists, Sutherland and Moore. I had seen such paintings before in museums, but never in a private, domestic setting, and somehow this made the act of looking at them much more intimate, more personal.

Jimmy Bomford was delighted by my obvious interest in his paintings and I became a regular visitor to his Saturday evening parties, where I met a seemingly endless stream of well-known writers, poets, critics and painters. And beautiful girls. Jimmy may have been obsessed with aesthetics, but he was also a devoted hedonist. I once described him as a truly Rabelaisian aesthete, and he replied that of course he was, because if one did not enjoy life, one could not fully enjoy art. And so the wine flowed, and the girls danced and we all played lunatic, children's party games.

It was during one of these games that I met the girl I was later to marry. I had spotted her across the room and fallen for her at first sight. It does happen. But to my annoyance, when it came to a crazy hiding game in which we all had to disperse over the many rooms of the mansion, I saw her being whisked away by a sophisticated young art critic from London. Then the lights were turned out and I had difficulty in following them to a darkened bedroom. After looking out of the window at the moonlight, they hid under the bed. All I could do was lie down on top of the bed, waiting to be discovered by whoever was supposed to be searching, as part of the game, which, as far as I could see, was largely an excuse for everyone to make for darkened bedrooms. They did not appear to be in any hurry to be discovered, and I decided to take action, so I carefully slid my hand down around the bed until I was able to clasp the hand of the girl below. I was sure she had seen me enter the room, and knew what was going on, so I was encouraged when, in response to a squeeze from me, she squeezed back. When I stroked her hand, she stroked mine and I was certain now that the art critic was losing ground. We held hands like this for some time and I was not sure quite what to do next, when, to my surprise, in the moonlight from the window I saw a convulsed form by the fireplace. In the dim light it appeared to be hugging itself and writhing in a strange way. Startled by this peculiar apparition, I twisted my head to get a better look, just as the figure by the fireplace lost control and exploded into laughter that could no longer be suppressed. It was the girl herself, who had quietly left her hiding-place under the bed and, for some time, had been watching the extraordinary spectacle of the art critic and myself each thinking that we were holding her hand and each imagining that we were making great progress. It is the only time that I have ever held hands with a London art critic, but it was one of the luckiest actions of my life. The critic was less than amused and soon left the scene, while the girl and I formed a bond of humour which has lasted for thirty years.

But all this happened at a much later Bomford party, after I had left the army and become a university student. While I was still in the Forces, lecturing in art, Jimmy Bomford was a constant source of help and encouragement, introducing me to many artists and giving me advice about the way to look at pictures.

Once, when I mentioned that I had to give a lecture on modern movements in European art, he told me it was no good showing people reproductions – he hated reproductions – and immediately took three paintings off his walls and bundled them into the back of my small car.

'Show them these,' he said, 'let them see the real surfaces of the pictures, it's the only way to understand.' I was terrified. The paintings were priceless – a Renoir, a Soutine and a Klee. What if they were damaged or stolen? He waved this away, saying that he knew I cared about paintings and would look after them. That night I hung them on the walls of my bedroom and lay in bed for hours looking at them, pretending they were mine. I was sorry to fall asleep.

Shortly after the lecture, which thanks to Jimmy was a great success, Mervyn Levy announced that an old school friend of his from Wales was coming to spend the weekend, and we should all go together to Jimmy's usual Saturday party. I was unable to go, which saddened me when I discovered that his old friend was one of my favourite poets, Dylan Thomas. I had all Dylan's published works and was fascinated by his imagery and his strange, musical use of words. The best I could do was to drive over to Mervyn's cottage at Aldbourne and spend the Sunday with them. When I arrived the poet was nowhere to be seen and Mervyn was muttering something about his mattress. It seemed that, at Jimmy's party, Dylan had imbibed so freely that he had been incapable of rising in the night to urinate and, as a result, the mattress was ruined. When Dylan finally appeared, putty-faced and tousle-haired, it was clear that he was not at his liveliest. In doom-laden tones, he complained of the poet's lot. One of my paintings happened to be lying against the wall of the dining room, where we were preparing to eat.

'Now look at that,' he boomed, 'you can sell that, can't you? The painter makes an object that can be sold. But not the poet.' And he took a scribbled poem he was working on and slapped it on to the wall, holding it there as if it were a picture. 'Now I can't sell that, can I? No one would buy that bit of paper, would they?'

How wrong he was, and how I wish now that I had challenged him and bought it on the spot, or swapped it for my painting.

After a drink he warmed up a little and when he discovered that I was interested in animals, announced that his two favourite jokes at the moment were about animals. The first was about two rhinos, and one said to the other: 'I wonder why I keep thinking it's Thursday?' And the second was: 'A mother hippo and her baby were standing by the water's edge and another female hippo came up and asked the baby, "And what are *you* going to be when you grow up?"'

This was not precisely the kind of soaring, breath-taking conversation I had envisaged in the presence of the great man. In my youthful innocence I had imagined that great men talked endlessly about their work, that artists discussed art in intense debate. Not a bit of it. I was to discover that such individuals were the exception rather than the rule. Most of the artists I met would talk about anything *but* their art. But all was not lost—their personalities shone through even their trivia, and over and over again humour played an important part. Dylan, for instance, was preoccupied with a very small man who had been at the party the night before. 'Fancy being that small,' he mused as he sat down to lunch. 'Such compactness. It deserves something grand to honour it. I shall compose a hymn, no, a prayer, for that unusually small man.' Skewering a large boiled potato with his fork, he raised it to his mouth like a B.B.C. microphone and intoned into it: 'Our midget which art in heaven, miniature be thy name ... ' and, without pause, playing with the words like keys on a piano, he proceeded to transform the Lord's Prayer into an ode to smallness, ending with the words 'For ever and ever, Tom Thumb.' Although, in his badly hung-over condition, he was operating at little more than the level of schoolboy humour, I was nevertheless stunned at the facility with which he could snatch exactly the right word from his memory and insert it precisely where he wanted it. I resolved then and there to spend more time playing with words, juggling with them like a verbal acrobat. It was a good lesson to have learnt and I was grateful to Dylan for it. On my way home I passed a large crowd and pondered on a succinct way of expressing the over-crowdedness of the planet. Eventually, in a notebook, before going to bed, I wrote down 'The penis is greater than the sword', and feeling unduly pleased with myself, fell asleep vowing to write more and paint less. At nineteen, there are so many directions to take.

With my spell in the army nearly over, the direction I did eventually take was towards Birmingham University's zoology department. It was the animals that reasserted themselves. I had toyed with the idea of going to art school, to learn from others more efficiently what I had supposedly been teaching for the past year. But at the time, in the late 1940s, the art schools were dead places, and the idea of endless drawings of nudes and still-lifes did not appeal to me. What I was always coming back to in my paintings were shapes based on organisms, and I argued that three years of drawing from the microscope would be the best art school in the world for me. The academic year was just starting and in a lightning transition I switched from being a military art teacher to a light-hearted, civilian science undergraduate. The change was intoxicating. I was suddenly free of responsibilities. I was no longer in charge of people, *they* were in charge of me. And so, with a brightly coloured, varsity scarf wound around my neck, and in a decidedly unscholarly, carefree mood, I sauntered off into an exciting new world.

3

A DINOSAUR IN BROAD STREET was the headline in the local Birmingham newspaper. And there, below it, was a photograph of two policemen struggling to force a strange object through the door of a police-car. It appeared to be a huge skull, so massive that it was clearly jamming in the open door. What it was doing in the centre of a busy industrial city was not clear. The paper played up the mystery angle and noted that a museum expert had been called in to identify it. The feature of the case that puzzled the authorities was that the skull had been found sitting quietly in a shop doorway early that morning. Nobody had seen it arrive and no one was claiming it. A crowd had gathered to stare at it and had caused an obstruction, requiring its removal to the main police station where it was awaiting an owner or an explanation. Neither was forthcoming.

I regret to say that the dinosaur incident reflects all too accurately my far from single-minded approach to my studies during my first year at university. True, I was attending lectures, taking notes, and making copious drawings from the microscope, but my preoccupations with the art world were still a major distraction. As soon as I had arrived in Birmingham I had set about exploring the local art scene and found, to my great pleasure, a thriving surrealist group centred on the home of the painter Conroy Maddox. Perhaps painter is the wrong word for him – he was (and still is) a theorist, an activist, a pamphleteer, and a writer, as well as an artist – in fact, the total surrealist, typical of and traditional to that movement. He was as much concerned with surrealist ideas as with the production of art-objects. Frequently it was enough simply to have an idea, without bothering to carry it out. Later, this approach came to be known as 'Conceptual Art', but at the time (it was 1948) it was merely a branch of the surrealist tree.

For example: one winter evening Conroy suddenly announced to the assorted group of students, painters and poets who, time and again, were drawn magnetically to his Birmingham home, that he would like to buy a piece of land and have a house built on it. It would be an ordinary-looking house, made of bricks. Ordinary except for one detail: it would be completely solid. Solid right through. No rooms — all bricks. And when it was finished, he would simply leave it there. There would be no announcements, no fanfare. It would quietly make its own statement.

I was one of those students who regularly attended Conroy's surrealist evenings in the late 1940s, and the irrational image of his solid brick house haunted me pleasantly for some time. It was only one of a flood of surrealist images that flowed incessantly from his fertile, eccentric brain. Some, like the house, remained no more than ideas; others, like his savage typewriter, with inverted drawing pins where the keys should have been, were actually constructed; still others were rendered as collages or paintings. For Conroy, the message was the message, and to hell with the medium.

Such was the intensity of his ambiguous, obscurely sinister visions, that it was inevitable that I should become eager to follow his lead. In my case, the medium most suited to my fantasies, other than paint, was film, and I set about writing the scripts of several surrealist scenarios that I was determined to realize, just as soon as I could lay my hands on a tame cameraman with a plentiful supply of celluloid. Having recently seen *Le Chien Andalou* by Bunuel and Dali, at the University Film Society, I was convinced that the cinema held enormous possibilities for the development of surrealist sequences, and I could hardly wait to get started. But with little money and no cameraman, I had to be patient; the scripts would have to be stored for the moment, to be sprung on an unsuspecting world at a later date.

In the meantime I wanted to make some kind of surrealist statement. And that was where the skull came in. Behind the zoology department there was a rubbish dump and on it, one day, I spotted a discarded elephant's skull. I was surprised that anyone would want to dispose of such an awesomely magnificent relic, but I was told that this one was in rather poor condition and no longer suitable as a scientific specimen. As far as I was concerned, its eroded surfaces rendered it even more remarkable, as a piece of natural 'sculpture'—what the surrealists referred to as an *objet trouvé*. I decided that such an object should inspire a sense of wonder and determined to bring it to people's attention. It was extremely heavy and I had to enlist the aid of a number of hefty helpers, who assisted me in carrying it down the road to the nearest tram-stop. The conductor refused to allow us to sit with it in the tram, insisting that it was 'luggage', and made us stow it under the stairs with a group of suitcases, where it was already beginning to take on a suitable irrelevancy. Since its huge teeth were in a bad state of repair I had decided to take it to one of the city dentists and leave it on a chair in his waiting-room. But it was so late by the time we arrived in the city centre, that I changed my plan to the simple act of leaving it sitting in a shop doorway in the main street. Nothing more was done—like Conroy's solid house, it was going to sit there quietly making its statement, reminding people that the world is full of strange and mysteriously beautiful objects.

It was the lack of any other purpose in its presence that was an important part of its surreal quality. I was slightly taken aback to read, in the following evening's paper, that my 'happening' had happened so effectively. It had never occurred to me that the object's impact would be so great as to draw a crowd that eventually caused an obstruction, to use the police term. And now there followed the inevitable desire on the part of society to find a logical explanation, so that the occurrence could be neatly filed away under some official heading, and forgotten. By refusing to come forward and claim the skull, I managed to keep the mystery going for several days, until the museum expert arrived and pronounced the 'dinosaur' to be nothing more than a rather dilapidated elephant skull of no particular value. After this, it was easy to write it off as a piece of dumped rubbish and the papers moved on to other, more topical items.

Years later, at the bottom of Julian Huxley's Hampstead garden, I saw another, much more splendid, elephant's skull, with small birds nesting in one of its gaping eye-sockets. 'Isn't that beautiful!' beamed Julian. 'One of the most beautiful objects I possess.' Since he also owned a magnificent Henry Moore sculpture, that put the skull into exalted company. And when Henry Moore himself saw the skull in the garden, he fell in love with it so passionately that Julian felt he had no choice but to give it to the great sculptor. Moore eventually used it as the inspiration for a wonderful series of 'skull' sculptures which, in my opinion, are amongst his most exciting works. What Birmingham missed, Moore did not.

Despite my surrealist adventures, of which the skull incident is the only one I wish to recall, I surprised myself by doing well in my first zoology examinations. The whole university atmosphere was so appealing after the military rituals and responsibilities I had left behind, that every day seemed like a childhood holiday. Children are always asking questions, and that was what we, too, were now supposed to be doing. I began to realize that the successful scholar is really only a sophisticated child, and that research is a kind of adult play. As soon as the sense of playfulness and curiosity goes out of research, it dies. To become an increasingly matured child was now my aim, and at a basic level this seemed to apply as much to art as it did to science. The games played in the two cases followed different rules, but the playfulness was there in both.

My problem was a conflict, not of mental attitude, but of time. When the spring vacation arrived in 1949, I was torn between making field trips to further my zoological studies, and working in my studio on new paintings. I tried to do both, but each suffered slightly in the process. Also, a new diversion entered the scene, in the form of the girl under the bed at one of Jimmy

Bomford's parties. There had been girl-friends before, of course, but this was to prove a stronger, more demanding relationship, of the kind that steals away one's thoughts at moments when total concentration is needed.

I have already told how we first made contact in a darkened bedroom, during a ridiculous party game. Before the night was out I had obtained a promise of a further, more private meeting, and was relieved to find that she was a local girl and not one of Jimmy's weekending Londoners. Her name was Ramona and she lived in the nearby town of Marlborough, where she was a star pupil at the grammar school, having just obtained a scholarship to Oxford. She was not due to go up to Oxford until the following autumn and had one more term to do at her Marlborough school. I was somewhat taken aback to discover that she was still a schoolgirl, a fact she was at pains to hide at the party. In her flamboyant, low-cut dress she looked more like an aspiring young actress, and the thought of her donning a school uniform again that summer was at once both erotic and mildly disconcerting. But nothing was going to stand in the way of the feelings that had been aroused between us, and we embarked on a headlong courtship that threw all caution to the winds.

Like me, she had grown up in the Wiltshire countryside and had developed a natural affinity with animals. She even liked snakes, and we went searching for them together in nearby Savernake Forest. While we were there I took her to visit an eccentric Dutch painter called Frans Baljon, who lived in a small cottage, right in the heart of the forest. Frans, a gritty, exuberant character who looked remarkably like his idol, Van Gogh, had fascinated me ever since I had first encountered him in my army days, when I used to take my art students to sketch trees in the forest. In Holland, before the war, he had been an eel fisherman who had lived in a church which he had converted into a studio. He used to sit in his pulpit painting intricate, botanical abstracts and would then take off in his eel-boat to earn his living. He was out on his boat when he heard on the radio that Holland had been overrun by the Nazis, so he piloted his vessel into a British south coast port to seek refuge. It was promptly requisitioned and he was suddenly penniless in a strange country. All he had were his nets and tackle and these he sold locally and then made for London.

Alone in the great wartime city, he decided that the only thing to do was to try and earn a living by his art. Seeing a shop that sold artists' materials, he went in to buy some charcoal for sketching. To his dismay, he was told that, as there was a war on, no charcoal was available. But he was not to be outdone by this. After a moment's hesitation, he replied:

'Then it is indeed fortunate that I happen to be an experienced charcoal-burner. Your troubles are over – I will supply you with all the charcoal you need from now on.'

The art shop was delighted. Of course, Frans had never made charcoal in his life, but desperate times required instant opportunism, and he immediately took a bus to Kew Gardens where a charming official told him all he needed to know about the process of charcoal manufacture. With a little ingenuity and a great deal of energy, he had soon set himself up in his little cottage in the forest as an 'expert' charcoal-burner and before long was supplying most of the art shops of southern England with all the artists' charcoal they needed. Now, although life was rather primitive, he could once again devote himself to the painting he loved.

One day he met someone from the aircraft industry who was bewailing the fact that there was a chronic shortage of dried pith that was badly needed in the making of lightweight aircraft instruments. The inevitable reply was:

'Then it is indeed fortunate that I happen to be an expert pith-maker. Your troubles are over – I will supply you with all the pith you need from now on.'

Back he went to the 'charming man' at Kew Gardens, who was only too pleased to impart to him the mysteries of pith-making. In no time at all, he was busily at work producing high-quality dried pith for the aircraft industry. This was more lucrative than the charcoal and he had remained in the forest after the war, still 'pithing about' as he put it, and still painting with a furious intensity, in an environment that ideally suited his richly vegetating abstract pictures. I had arranged an exhibition of his work for him and, in gratitude, he agreed to paint Ramona's portrait. While she sat, I worked quietly in a corner with a binocular microscope that I took with me to examine the insect life of the forest floor. We both felt that he was somehow a magical character – a rumbustious old witch of a man – full of extraordinary stories about the bizarre happenings in Van Gogh's private life, stories that had never found their way into any of the art history books, largely because most of them were unprintable. Hilarious epigrams poured from his mouth and his childlike sense of wonder impressed me deeply. His guttural laughter echoed through the forest, accompanied by a joyous flood of Dutch obscenities rendered harmless by their incomprehensibility. In fact, he died laughing. Several years later, he went to the local cinema to see a comedy and laughed so much that he died then and there in the darkness of the balcony.

Old Frans Baljon made the forest into an enchanted place for us, as young lovers, and we spent hours wandering in its under-growth, lying in one another's arms amongst the ferns and long grasses. And all around Marlborough there were magical places – the great stone circle of megaliths at nearby Avebury; the monu-mental earth mound called Silbury Hill whose function remains unknown to this day, its 4,000-year-old secret still defying the archaeologists; the magnificent remains further south at Stone-henge; the mysterious long-barrow at West Kennett; and the huge White Horse scarred into the chalky slopes of a hillside just outside Marlborough. We prowled them all and talked endlessly about schemes and projects and ambitions.

One small project of mine, with which I needed help, concerned the wild rabbits that infested many of the Wiltshire fields, in those pre-myxomatosis days. Someone had told me that wild rabbits were untameable and that they died of shock if you caught them and tried to keep them in captivity. This I could not believe, because, after all, the rabbits were not indigenous to Britain, having been introduced by the Romans as food animals. If the Romans had brought them over, then they must have been tame-able and I wanted to prove this by keeping a wild rabbit in an enclosure at home.

Ramona did not quite approve of this idea, reminding me that I had lectured her about the need to *watch* animals, rather than interfere with their natural lives, and I was at a loss to answer this. She was right, of course, and I was going against one of my basic beliefs, but my new role as a zoology student had set up a contradiction within me. I still believed in my long-held dictum about being a watcher rather than a keeper, where animals were concerned, but my recent zoological training had forced me to realize that without some degree of interference it was impossible to answer many questions. In fact, this problem was beginning to worry me at Birmingham, because I could not see how I could develop my zoological studies without conducting experiments. I knew I would never be capable of taking experimental work to the extreme of operating on animals, and I was not sure how to find an outlet for my zoological passion which would minimize the degree of interference with my animal subjects. Later, as it turned out, I was to be lucky in this respect, by channelling my studies into the direction of animal behaviour, but this was some time in the future. For the present, I had to admit to her that there was a contradiction, and that I was unhappy about it, but my scientific curiosity was too strong to be ignored. Reluctantly, she agreed to help.

The problem was catching the wild rabbits without harming them. I had noticed that, when we drove slowly down a country lane near Marlborough at night, the rabbits scampering across the road, from one field to another, were momentarily 'hypnotized' by the light from the headlamps. If I stopped and leapt from the car to chase them, it was always too late. It gave them time to recover and dash off into the darkness. What I needed was some-one sitting on the front of the car who could jump off as soon as I braked and grab the rabbit before it had time to come to its senses. This, I explained, to Ramona was where she came in.

Most girls would have refused, but Ramona accepted without question, and I think that was the moment at which I decided we were truly compatible. Greater love hath no girl than that she is prepared to be flung from the bonnet of a car on to a wild rabbit.

We set off down the narrow lane with Ramona perched over the radiator grill, as if someone had replaced an ordinary car mascot with a ship's figurehead. At the sight of the first rabbit in the road, I jammed on the brakes and Ramona was jettisoned forward in a kind of flying rugby tackle. Unfortunately, we had been going too fast and she overshot the animal, which bolted under the car and vanished. We tried again, taking it more gently this time. Lunging forward in the glare of the headlamps, she disappeared from my view. I leaped out and found her grappling with a kicking, struggling rabbit. It was a very large one and seemed to have the strength of ten domestic rabbits, but she held firm. I managed to take it from her and pop it into a grass-filled box on the back seat of the car, where it continued to thump and kick for a while, before quietening down.

'Poor thing,' she said, ignoring her scratched arms. But at the same time she was quite radiant at her success, which had so obviously filled me with admiration. I encouraged her to try for a second one.

After a number of failures, we managed to acquire a medium-sized rabbit that struggled much less than the first, giant one, and later a rather small one that hardly struggled at all. The evening had been a triumph as far as I was concerned, and Ramona was now able to project herself like an arrow from a bow whenever I braked.

I took her to her home and then sped back to Swindon with my trio of wild rabbits. There was a large, empty aviary in the garden in which I had constructed a set of burrows from rocks covered with earth, and I wanted to decant the animals into this as quickly as possible. When I carried the box into the enclosure and opened it, the two smaller rabbits were easy to remove, but as I reached forward to pick up the large one, it started to writhe and kick and, to my horror, began to go into convulsions. In less than a minute it was dead from shock. I knew Ramona would be upset and I dreaded having to tell her. The medium-sized rabbit

died a few days later and I was beginning to think that I was wrong.
The view that they were untameable was sadly being supported
by the facts before me. But the third, smallest rabbit went on to
flourish and eventually became almost as tame as a domestic
animal. It dawned on me, too late, that the Romans had obviously
caught and transported only young rabbits, from which they had
been able to start breeding captive animals and eventually produce
fully controllable stock – the ancestors of the modern domesti-
cated rabbits.

So I had learned a lesson – which I suppose I should have known
already – and it had cost the lives of two rabbits. True, they were
only pests and would probably soon have died, full of farmer's
buckshot, or caught in a wire snare, but it left a nasty taste in the
mouth all the same. And Ramona, predictably, was not happy
about the outcome. Her main concern seemed to be that, thanks
to her, the surviving rabbit was now suffering from enforced
celibacy. She agreed that it could be kept long enough for me to
film it as part of a surrealist project that I had at last got off the
ground, but after that, pest or no pest, it had to be released. And
so it was; the first of many animals to come under her 'personal
protection', as she put it.

The film project was also to involve Ramona. I had written a
script called *Time Flower* and was fortunate enough to find a local
cameraman, Christopher Simpson, who was prepared to finance
the shooting of it. He clearly did not understand much of what
was going on, but enjoyed the novelty of the scenes he was recording, and never questioned a single thing. His wife was even more
puzzled and at one point plaintively asked me, 'Why is the stuffed
sparrow exploding on the stringless violin?' I replied that it was
symbolic, which seemed to satisfy her. In fact, everything in the
film was so heavily symbolic that even the symbols had symbols,
and the whole sequence of events became confusingly cyclical,
returning again and again to the same bizarre images. All I can
recall clearly from a distance of thirty years, is a scene in which
Ramona had to be cut loose from a giant web and insert two over-
ripe plums into the eye-sockets of the skull of a horse, and a scene

in which, following the injection of a carnation in my button-hole, I slowly opened my lips to reveal a glass eye staring out at the world. Every time I blinked my real eyes, I blinked my lips as well, in a three-eyed gaze, an image that haunts me still, not only for its visual impact, but because I remember the fear I had of swallowing the glass eye while I was being filmed. But since I wrote the script I had only myself to blame.

To my amazement, the film won some amateur award—largely I think because nobody could understand it—and was even shown on television. We made a sequel called *The Butterfly and the Pin*, which I felt was a failure, but the two films were later to play an important part in acquiring me a post as head of a film unit, not because of their content, but because they revealed that I did, at least, understand the business of film-scripting and editing.

Ramona and I were becoming inseparable and it was with a sinking heart that I learned she was soon to be whisked away for a lengthy summer visit to France to improve her French. As soon as she had gone I realized that I wanted to marry her and immediately set off in pursuit. I knew she was changing trains in Paris on a particular date and I prowled the station all that day, watching for her. Unfortunately I had made a mistake and was at the Gare du Nord instead of the Gare St Lazare, where Ramona was sitting for several hours patiently waiting for her train. Eventually we met up again in England, just before she went up to Oxford, and became engaged. We could not get married until after she had obtained her degree, since the university did not permit married female undergraduates, and so there was a three-year wait ahead of us. But at least there seemed to be less chance of losing her now, to the bright young men of Oxford.

Birmingham suddenly seemed less appealing to me and, when I returned to my digs in Selly Oak for my second year, I felt horribly excluded from Ramona's glittering new social scene. Reading history at St Hilda's, she soon became caught up in the seemingly glamorous world of Oxford Highlife. Her letters, full of innocent enthusiasms, seemed to me to signpost a growing gulf between us. Whenever I contrived to escape from Birmingham for a few days to visit her, I felt increasingly like an outsider, unable to keep up with the brittle verbal cross-fire of her new friends. Although it was against my nature, I found myself sinking into a mood of sullen resentment. But then the vacations would come along and we would be together again, our bond as strong as ever. With each new term, the problem arose once more, until I was determined to take some kind of drastic action to resolve the situation. Somehow I had to get closer to Ramona, but how?

The answer came unexpectedly in the form of an invitation to a special lecture at the Birmingham Medical School. The professor there, an extraordinary South African called Solly Zuckerman, had organized a series of talks by outside speakers, covering many aspects of animal behaviour. He had originally made his name with a book entitled *The Social Life of Monkeys and Apes* (its first title had been *The Sexual Life of Primates*, until the church authorities objected) and he had been instrumental in setting up the Society for the Study of Animal Behaviour, just before the Second World War broke out and diverted him into more military researches. He was now the Professor of Anatomy at Birmingham, but his interest in behaviour studies still survived, hence this programme of special lectures.

My own professor, Peter Medawar, knew of my keenness in the behaviour field and suggested I accompany him to the next talk, which he considered to be a particularly important one. It was by a Dutch ethologist called Niko Tinbergen, and he was speaking on the latest advances in animal behaviour research. I was flattered that Medawar was taking the trouble to help me in this way. He was frantically busy at the time, working on a new line in immunological studies. As he drove me across to the Medical School, I apologized for taking up some of his valuable time, but he brushed this aside, saying he would have gone to the talk anyway. Tinbergen, he insisted, was leading the way towards an exciting new approach to experimental field-work. In the past, he explained, there had been charming natural historians who had pottered about in woods and fields, gazing rather ineffectually at Mother Nature, and there had been white-coated laboratory psychologists who were so isolated from reality that they would not know a field if they saw one. The first lot were good observers, but did not know what to do with their observations, except keep little lists, and the second lot were good experimenters, but had no idea which tests were relevant to the life of an animal and which were virtually meaningless. Tinbergen, it seemed, was correcting this situation by first making a broad study of the whole of an animal's behaviour repertoire, and then by carrying out simple experiments *in the field*, where their relevance or non-relevance became immediately obvious. This new approach, which had started to develop in Holland, Germany and Austria during the 1930s, had been rudely interrupted by the Second World War and was only now beginning to gain a new momentum, at the end of the 1940s.

In Medawar's far-from-humble opinion, Niko Tinbergen was a force to be reckoned with, and my respect for Medawar's brain was such that I entered the lecture hall that day with dangerously high expectations – so high that I was almost bound to be disappointed. Nobody could be *that* inspiring. But I was wrong and Medawar was right. One hour later, when I emerged from the lecture, my scientific life was totally transformed. No religious conversion could have been more dramatic. Here at last was precisely the kind of approach to zoology I wanted. Tinbergen had shown me, in sixty minutes that seemed like five, how it was possible to conduct serious, rigorous research without having to turn one's back on the natural world of the living animal. My lifelong obsession with wild animals could at last find a scientifically respectable outlet. I was overjoyed, but dubious about my chances of graduating to a research posting after taking my degree. It seemed to me that I had spent far too much time in the art world, painting and filming, to be able to achieve a high enough examination standard.

I was deep in thought as Medawar gunned his car, at his usual terrorizing speed, back down the road towards the zoology department.

'The maestro was on form today,' he announced, as he swung

into the car-park. Maestro was right, but he was a curiously gentle, soft-spoken maestro, all the same, and I made some remark to this effect. 'Yes,' sighed Medawar, 'he's pathologically modest. It's ridiculous, but don't let that fool you. He's important, very important, and you should think about the possibility of joining his research group at Oxford. He has just moved there from Holland, to introduce ethology to the English-speaking world.'

I could hardly believe my ears. Not only had I found my perfect kind of zoology, but its headquarters were situated at the very university where Ramona was beckoning me for quite other reasons. The combination was too good to be true. I spluttered something about having to work harder in the months ahead and, with Medawar's good wishes, took myself off to contemplate the problems now faced.

The main obstacle was that, in order to be accepted at Oxford, I would have to obtain a First Class Honours degree. Frankly, I did not think I was good enough, and I was fairly sure that, in my case, the modesty was justified rather than pathological. Then again, even if I worked like a maniac in my remaining terms, would Tinbergen take me? Would he have a place for me?

Despite my doubts and fears, and the danger of a major disappointment if I failed, I decided to set my sights firmly on the Oxford research goal. This meant severely curtailing my activities in the art world, which was difficult for me to do. I had recently held my first one-man show in London, and the signs were encouraging. There was pressure on me to continue painting and exhibiting. My work was being shown at an arts festival in Europe and I was loath to lose this early impetus. But my rather cavalier approach to my university studies in the early days at Birmingham meant that I had to make up for a great deal of lost time. In effect, I had to do two years' work in my final year, if I was to obtain a good degree.

I was aided in my conflict by the exceptional personality of my head of department. Peter Medawar had been made a full professor when only thirty-two and was still in his early thirties. His brain was at its zenith and there was no escaping its influence. He carried with him, minute by minute, that contradictory, relaxed intensity of a man whose superiority requires no feedback, no enforcement and no contrived display. His lectures were a revelation, not so much in content as in style. Here, I realized, was an intellect of supreme elegance, floated along by a current of sweeping confidence bordering on the arrogant. But his insults were always muted with humour— and they were never aimed at us, only at certain of the great names of science.

Above all, he made scientific research seem immensely significant and important, and created exactly the right atmosphere in the department to encourage my new single-mindedness. But motivation was not enough. There had to be knowledge as well— knowledge of thousands of names and terms, and the textbooks could no longer be avoided. I started a routine of late-night working that was later to become an adult habit. I am too easily distracted during the day, and only after everyone else is asleep can I operate at my desk at full intensity. From 10 p.m. to 4 a.m. non-stop is my standard work-stint, and I began to move into this nocturnal pattern during my final terms at Birmingham. Nowadays I tend to sleep late to achieve a balance, but then, as a student, I had 9 a.m. lectures to attend, and before long my health began to suffer. At the end of one term I arrived home for the vacation and collapsed into bed. I was running a high fever and the doctor was called. He was startled to find me lying moaning in a bed placed in the dead centre of an entirely black bedroom. In an early moment of surrealist abandon I had painted all the walls, woodwork, ceiling and doors of my bedroom jet black. It was part of some foolish conceit I had about falling asleep in the total absence of colour, as a means of clearing my mind for intense dreaming. The startled doctor was clearly under the impression that I was preparing for a lying in state and was so distracted that he hardly seemed able to concentrate on my symptoms. His prescription did little to relieve my condition and I lay in bed for days, groaning and sweating.

Whether it was the blackness of the bedroom at last having its effect, or whether it was the ridiculous degree to which I had over-burdened my brain with a mass of zoological facts, I am not sure, but my fever-dreams were the most vivid and compelling of my life. One, in particular, so fascinated me that I scribbled it down before it faded. The scene was as clear as if I was sitting in a cinema watching a giant screen. I was too feverish to read through the notes I had written, describing the dream, until some days later. Studying them then, I discovered that what I had recorded was both a summary of the present and a curious prediction about the future. The first few sentences read:

'It's no good, they won't go away, they are following me into the studio and grazing all over the canvases. There is one enormous creature I can see just out of the corner of my eye, perched on one of the highest branches of the tree that hangs close over this glass roof. Without looking straight at it, it seems different from the rest. It has a single claw and a red head with big teeth fixed all around it, which, strangely, seem quite sad. Going out through the door ... '

The dream notes went on and on and seemed to record the fact that unconsciously I had accepted that animals were going to dominate my life. And there was something more. In the dream, after I had moved outside the studio, I lay down in the grass and gazed up at the strange creature in the tree above my head. As I did so, it began to fall, very slowly, down and down, and I shut my eyes tight as it fell on top of me. I blacked out and when I came to, I could feel the swish of leaves against my body. Opening my eyes carefully, I looked down at my feet to see with surprise that they had become a single, large claw, clinging to a branch.

I had become the creature in the tree. Through the glass roof of a studio I could see a young man painting, surrounded by a circle of watching animals. As I stared at him and recognized my own features, he caught sight of me and stopped painting. Gazing up into my tree, he rose and walked out on to the grass below, where he lay down, looking up at me intently. Slowly, I began to feel myself toppling forward and falling, falling ...

That was the end of the dream. It was a strange little scenario.

Not only was I surrounded by animals, but I changed into one myself. In essence, this was what was going to happen to me in my future research, when I became a full-time student of animal behaviour. With each animal I studied, I *became* that animal. I tried to think like it, to feel like it. Instead of viewing the animal from a human standpoint—and making serious anthropomorphic errors in the process—I attempted, as a research ethologist, to put myself in the animal's place, so that *its* problems became *my* problems, and I read nothing into its life-style that was alien to its particular species. And the dream said it all.

In the final terms at Birmingham, I continued to drive myself hard and was slowly getting on top of my subject. In the May of 1951, with only a short time to go to my final exams, I received a telephone call from an old Swindon friend, John Trehearne, who was now in the zoology department at Bristol University. He knew of my interest in animal behaviour and urged me to drop everything and get the next train to Bristol. The Father of Ethology, the great Austrian zoologist, Konrad Lorenz, had arrived unexpectedly at the department and was about to give a series of impromptu lectures.

It meant breaking into my routine studies, but it was an opportunity I could hardly ignore. I had heard so much about Lorenz and how, with Tinbergen, he was the spearhead of the new, naturalistic approach to animal behaviour research, that I packed a suitcase and headed south immediately. I was well rewarded.

Konrad Lorenz was an imposing, even majestic, figure and his style was as flamboyant and colourful as Tinbergen's had been gentle and persuasive. Looking like a cross between a Victorian God, a great orchestra conductor and a magnificent husky dog, he launched into a *tour de force* that was irresistible even to those of his audience who clearly disapproved of him. Their disapproval stemmed largely from his non-experimental approach to his subject. They were used to neat laboratory procedures, carefully controlled tests and elaborately quantified analyses. Lorenz, by contrast, was concerned with ideas, concepts and observations.

Often he was unashamedly anecdotal, and tables of figures were nowhere to be seen. (To this day, I have been unable to find a single table of figures anywhere in Lorenz's voluminous writings — a remarkable achievement for a modern scientist who was to become a Nobel Laureate.)

Compared with the typical laboratory-worker, Lorenz was almost a poet. Epigrams swirled around us like confetti. It was as if the great master of animal behaviour studies was constitutionally incapable of uttering a boring sentence. Even when you disagreed with what he was saying, you had to admit that he said it beautifully. But most of the time you just agreed, and wondered why you had been so blind as not to have seen it that way before.

Talking to a few of us after one of his lectures, he was amused when someone asked him about his scientific method. He subsided into a brief, thoughtful silence, puffing paternally on his drooping pipe.

'Contrary to your Shakespeare,' he proclaimed suddenly, with disarming theatricality, 'there is madness in my method.' And so, we had to admit, there was. If a group of typical, cautious, orthodox scientists were to make a careful examination of the Lorenzian 'scientific method', it is unlikely they would ever recover from the experience. For Konrad Lorenz is the living proof that eccentric, inspired guesses are frequently the basis of scientific progress. His whole life-style seemed to be an animal-infested chaos. Like some kind of modern Noah, he lived surrounded by fish, reptiles, birds and mammals of every shape and colour. There were endless mishaps and it was often from these that Lorenz learned his most valuable lessons.

For instance, he was out walking with a tame raven one afternoon. The bird was free-flying and, in order to keep it close to him, Lorenz had taken the precaution of filling one of his pockets with small pieces of raw meat. Every so often, he would call to the bird (he was fluent in Raven) and as it approached, would put his hand into the meat-pocket, take out a strip of meat, and feed it to his great, black companion. This procedure meant that, although the raven would zoom off into the sky, it always kept a bright, corvine eye on Konrad's movements, as he wandered across the summer fields.

They continued like this for several hours, with the bird returning regularly to Lorenz's side for a further tidbit. As it was a hot day, Lorenz had drunk copiously at lunch-time and now needed to relieve himself. As there was nobody about, he moved near a hedge, undid his trousers, and started to do so. The raven's sharp eye had observed Lorenz undoing his trousers and assumed that he was opening another pocket to extract a fresh piece of meat. Swooping down with a raucous cry, the great bird seized this new piece of meat, clamping down tightly on it with its massive powerful beak. Lorenz let out a roar like a wounded bull and began leaping dementedly about in the corner of the field. The raven was nonplussed by this extraordinary behaviour and could not understand why its human friend was so reluctant to hand over a piece of meat that was so plainly meant for its consumption. Placing its huge feet firmly on Lorenz's body, the bird started to tug fiercely at the stubbornly resistant food-offering, like a blackbird trying to pull an earthworm from a garden lawn. Lorenz claims that he nearly fainted from pain and loss of blood, but it is more likely to have been shock.

Despite this unfortunate incident, Lorenz was far from critical of the bird's behaviour, claiming that the raven had been intelligent and that it was he who had been stupid. And he had learnt another valuable lesson. He had always been interested in 'intention movements' – small, incipient actions that during the course of evolution can easily become developed into exaggerated animal signals. Animals, he explained, frequently respond acutely to the first tiny element in a behaviour sequence, without waiting for the later stages. When a bird is alarmed and flees, the first element of its take-off is a slight crouching of the body, with the head bobbing downwards. From this sequence, the head-bob alone can be enough to signal alarm and eventually an exaggerated head-bob will develop as a special danger signal. In the case of the raven, the movement of Lorenz's hand towards his clothing had come to act as the 'intention movement' signal that food was on

the way and, as the bird became more experienced in this procedure, it did not need to wait for further information, but came
swishing down out of the sky to claim its reward. As Lorenz put
it, the mishap that had then occurred left a deep impression on
him of the vital importance of intention movements in animal
reactions.

Sadly, not all his mishaps carried a useful message. He was once
nearly knocked out by an exploding fish-tank, from which he
learned only that very large aquaria require very thick glass. The
incident occurred when he had moved his research unit into an
old castle in Germany. It was one of his rules that there should
always be a tank of fish in front of his writing desk, so that even
when he was working on his papers he could continue to make
observations. He was partial to large tanks because, in them, he
could create a more natural social environment for his favourite
cichlid fish. Unfortunately, in this case, the glass wall of the tank
facing his desk was much too thin for the weight of water behind
it. As he sat staring into the tank one morning, the front glass
gave up the struggle and with a loud bang disintegrated on to
Lorenz's head, followed by a cascade of water, cichlid fish and
water-plants. Lorenz was thrown backwards by the force of the
explosion and found himself on the floor, draped in aquatic
plants and struggling fish, and festooned in fragments of glass.
Sloshing wildly about, half stunned, he tried desperately to rescue
his stranded cichlids. The good news was that the old castle floor
sloped steeply to one side of the room, so that most of the water
and most of the fish were swept across into a shallow pool that
formed against the far wall. The bad news was that this wall was
the one against which there stood a vast, antique wardrobe that
would have required an army to move it. So the pool had formed
beneath the wardrobe and was almost inaccessible.

Luckily, cichlids are remarkably tough fish, tenacious of life,
and they survived the ordeal, but Lorenz recalls the minutes that
passed during the desperate rescue operation as being like hours.
For him, there was no austere, scientific coldness in his relations
with his animals. They were all personal friends, and aroused

strong protective emotions. For some people this would have led
to the danger of anthropomorphism, but not Lorenz. He knew
too much about the lives of his animals ever to make the mistake
of seeing them as caricatures of human beings. Well, hardly ever
– he tells one amusing story against himself on this score. He had
been breeding geese for many generations and had kept records of
all their matings and social relationships. One day he asked a girl
assistant to check the pairing records of the geese to see if they had
all been sexually faithful to their mates, as geese are supposed to
be. The girl returned some time later to inform him that, to her
surprise, a certain percentage of them had in fact been unfaithful
to their mates. Lorenz looked rather perturbed at this news, but
roared with laughter when the girl tried to cheer him up by
saying:

'Never mind, Professor, after all, geese are only human!'

His concern for the well-being of his animals often led him into
trouble. Many years later, when he had a splendid new research
institute at Seeweisen, near Munich, he once again insisted on
having a large aquarium in front of his working desk. But this
time it was to be constructed with great care and efficiency.
Instead of a simple tank, standing in the room, it was a massive
structure built in to the wall of his study and looked like a huge,
living painting above his book-littered desk-top. A small door
near by led to a hidden servicing room, from which the tank
could be tended and the fish fed. Instead of a few loose rocks in
the water, the whole of the concrete back of the tank had been
sculptured into naturalistic contours with nooks and crannies and
little caves as hiding-places for the smaller fish.

It was in one of these small rock-caves that a particular fish was
now lurking. It had become a trouble-maker in the tank and
Lorenz knew that it had to be removed, for the safety of the other
fish. The trouble was that the tank was so big that the fish in
question had eluded all attempts to net it from the service platform behind. Lorenz was sitting in front of the aquarium one
afternoon, pondering how to deal with this delinquent specimen,
when his secretary entered to remind him that, in half an hour, he

was due to receive a group of civic dignitaries who were arriving to present him with a statuette – some high award he had recently won. He assured her he had not forgotten and returned to puzzling over his fish problem. Suddenly it dawned on him that the huge tank was big enough for him to get right into it himself and that he could then catch the trouble-maker at close quarters. He looked at his watch. There was just enough time. Hurrying into the service room behind the aquarium, he quickly stripped off his clothes and climbed over the edge of the tank, lowering himself carefully into the warm water. Grasping a small hand-net, he slowly submerged beneath the surface until he was crouching down near the small cave where the fish lurked. It was difficult to manoeuvre in the space of the tank, large as it was, and he had to push himself backwards until his behind was firmly pressed against the front glass.

It was at this point that the local dignitaries were ushered into the study to make the presentation of the award. Finding it empty, they wandered around admiring the pictures on the walls. An elderly lady in the group moved across to the desk, to examine what appeared to be a strange, abstract picture above it. Peering closer at it she let out a stifled scream, which brought the others running across the room. As they watched, the large, naked bottom slowly rotated, to be replaced by the Neptune-like, submerged head of the great professor. Lorenz blinked through the glass of the tank at the distorted cluster of horrified faces and, as the awful truth dawned, shot up out of the tank like a Polaris missile being launched from a submarine. Frantically drying himself and throwing on his clothes, he tried desperately to think of a suitable apology. But none was needed. When he emerged through the service door into his study, it was empty. On his desk there stood the small statuette. The dignitaries had fled.

It takes a man of great warmth and with a rich sense of humour to tell stories like that against himself. But I must not give a one-sided impression of him. He is also intensely serious about his work and a profound thinker who is widely read in philosophy as well as zoology. He once told me he thought of himself as a lazy man, but his laziness only extends to the inessentials of life. True, he is an erratic correspondent, and there is no telling when he will answer a letter and when he will ignore it, but that is only because his priorities demand that he shall spend hour after hour with his animals, sitting, watching and analysing the meaning of their behaviour patterns.

In that first series of lectures of his that I attended in Bristol he made a relevant point. MacDougall, he reminded us, had a phrase, 'The healthy animal is up and doing', but we should remember that a healthy python is 'up and doing' when it lies perfectly still waiting for its prey. There are, of course, a number of such 'waiting' animals and, in a sense, Lorenz is one of them. When he sits quietly for hours watching the animals he has collected around him, he, too, is waiting, but his 'prey' is an exciting new observation. There is nothing lazy about the way Lorenz watches animals.

During his lectures, it became clear that the range of animals he had studied was enormous. Most modern zoologists specialize in one small group of animals, but Lorenz insisted that his comparative approach required 'analysis on a bold front'. This applied not only to the number of species, but also to the variety of behaviour they performed. One has to know the whole animal, he said, echoing Tinbergen's approach. And he went on to discuss feeding behaviour, fighting, nesting, cleaning, mating, imprinting, rearing, and virtually every major aspect of animal life. He gave us examples from lemurs and lizards, jackdaws and jewel fish, seals and starlings, apes and ants, ducks and dogs, geese and grebes, and mice and men. He seemed positively Darwinian in his range of knowledge and his insistence that nothing should be considered as outside the scope of investigation.

People who talk of a 'vital life force' which is beyond analysis, he commented, 'have the infernal cheek to think they know what is not explicable'. How do they know where to draw the line, he demanded? If there were wonders, nature would be much less wonderful.

It was hard to wrench myself away from Bristol, but I forced

myself to leave before the end of his short lecture course and
return to my examination syllabus at Birmingham. Fortunately I
had already heard enough for the Lorenzian approach to have
made its impact. If Tinbergen had baptized me as an ethologist,
Lorenz had confirmed me. All I needed to do now was to pass that
wretched exam well enough. I was further encouraged by the
news from Oxford that, if I obtained a 'First', Tinbergen had
agreed to find a place for me.

At last the weeks of feverish scribbling in tension-filled examination halls were behind me, but I was far from pleased with my
performance. In a letter to Ramona at Oxford I wrote: 'The last
paper could have been worse, but I now know that I have missed
my "First" ... I feel quite lost.' But in my longing to get to Oxford
I must have been setting my standards too high and happily my
self-criticism was unjustified. After an agony of waiting, the First
came through. Early in July 1951, Tinbergen wrote me a brief
note of congratulation and asked me to come to Oxford at the
end of the month 'to make concrete plans'. The long sweat was
over. I was as thin as a rake and felt totally drained, but after a few
weeks of summer vacation with Ramona on the south coast I was
raring to go again, and drove off to my meeting at the Oxford
zoology department with the eagerness of a child rising on
Christmas morning.

4

THE MAESTRO WAS SITTING ON A WOODEN CRATE. It was the first thing I noticed as I entered Niko Tinbergen's room in the department of zoology at Oxford. It seemed strange to me to be offered a comfortable chair while, across the desk from me, the great man sat on that old box. Later, when I knew him better, I understood. No matter where Niko happened to be, his heart was always in the field, out on some undulating sand dune, or a wind-swept cliff-top. His natural habitat was the field camp and, even in his Oxford laboratory, he needed some reminder of that world. The rough wooden crate provided that reminder.

He had just returned from watching a gull colony on Scolt Head Island and in the corner of his room was a crumpled pile of canvas hides awaiting repair. Behind me were fish tanks containing sticklebacks. Like Konrad Lorenz, he had to have animals somewhere in his line of vision. On a bench there was a mass of camera equipment and on rows of shelves there were hundreds of numbered box-files containing his massive collection of scientific reprints. The room was austere, as if Niko was camping briefly in civilization before returning to his true home in the wild.

I noticed that in the centre of the desk there was an old Royal portable typewriter identical to the one on which my father had written all his boys' stories in the 1930s – a machine which I was still using myself. Niko was typing furiously as I entered, and pulled out a long sheet of foolscap which he handed across to me. On it he had written the names of five animals, with notes against each one. He explained that these were five suggestions of his for suitable research topics for me. I read down the list: Drosophila (the fruit fly), Chaffinch, Ducks, Bumble-bees, Ten-spined

Stickleback. While he rolled himself an incredibly rumpled, emaciated cigarette, we discussed the relative merits of his five proposals. After a while, he broke into the discussion to enquire whether I smoked. When I said I did, he apologized for not offering me one and then began searching around in one of his desk drawers until he found a packet and offered me one. Again, the same contrast: I was sitting on the chair, he was sitting on the crate; I was smoking a tame, packet cigarette, while he was puffing on a wild, hand-made one. I mentioned this observation to one of his older students, who laughed and said that if I had been given a cigarette from a packet, that meant that I still rated as a stranger. When Niko knew you better, it seemed, you rose to the status of being offered one that he had rolled himself, but with the gummed edge still unlicked. You then licked it yourself and completed the rolling process. The final stage, when you became a close friend, involved Niko rolling the cigarette, licking the gum and sticking it down himself, before handing it to you.

The animal I chose from the list of five was the ten-spined stickleback. I had already kept the more common, three-spined species and had briefly studied its extraordinarily complex breeding cycle, so that I felt I had a head start with sticklebacks. I would find the practical problems of setting up research aquaria comparatively easy and, furthermore, I happened to know an excellent ten-spined stickleback river — the Kennet, which flowed through Ramona's home town of Marlborough, only an hour's drive away. So collecting them would present no problems.

There was the added advantage that Niko himself had already made extensive studies of the three-spined fish, which would enable me to carry out a comparative investigation — seeing how and why the two species differed. It was agreed that I should become a sticklebacker.

I was allocated a basement room, because it was suitably cool for the fish, which I shared with Philip Guiton, another new student of Niko's, who was also going to do his D.Phil. studies on sticklebacks. Together we set up row upon row of aquarium tanks until there was hardly room left for us to move about.

Surrounded by about fifty of these tanks, we had to slide our way around between them, planting water-weeds, fitting aerators, and adjusting lighting covers. Then we set out in the departmental Land Rover on collecting trips, stocking our fish room until it was almost as if we were living submerged in a densely populated river. With fish-watching, it was difficult to take the laboratory into the field, so instead we brought the field into the laboratory.

The problem with sticklebacks was that they were carnivorous and Niko insisted that we feed them on minced-up earthworms. He persuaded us to dig a huge worm-trench outside our basement window, fill it with kitchen refuse from nearby Keble College, add a parent stock of worms, and then cover it with earth. In no time at all, he promised, we would have all the fish-food we needed, right outside our door. He himself provided the earthworms to start us off, digging furiously for them in his garden, where we collected them from him by the jarful.

Chopping the worms into pieces small enough for the sticklebacks to swallow was a long and tediously messy business, but it had about it the arduous quality of a field-camp task that clearly appealed to the maestro. Although he never mentioned it, I think he was mildly disgusted when I found a much lazier, more efficient, method of filling the bellies of our army of small fish. There was an excellent aquarist's shop in Oxford which sold tubifex worms — minute red worms which one bought in a squirming lump and kept in the sink under a gently running tap. Tubifex were exactly the right size for the mouth of a stickleback and they required no messy preparation. You simply plopped a small ball of them into each tank and the fish devoured them quickly and easily. It was the obvious answer for us, but for Niko it lacked the dignity of labour. Buying the food was somehow cheating. But he never complained openly about it.

In fact, he was a remarkably tolerant supervisor — immensely helpful and rarely dogmatic. The one thing he did insist on was that we should exercise extreme caution in making any statement about an animal's behaviour. Was it really justified? Had we tested all the possibilities? Were we rushing ahead too fast? 'So far as we know' was his favourite phrase, and he always wanted to know more. Caution was not my strong point, and his insistence on digging deeper into every problem provided a valuable discipline for me. 'Konrad Lorenz is a spreader,' he once said, 'while I am a digger. Konrad is like a farmer, surrounding himself with hundreds of different animals, while I am more like a hunter, pursuing one animal at a time, further and further, until I know all I can about it.' He sensed that, by nature, I was a 'spreader', too (and, in fact, by the time I had obtained my doctorate, no fewer than eighty-four different species had passed through my Oxford laboratory) so that he felt it was particularly important in my case to keep me digging deeper into each problem I tackled. In the case of the ten-spined stickleback, he succeeded, and I persisted with my studies of that fascinating small fish for the full three years of my D.Phil. period, while other species came and went to satisfy my urge for variety.

During my first winter in Oxford I read up all the existing literature on the stickleback and in the laboratory examined its winter shoaling behaviour. Then, in the following spring, came my first major research phase, as the breeding season approached. My main task was to analyse the reproductive cycle of the species and this was condensed into a period of a few months, starting in late February and extending through March, April and May, and petering out in June. It was a time of frenzied activity for the sticklebacks in my tanks and a time of endless hours of crouched watching for me. My facility for fast typing was a godsend, as I could sit in front of my tanks thumping out a running commentary of the behaviour sequences while they were actually occurring.

My initial task — and one that Tinbergen always insisted on — was the compilation of an 'ethogram', that is, a comprehensive list of every action my fish were capable of performing; in other words, a complete behaviour repertoire. It was part of the Tinbergen creed that no one should attempt to analyse any one aspect of an animal's behaviour until he had first spent a whole year familiarizing himself with its complete range of activities and had described each action in detail. Although, for some, this seemed like a slow beginning to a research project, Niko claimed that without it, it was impossible to understand the true life-style of an animal. Animal psychologists came in for a great deal of harsh criticism on this score. How could a man study a white rat when he had never seen it make a burrow, for instance? The burrow was the very centre, the core, of the rat's existence. And how many of the hundreds of 'rat psychologists' had provided burrowing facilities for their animals, and watched them at work constructing their natural home base? The answer was simple: none. So much for psychologists who claimed to study animal behaviour. As budding ethologists, we had no time for them.

The main difficulty I encountered in recording the various actions of my sticklebacks was the speed at which they were performed. In one ninety-minute observation, for instance, when I introduced several females into a male's tank, he performed no fewer than 1,925 actions. This required something more than fast typing – it demanded a special code of shorthand. I had isolated forty-five stickleback actions and gave each one a symbol of one or two letters. This code then streamed out across the page: PF3 GclockP ZZ B ZZZZZ BB ZZZZ SHW SHV BBBB PF2 ... and so on, leaving me with countless hours of decoding later in the day. But from all of this I was beginning to assemble a picture of what it was like to be a sexy stickleback in the spring. I was amazed at how many questions there were to answer. Someone had once written that 'Fish are such incredibly boring creatures that I feel sure they must go to heaven when they die.' In that case, I thought, my sticklebacks will certainly go to hell.

The most exciting discovery I made during that first spring season was that some of my male sticklebacks appeared to have strong homosexual tendencies. This was totally unexpected and gave me the subject for my first scientific paper, which appeared in the journal *Behaviour* in 1952, with the unlikely title of 'Homosexuality in the Ten-spined Stickleback'. Briefly, what I observed was this:

With the arrival of the breeding season, male ten-spined sticklebacks cease to swim in shoals and begin to space themselves out among the water-weeds, each one defending a territory against the others. Their bodies become jet black in colour and they start to construct a small nest of plant filaments, lodged carefully in a clump of weeds. They bore a tunnel into this nest and then start to look for a ripe female, swollen with eggs. On seeing her, they perform a vigorous, head-down dance, zig-zagging their way slowly towards the nest-site. If the female is nearly ready to lay her eggs, she follows closely behind the dancing male and pushes her nose into the nest entrance. The male hovers above her, pointing to the nest entrance with his nose. If she then enters the nest and lies quietly in the tunnel, he moves down a little and begins to shiver his nose against her protruding tail. If she leaves the nest by the tunnel exit without laying her eggs, he then pursues her and bites her savagely, before starting to court again. If, on the other hand, she lays her eggs in the nest before leaving, the male then follows her quickly through the tunnel and fertilizes the eggs. After this, he guards and cares for the eggs day after day until they hatch, the liberated female stickleback taking no further interest in her offspring.

That is the typical sexual sequence, but some of my males behaved in a very different way. Seeing a courtship in progress, they would creep stealthily across the tank and compete with the female to squeeze into the nest tunnel. If the female then gave up and left, one of these 'pseudofemale' males would then sometimes take over her role, following the nest-owning male closely when he danced and going through all the motions of the female courtship sequence, even to the extent of lying inside the tunnel, as though laying eggs. In fact, they were seen to do everything the female did *except* lay eggs. This was most common when they themselves were in a tank where there was slight over-crowding of the males, and where the pseudofemales had not been able to establish the ownership of a clump of weeds in which to build a nest. In other words, a sexually frustrated male, who could not perform the usual masculine courtship actions, was sometimes driven to express himself sexually by adopting the female role.

This first paper of mine was well received and I was so encouraged that I began to branch out, filling my laboratory with many different species of fish, birds and mammals, writing short papers on a variety of subjects, while continuing to work on the long-term, three-year stickleback thesis. I was too impatient to wait for that major publication to appear, and suffered from an immodest urge to see my name in print as often as possible. Niko was delighted at my energetic approach to ethology, but repeatedly had to warn me of the dangers of spreading myself too thinly, and of neglecting the main project.

Somehow I managed to maintain a balance, but I was over-working and my domestic life was primitive, to say the least. I had rented a room on Folly Bridge in an unusual house right on the river Thames. My room was on the ground floor and the river actually passed beneath it, so that at night I could sometimes hear the ghostly hissing of swans below my floorboards. The place was cluttered with about two hundred of my paintings, my easel and painting table, a bed and a few chairs. On the mantelpiece there was a large glass case that had once held a stuffed fox. I had removed the fox, not wishing to see a species that was an old friend of mine frozen into such an undignified immortality, but I had left the artificial, hollow mound on which he had been standing. This had been carefully painted by the taxidermist to look like a small chunk of fox-habitat and was festooned with dried grasses and mosses. It seemed to me to be the perfect place to house a pet hamster, so I cut a small hole in the top of it and half-filled it with earth and hay. I then introduced a charming golden hamster, whose hoarding behaviour I had been studying in my laboratory, and he immediately took to his new home, coming up in the evening for his food and drink and peering out of the case at the room beyond. I had not realized the consternation he would cause until, one evening, I heard a guest let out a scream. Jumping backwards, she fell over my painting table and descended to the floor in a cloud of tubes of paint, turpentine and linseed oil. What had happened was that, as we entered the room and I switched on the light, the hamster had frozen in alarm, like a statue. As my guest approached the fireplace to examine the 'stuffed animal' in the glass case, she had come too close for the hamster's comfort and, recovering himself quickly, he promptly scuttled off and disappeared down his hole. My guest, a female relative who was visiting me to see how I was 'getting along' at Oxford, found this sudden animation on the part of an apparently taxidermized animal so unnerving and the chaos of my room so appalling that she left shortly after she had been cleaned of paints and oil, no doubt to regale my other relatives with tales of Oxford decadence and decay.

And she was not far wrong, as far as decay was concerned. A week or so earlier I had decided to undertake my very first meal as a host. Having no suitable crockery, I went to a local saleroom and bought for three shillings a huge pile of ill-assorted plates and dishes. These I covered with a variety of cold foods, taken mostly from tins, bought a few bottles of cheap wine, and awaited my dinner guests with a feeling of vast culinary achievement. Ramona, being in the final throes of her history degree at St Hilda's College, was too busy to help, and I was rather proud to have done all this on my own.

The mixture of food I was offering my research friends was unbelievably horrid to even the most undiscerning palate and they politely left most of it untouched and concentrated on the wine. Despite their hunger, it was a pleasant evening and the wine and the talk flowed on until the early hours. Unable to face the task of carrying all the plates round to the small shared kitchen, which was some distance away, I opened up some empty cavernous cupboards that were built into the walls on either side of the fireplace and piled all the gruesome, food-covered plates inside. Forcing the cupboard doors shut on the squelching mountains of crockery and mushy salad, I collapsed into bed and slept off the wine.

Next morning I was late for a timed test at the laboratory and raced off without thinking of the horrors in the cupboards. After that, I forgot all about them until, two weeks later, Ramona

managed to snatch a few minutes from her studies to visit me at
Folly Bridge. 'What,' she enquired, 'are those strange green
whiskers creeping out of the cracks of your cupboard doors?' A
woman's eye seems to be unerringly attracted to such phenomena.
I had now completely forgotten about the plates, having decided
to give up my new-found role as a culinary host, and I was as
puzzled as she was. We peered closely at the protruding whiskers.
I said I thought they were rather beautiful. All she said was: '*You*
open it.'

Forcing back the cupboard doors I was met with a sight that
would have warmed Lon Chaney's heart and brought a benign
smile to Bela Lugosi's fangs. The whole interior of the cupboard
(both cupboards) was a mouldering mass of yellow and green
decay, festooned everywhere with dense strands of olive and
turquoise filaments, like the dead hair of something from outer
space. Ramona was horrified and, to this day, always eyes me
with deep suspicion whenever I enter her kitchen. (The great
bonus, of course, is that in a quarter of a century of marriage she
has never allowed me to do the washing up. Traumas can have
their uses.)

After that, she took valuable time off from her studies to visit
my room regularly with small food offerings. I tried to stop her,
feeling guilty at interfering with her work, but she insisted that
I looked so thin and wan, that she had to feed me to ensure that I
was still alive for our wedding, which was due to take place that
summer, immediately after her final exams. And I am ashamed to
say that I was too selfish to demand that she ignore me.

Despite these distractions, she managed to obtain her degree
and the wedding was set for July 30th, 1952.

Since he had been responsible for bringing us together, Jimmy
Bomford organized a wild stag-party for my last night as a
bachelor. He imported some young actresses from London and
late at night, after the wine had been flowing even more freely
than usual, we all decanted from his house and descended on a
fair that was being held in the local village. Bravado demanded
that I launch myself on to every fiendish device known to fair-

ground inventors. It was on the chairoplane that I realized I was not going to survive and, as the village lights spun round me in a blur, I would have given anything to be at home in bed, instead of engaged in this primitive *rite de passage*. I was horribly sick and the next morning arrived for the church ceremony feeling embalmed.

The cameraman who had filmed my surrealist fantasies had been asked to make a film of the wedding, and the first scene shows me, white-faced and in full morning dress, falling over a dustbin. In my confused state, I had approached the church from the wrong direction and was squeezing down an alleyway, where the camera caught me at just the wrong moment. Worse was to come. In my befuddled condition I had a fixed image in my mind of the bride and groom running happily away after the nuptials, while cheering guests pelted the smiling pair with confetti. The scene was so implanted in my brain that, as soon as the vows were over, I grabbed an astonished Ramona by the hand and took off down the aisle at a gallop, wondering why the assembled guests were staring at me instead of hurling handfuls of confetti. Ramona did her best to slow me down and at the same time struggled to control her long flowing gown. The cameraman was waiting outside the church door to film the dignified emergence of the radiant couple. What emerged were two young people arguing furiously with one another over the niceties of wedding procedure. On his film this followed immediately after the opening shot of me falling over the dustbin and he was beginning to wonder if I was intent on producing a sequel to my surrealist efforts of the previous years.

At the reception afterwards I had to face the ordeal of a wedding speech, during which everything I said seemed to have a double meaning. The harder I tried the worse it got, much to the delight of those of my friends who had enjoyed the previous night at Jimmy's party, and who knew perfectly well the fragile condition in which I was now barely surviving.

It was with the most enormous relief that I finally drove Ramona away – confetti-covered at last – to begin a long, lovely honeymoon. But in retrospect I am glad we went through the elaborate ritual of marriage, despite the hazards, because I have become more and more convinced that occasional ceremonial performances are a vital part of social life. They establish important personal landmarks, even if, at the time, one's brain is in no condition to appreciate the fact.

Back in Oxford after the honeymoon, we set up home in a small suburban house with a pleasant garden. Niko Tinbergen gave Ramona a part-time job assisting with the ethology group. One of her first tasks was to act as secretary for the Second International Ethological Conference in the autumn of 1952. The first one, held in Germany two years previously, had been organized by Erich von Holst, a colleague of Konrad Lorenz. Von Holst felt that conferences were always too formal and too pompous (a surprisingly un-Germanic idea) and that, if there was to be a true exchange of thoughts, the proceedings should be as informal as possible. As he put it: 'half-baked' ideas should be discussed, and no report should be published. In that way, he hoped, people would speak more freely, even about problems they were still struggling with, because these were the ones that would most benefit discussion. It was an excellent approach and was to be the start of a long series of such conferences that have taken place every two years, ever since. Sadly though, as ethology has gained ground and the numbers attending have risen to huge figures, the original informality has inevitably been lost. Today the International Ethological Conferences are as formal and useless as those of most other scientific disciplines.

Back in 1952, however, the mood was perfect for the gathering in Oxford. We still felt ourselves to be part of a pioneering movement invading the sphere that had been dominated for so long by the laboratory-bound psychologists. Ethology had yet to reach America, but there were delegates from many European countries and the exchange of ideas and information was intensely rewarding. In keeping with the friendly atmosphere of the occasion, Niko Tinbergen had decided that the last evening was to be a light-hearted entertainment, and I was given the task of organizing this. I decided on a satirical approach and chose as my victim a German theorist who had produced a concept of brain function based on the analogy of water-flow. Nervous energy was seen as water trickling from level to level, being dammed up here, seeping out there, or being released in a sudden flood when an appropriate stimulus was applied. The analogy had been initiated by Konrad Lorenz. In an early paper, he had shown a drawing of what looked like a lavatory tank, releasing water when the flush was pulled. It was meant to illustrate the way in which a particular urge in an animal could build up and up, until even a minor stimulus could release it in a flood of activity. As a crude analogy it was effective enough, but as with many such 'parables' in science, it could not stand refinement or undue elaboration. This was the error that the victim of my satire had made — he had tried to take the analogy too far and, in the process, had made it look ridiculous. Complex plumbing was not the way to view the workings of the brain. Nervous impulses did not flow like water through pipes, and I set out to ridicule this concept before it became too entrenched in ethological thinking and caused real damage to the advancement of our ideas about the way the brain worked in real life.

We had christened this plumbing analogy 'psycho-hydraulics', and I decided that we would construct a vast psycho-hydraulic machine which we would unveil on the last evening of the conference. With the help of several friends, I began to collect a mass of outlandish equipment and we assembled it in secret in one of the laboratories. While all the conference delegates were at their final dinner, we laboured feverishly to transport it into the main lecture hall, where it was covered by an enormous tarpaulin, acting as a curtain.

Niko had announced that there would be a final, farewell lecture by a Dr Fink, but had made no mention of the nature of this talk. The delegates all filed in and sat, rather puzzled, in front of the bulging tarpaulin. I delivered a totally incomprehensible speech about the Fink, Fink and Smith Psycho-hydraulic theory and the tarpaulin was then lowered to reveal our monster machine.

It was designed to demonstrate every popular ethological principle then in vogue, and to do it by means of coloured liquids. I cannot now recall every detail, but I do remember a row of very large balloons which slowly filled with coloured water until they dangled obscenely, high over the front row of senior delegates.

Seated beneath an umbrella, at a steering wheel on top of one end of the machine, I yelled to the second Dr Fink (Aubrey Manning, now Professor of Zoology at Edinburgh University) to switch off the water supply. The body of the machine contained such a mass of taps and tubes, all bubbling away with streams of coloured liquids as in the best horror movies, that he was clearly having trouble stemming the flow. 'Fink, Fink!' I shouted. 'I am finking,' was his memorable reply. I was now becoming alarmed because the balloons were assuming monumental proportions and, as they were representing the reproductive organs of the machine and were about to be fertilized by giant sperm, I was terrified about the effect this was going to have on the distinguished front row.

'Fire the sperm!' I bellowed to our accomplice who was crouched at the back of the lecture hall. There were almost invisible threads stretched out over the heads of the audience and down these threads the gigantic mock sperm sped unerringly towards their goal, exploding the balloons and drenching at least the first three rows. Smith appeared at this point carrying a complete lavatory with its tank, to demand a return to the simpler model, and our demonstration came to a soggy if triumphant end. They don't make ethology conferences like that any more and, for the front rows at least, it must be a great relief.

The following day, with the delegates departed, Niko insisted on photographing the somewhat skeletal remains of the giant machine. Aubrey Manning was in the field with his bumble-bees, but David Blest (alias Smith) and I did our best to reconstitute it from the wreckage and it was duly recorded for posterity. I was relieved that Niko was still able to see the joke. I had feared that he might have felt we had slightly over-stepped the mark in our attempt to provide an amusing conclusion to the important conference. But there was not a trace of criticism as he busied himself with his camera. Like Konrad, who had roared with laughter during the demonstration, Niko had a rich sense of humour. Despite the fact that both men promoted ethology with an almost evangelical fervour, neither suffered from the curse of undue solemnity.

Niko's personality, I was beginning to discover, was far more complex than I had at first supposed. His extreme modesty, of which Peter Medawar had spoken, was balanced by a steel-hard determination to further his research ideas. When I taxed him about his modesty, he shrugged it off as 'necessary caution' appropriate to a scientist and insisted that he also had a streak of arrogance. But this arrogance seldom surfaced, except in his firm conviction that many zoologists were poor observers and ignored the need to study an animal in its natural environment. Many farmers and hunters, he claimed, were better zoologists than the armchair professionals who never got their hands dirty or their boots muddy. As a zoology student in Holland he had often been the despair of his professor because of his lack of interest in the traditional dissections and laboratory routines. At every opportunity, he was off into the Dutch countryside, to the canals, the lakes and the sand dunes, and even when not engaged in natural history pursuits, he was out of doors playing hockey, pole-vaulting, or skating. When he married, he took his young bride, Lies, on a field trip to the Arctic for her honeymoon, to live among the Eskimos of Greenland. A more rugged honeymoon it is hard to imagine, but Lies was well aware of the kind of man she was marrying and took it all in her stride, even when she nearly drowned upside down in an Eskimo canoe.

When the Nazis invaded Holland the Tinbergens already had a family of small children and Niko himself was by now a professor at Leiden University. One of the first acts of the invaders was to remove all the Jewish academics from the Dutch universities. Niko, along with many other professors, refused to teach unless these Jews were restored to their rightful places. The immediate result of this was that Niko and the other protestors were thrown into a Nazi concentration camp. Whenever the Dutch underground killed a German, a batch of professors was taken out and shot in reprisal. Konrad Lorenz, in Germany, learned of his friend's plight and offered to intervene on his behalf, but Niko refused, thus being put in the extraordinary position of being a voluntary inmate of a concentration camp. Such was his strength of character, that he actually wrote a book for his children while under these horrifying circumstances. He was only allowed to send a one-page letter home each week and, as he had no news worth telling, he made each letter into one page of the book. It was called *The Tale of John Stickle*, and told the life story of his favourite sticklebacks. An English edition of the story was published by Methuen in 1954 and, because of its extraordinary history, I value my inscribed copy of it as highly as any of Niko's more important scientific works.

After the war, Niko found it hard to visit Germany again, but when he and Konrad met up once more, in England, their old friendship quickly re-established itself and together, in the post-war years, they took ethology on to higher and higher levels of success, culminating with their joint triumph in 1973 when (along with Karl von Frisch) they were awarded the Nobel Prize for their achievements. This award brought Niko's modesty to the surface again. He was surprised to find himself chosen for such a high honour but was delighted 'for ethology', because it gave recognition to the scientific discipline that he had struggled so hard to foster.

An interesting sidelight on the Nobel award was that it gave Niko's mother a unique distinction, making her the only woman in history ever to give birth to two Nobel Prize winners, since Niko's brother Jan (a famous Dutch economist) had already become a Nobel Laureate some years earlier. This is a maternal feat which should surely be in the *Guinness Book of Records*.

Niko's combination of cheerful, boyish enthusiasm and total dedication worked wonders with those of us who were fortunate enough to be his students in those early Oxford days, in the 1950s.

It even started to rub off on Ramona, who suddenly developed an unexpected passion for the common carrion crow. It all began one spring afternoon when I arrived home from the department of zoology with a young crow that had been prematurely introduced to the art of flying by a woodman's axe. The axe had chopped down the tree in which the bird's nest had been situated and the nestling had somehow managed to flutter to the ground, where it was found wandering about in a garden. It had been taken to the zoology department where I had found it housed in a rabbit cage awaiting a helpful owner. Since it was begging hungrily for food, I decided that it would stand a good chance of arousing Ramona's maternal feelings, so I popped it in a box and headed home.

As she recorded later: 'I was reclining peacefully in a deck-chair on the lawn when I saw him approaching, carrying a large cardboard box. On his face was a special smile which I knew too well. It was an attempt to convince me that I would be delighted with what he was bringing me … Placing the box ceremoniously on the ground, he stood back and waited while I opened the lid. The first vision I had was of a large, gaping, pink mouth. Surrounding this mouth, but completely dominated by it, was a black body which eventually stumbled on to the lawn and tottered uncertainly off towards a flower-bed.' Ramona claimed that I tried to pass the bird off as a fledgling, simply because it had flown when its tree had been chopped down, when in reality it was no more than a nestling and was going to mean weeks of hand-feeding and endless trouble. She was quite right, of course. I knew that once she had become involved with the wretched bird's plight, she would do anything for it, but I also knew that she was wary of undertaking long-term rearing tasks, which so often end in disaster. But before long, the infantile signals of the squawking bird had worked their magic and Ramona was busily cramming minced meat down its ever-open throat. This she continued to do, every few hours for several weeks, until, now a proud crow-mother, she took her clumsy offspring out for its first flying lessons. She had trained the bird 'to arm' like a falcon, and could be seen stumping about talking to it like some apprentice witch, every so often flinging her arm into the air and watching anxiously as the heavy bundle of black feathers zoomed crazily down to the earth, making a three-point landing with its beak stuck in the ground. After countless, patient sessions she was rewarded by the sight of strongly flapping wings and her offspring disappearing over a whole series of garden fences to crash-land in an immaculate flower-bed belonging to a bird-hating neighbour.

But true flight was at hand and her long weeks of maternal devotion were shortly to be rewarded. Two months after the crow's arrival there was a terrible storm and the garden shed where it lived was buffeted all night. In the morning we found the door of the shed torn from its hinges. The crow had departed and was never seen again. Ramona consoled herself that she had, at least, given it a fair chance of survival whereas before it had had none. But in the process she had become deeply attached to crows and angered by the cruel treatment which they received from almost everyone who encountered them. She pointed out that for every misdeed, they performed a good deed, as far as the farmer or gardener were concerned. For every object of value they ate, they devoured a whole collection of harmful insects and other pests. But nobody gave them any credit for this. She also claimed (rightly, I think) that they are the most intelligent of all birds, and became determined to pursue her crow studies further.

Her opportunity came when I spotted a large black form sitting on a garden fence not far from our house. At first I was convinced that it must be her original crow returned, but it emerged that this was a tame bird that had originally belonged to a group of school-children in a nearby village, until it was attacked and bitten by the vicar's dog. With a crippled wing it had stumbled off, leaving the village for good, and was now terrorizing the local gardeners. Despite its poor flight, it proved extremely hard to catch. In the end I had to employ a special net-trap. Bait was placed on a lawn and then, as it approached, I pulled a cord and the net flew up and over the startled crow.

We decided to build a large aviary for it in the garden, but while this was being done, the bird would have to go into a big cage on top of the zoology department. Once our own enclosure was ready, we went to catch it up, but to our horror it flew out through the door of the cage and up into a tall tree. There it was brutally attacked by two crows who considered all trees near the department as their personal territory. We did our best to drive them away, but when darkness came we had to abandon our efforts. The next morning the tame crow was gone and we were left with a brand new aviary that was suddenly rather point-less.

Ramona was so upset by the loss that I decided to try and find a replacement for her. I went over to the Ornithology Institute to ask for their help in locating one. As I entered, and before I had spoken, a girl asked me if I had come about the bird. When I looked puzzled, she explained that the crow had already been sent over to the zoology department for me. There seemed to be some sort of telepathy at work, because I had yet to mention the reason for my visit. It turned out that that very afternoon a starving crow had been brought in and, because it was known that we kept crows, someone had kindly taken it round to my room for me. I imagined that it must be Ramona's first crow or, more likely her second one, but when I looked at it I saw that it was neither. It was a most unusual bird, having white wings that contrasted strikingly with the black of the rest of its plumage. It was a common crow, however, and not some exotic species that had escaped from captivity. Being a black-and-white mutant, it had probably been attacked by other crows and driven away to fend for itself at a stage where it still needed to be fed by its parents. It was pitifully thin and I hurried it back to an eagerly maternal Ramona who proudly installed it in the waiting aviary. After days of cramming food down its throat, she had just restored it to a suitable corvine plumpness when her second crow reappeared on the scene. It had been caught by one of Niko's ethology students in the centre of Oxford, where it was being tormented by a large group of children. Now there were two crows in the aviary and she was able to study their reaction to one another

which, despite some initial threat displays, was soon reasonably
amicable.

And so began Ramona's study of crow behaviour—their calls
and postures, their food-dunking and hoarding activities, their
water-bathing routines and their sun-bathing. The strangest
moment came when we heard someone talking in a very cultured
voice at the bottom of the garden. We rushed out to see who it
was, but nobody was there. It happened again and again until,
one night, she discovered that it was her second crow who was
doing the talking, speaking in a perfect human voice that would
have put any parrot to shame. 'Go away, go away!' it would
shout at no one in particular. We decided that during its sojourn
in Oxford it had repeatedly heard these words spoken as it
invaded the gardens of Oxford dons, in search of food. Hence its
cultured, Oxford accent.

There was something charmingly bizarre about owning a crow
with an Oxford accent and Ramona went to great pains to teach
it more words. It used to mutter under its breath when she went
to feed it and, little by little, she trained this muttering into words
of greeting. The strange thing about its talking was that, as it
uttered its beautifully articulated words, it threw back its head
and closed its eyes. It did not close them in the usual way, by
bringing the upper and lower lids together, but instead flicked
across its nictitating membrane—its pale-coloured, third eyelid.
This gave it the strange look of a suddenly blind crow and for
some reason it was only in this curious, neck-stretched posture
that it would deliver its verbal messages.

Eventually, when we left Oxford and moved to the London
Zoo, we took our old talker with us. The black-and-white bird
was never fully tame and was now strong enough and mature
enough to fend for itself in the trees near our Oxford home,
where we released it before our departure. The older bird, with
its crippled wing, was never going to be a really good flyer, we
thought, and so we kept it at the zoo in a spare aviary, behind
the scenes, until one day it escaped yet again and took off into
Regent's Park where, for years afterwards, it would startle sun-

bathers in the park by hopping down on to the grass and saying in perfect Oxford tones, 'Hallo, old boy', or 'Go away, go away', as the mood took it. There was always plenty to eat and its powers of flight seemed to be much greater than before, so we made no attempt to pursue it and it lived out a long life in the centre of the great city, where there were no country-folk with their traditional crow-hatred to persecute it.

Ramona's involvement with her crows had brought her much closer to the zoological world, and she helped me more and more with my investigations into animal behaviour. I had completed my stickleback thesis and gained my doctoral status, but I was not yet ready to leave my Oxford 'nest'. There were many new problems I wanted to tackle and I was allowed to construct a whole series of aviaries on the roof of the department. In these I installed large colonies of small finches and began a lengthy, post-doctoral research project, analysing their social behaviour.

My main interest in this work was to study the behaviour of many closely related species and to use behaviour differences as a key to understanding the evolution of the whole finch family. It was an arduous process involving many long hours of observation crouched at tiny viewing slits that overlooked the aviary enclosures. The birds were too shy to permit open viewing and there were times when I thought I would never be able to unbend my body again. But there were several side-benefits from this research. As often happens, the most intriguing discoveries come, not from the central plan of a project, but from lucky accidents that happen along the way – the serendipity principle.

It was just such an accident that led to the unexpected possibility of studying 'divorce' proceedings among birds. The birds in question were zebra finches – delightful little multi-coloured birds from Australia which have recently become very popular among aviculturists. I was breeding these birds in my aviaries and writing a paper on their reproductive behaviour. Being a pair-forming species, I kept them in pairs in separate aviaries, but some of the aviaries had partition doors, so that I could open them up to make double-sized enclosures. In one such double-aviary I had a successful, parental pair on the left and an unsuccessful pair on the right. The parental pair had managed to rear four chicks to independence. The other couple had merely produced a messy nest and gone no further. I took away the 'bad' female to try her with another male elsewhere, leaving her mate alone in his aviary, eyeing the parental pair next door. Then, on a whim, I opened the partition door to see what effect a 'triangle' of adults would have on their relationships.

To make the description easier to follow, I will call the three birds the husband, the wife, and the lover. The lover, who was now badly in need of a female, was a fine young bird with sleek, silky smooth feathers. The husband was a ragged, dishevelled old bird. The wife was a plump, active little thing who clearly had great bird-appeal. With this cast, the drama was not long in coming.

The lover, seeing the open door to the adjoining cage, wasted no time in hopping through it and made straight for the wife, offering her his most vigorous courtship display. She promptly attacked him and drove him away. Her faithfulness to her husband became intense to the point of savagery roughly four hours later. She had just gone into her nest (a ball-shaped affair with an internal chamber) and was usually followed, when she did this, by her fledglings. On this occasion, however, the lover shot in after her, scattering the fledglings as he went. For a moment it looked as though the nest would explode, then a whirling, feathered bundle emerged from the nest-hole and fell to the floor. It was the wife and the lover locked in battle. When the lover escaped, he did so at the cost of a large bunch of his fine feathers, which the triumphant wife still held in her beak. This encouraged the decrepit old husband to launch an attack, while the going was good, and he proceeded to chase the plucked lover from branch to branch in a frenzy of pecking.

I expected to see the lover retreat to the safety of his own aviary, but to my surprise he was determined to stand his ground and, with both members of the pair still harassing him, he cowered in the top far corner of their enclosure. He held his ground there

and bided his time. He was still there the next day and was making
mild attacks on the fledglings. When the wife called her offspring
to her nest, the lover mixed in with the group and tried to get in
with them, but she quickly spotted him and threw him out again.
At this point the wife did something strange. She flew over to
her husband and approached him assertively. The ragged old
male then gave the *female* display inviting copulation and his
wife promptly mounted him like a male and mated with him.
Her aggressive treatment of the intruding male seemed to have
given her the upper hand in her relationship with her own male,
and she expressed her upper hand by being the upper body in the
mating act. In so doing she had relegated her poor old husband
to the subordinate female role and this was the start of his undoing.

A few days later, the husband tried to reassert himself and pursued his wife with the full zebra finch male courtship display,
inviting copulation. She ignored his advances and hopped in
amongst her fledglings. When she finally managed to avoid him
and flew off to another part of the enclosure, his reaction was to
try and mount one of his own offspring, regardless of the fact
that the fledglings were still in their juvenile plumage. Desperation
appeared to be setting in. His courtship singing brought the lover
darting in from his own aviary, where he had temporarily
retreated. To my astonishment, the husband's response to the
intruder was not to attack him, as before, but instead to crouch
down in the full juvenile begging posture, with gaping beak and
waving head. The lover appeared somewhat taken aback by this
infantile behaviour, but then ignored the pathetic husband and
started to court his wife with great verve and vigour. When he
did this, the husband flew up, pushed himself between them, and
started begging at the lover again. It was hard not to see this as the
dejected husband begging the strident young lover not to court
his wife.

The wife was now clearly entering a stage of divided loyalties.
She still had a bond with her broken-down old husband and yet
she had stopped attacking the young lover. When she moved
over to sit next to her husband on a branch and started preening

his head feathers, as mated birds will, the lover sidled up to her and began preening *her* head feathers, from the other side, at the same time. After a while, she gave up nuzzling her husband and turned round and began to preen the young lover's head instead. The husband promptly gave up and went to sleep.

Later that afternoon, the lover tried courting the wife again, but without success. In his frustration he launched a savage attack both on the husband and the young fledglings. He was now able to beat the husband, who was looking increasingly dishevelled and dejected. Even his wife was no longer interested in him and pecked him when he came close to her. Seeing this, the lover rushed over and performed the special pair-formation display of the zebra finch. He then flew off and entered the old nest belonging to the original pair and the wife followed him into it. Inside, instead of the ball of fury that had formed on his first intrusion, there was the sound of soft tweeting and cheeping. A new pair was being formed.

Nine days after the first arrival of the lover, the struggle was over. The wife had a new husband and her old mate was now attacked and beaten by both of them. She now gave the full invitation display to her new spouse and they were mating repeatedly. The new husband occasionally attacked and drove away her offspring by her old husband, but she never joined in on these assaults. The fledglings were almost adult by now and fending for themselves. The old parental nest was now the love-nest of the newly formed pair. The wretched old male who had been displaced still occasionally hopped up and begged at the new husband when he started courting the wife, but he was largely ignored. Finally, he gave up and moved away altogether, and the new husband set about building a fine new nest for his wife, in which they started a new breeding cycle.

Later on, I saw a similar divorce sequence in which the triangle consisted of a male and two females. The details were much the same. I could not help thinking of Konrad Lorenz's joke about 'geese are only human' – referring to the imperfections in their pair-bonds. I have told the story of the bird divorce at some length because it does have an important implication for human behaviour. When I wrote *The Naked Ape* in the late 1960s and took a long hard look at the human species, as if I was studying one of my birds or fish, I was forced to the conclusion that man is a pair-bonding species. Some authorities disagreed with me, preferring the view that pairing in man is a cultural device, rather than a basic biological feature of our species. One of their main arguments was the high failure rate of marriages, and the commonplace occurrence of adultery and divorce. How different, they said, from the lifelong pairing of birds, with their utterly faithful devotion to their mates. How stupid to compare the rigid pair-bonding of other animals with the hazardous relationship involved in human marriage. But I had studied the pair-bonds of other species and they had not. Theirs was a fairy-tale view of the animal world, and if they compared *that* with human relations they were naturally going to come to the wrong conclusion. The truth is that the pair-bond is always a vulnerable state and there are few basic differences between the pairing of two birds and two humans. If Konrad's geese were 'only human', I could also argue that, where pairing is concerned, people are 'only zebra finches'. In both cases, the function of pair formation is essentially the same – the combined effort of the pair ensuring the successful rearing of the young. Wherever you see a heavy parental burden for a species, there you are likely to find the male and female staying close together and helping one another out. And nowhere in the animal kingdom is there a heavier parental burden than in our own species.

Another lucky accident led me into the intriguing world of 'supernormal' stimuli. In his field experiments with gulls, Niko had found that he could improve on nature. The young gull chicks pecked at a red spot on their parent's bill when they were begging for food. The bill of a herring gull is bright yellow, with just one vivid red spot near its tip. This spot acts as a stimulus to the nestlings and when they peck at that region, the parent bird responds by regurgitating fish, which the young birds then gobble up greedily. Niko discovered that he could make a simple cardboard model of a gull's bill and if he offered it to young chicks, they would peck at this just as vigorously.

On one of his cardboard bills he decided to see what would happen if he painted three red spots instead of one and, to his surprise, found that the young birds responded to this model even more keenly than to the real thing. He had made a supernormal bill.

Human civilization is full of such tricks. We are constantly supernormalizing ourselves and our objects to make them more attractive. But I had often wondered whether it would be possible to demonstrate a supernormal stimulus occurring in nature, without human intervention. If the red breast of a robin was a valuable threat display, then was there, perhaps, a super-redbreast somewhere, scaring the daylights out of every rival in sight? The obvious answer was *no*, because every animal is a system of compromises. If that system is unbalanced, then one aspect of survival suffers. The robin that gets *too* red becomes too conspicuous and runs the risk of attracting predators. Over thousands of generations, each species arrives at the best survival compromise for its particular way of life. And that is the way it stays until there is a major shift in its environmental condition.

So it was stupid of me to look for natural supernormal signals. Or was it? In an old natural history book I came across an extraordinary photograph of a small bird feeding some carp. The bird had its beak stuffed full of insects it had obviously been collecting for its nestlings. No doubt it had been catching some of the juiciest of these at the water's edge. But there in the pond were some huge, tame carp which had been conditioned to come up to the surface when they saw any movement and gape their great mouths out of the water in anticipation of tidbits. The small bird was programmed to respond to the large gaping mouths of its nestlings by ramming food down them as hard and as often as possible. Seeing these supernormal gapes at the edge of the pond, the poor creature had no choice but to stuff its painstakingly collected food hoard down them as fast as possible. The gapes were so big that they proved irresistible.

I had to admit that this situation was only 'semi-natural', in that man's hand had been involved indirectly, in taming the fish in the first place. But, at least, no human intervention was occurring at the moment of the interaction in the photograph. It was just such a semi-natural example of supernormal stimulation that I was about to discover on the roof of the zoology department. The accident that led to it was an unpleasant one. An owl had been swooping down on the wire of the largest of the roof aviaries, in the night, and panicking the inmates. When they panicked, they flew wildly about and ended up clinging to the wire. There the owl grabbed at them and tried unsuccessfully to pull them through. Mortally wounded they dropped to the floor, where I discovered them the next day. I had no proof that this was happening, beyond the damaged corpses I found on several mornings, so I determined to keep watch on the aviary the next night. There was a small wooden 'hide' at one end and I settled down in this at dusk, to await events and, hopefully, to devise a way of preventing them. (A stuffed owl to frighten off the real attacker seemed to be the answer.) What I did in fact see diverted me from my original task and set me a fascinating new problem.

In the aviary there was a mixture of species, including some beautifully coloured necklace doves and some rather gaudy little Java sparrows. The doves were much larger and plumper than the little sparrows and even in the half-light it was easy to distinguish between them. The birds were settling down for the night's sleep and a pair of the doves were roosting next to one another, on a branch quite near to me. They appeared to have hiccups, their rounded bodies jerking up and down from time to time, and I peered closer to see if they were ill. As I did so, I made a slight noise. To my astonishment, I saw the startled head of a Java sparrow emerge from the chest plumage of each of the doves. The small heads looked around to see what had made the noise and then withdrew again and disappeared.

Perhaps I needed a rest. I had been looking at birds for hour after hour, week after week, and was obviously beginning to have hallucinations. Worse was to come. Another dove, roosting alone on another branch, was also crouched down and fluffed out ready for the night's slumber. As I watched, I saw with disbelieving eyes a Java sparrow approach it and then start to play leapfrog over its back. It hopped up, sat at right-angles across the dove's back, then hopped off the other side. Then back again, and so on, several more times. The dove looked faintly put out by this extraordinary behaviour, but was not sufficiently irritated to move from its roosting position. Then the little sparrow did something even stranger. It flew down underneath the dove and suddenly thrust itself up between the bigger bird's legs. At this, the dove did stir itself, stretching its legs and squinting down at the small object trying to squeeze itself into position between its feet. Pushing and struggling, the sparrow finally achieved its goal and crouched down on the branch, as if satisfied at last. The dove still did not move away. Instead, treating the small invader of its privacy as if it were an egg to be incubated, it settled itself slowly down on top of the contented sparrow, which disappeared almost completely from view.

On yet another branch, I caught sight of a dove being preened by a Java sparrow that was clumped tightly to one side of it. After a while they both closed their eyes and fell asleep, cosily pushed up against one another. A few minutes later, another Java sparrow arrived and tried to join them, but the first sparrow quickly woke up and attacked the newcomer, driving it away with sharp pecks.

I was so puzzled by what I had seen that I spent many nights watching this curious roosting activity and gradually began to understand what was happening. A valuable clue came when I was looking at some of my other birds and noticed that if one of them was sick, it sat with fluffed-out feathers and crouched low on its perch, while its companions were sleek and active. If there were two species of finch housed together, they normally only clumped with their own kind when roosting, but when there was a sick bird present I saw that it might be 'clumped with' by a bird of the wrong species. In other words, a fluffed-out bird of the wrong species was more attractive as a sleeping partner than a sleek bird of your own species. This meant that the fluffed-out rounded shape of the sick bird was such a powerful invitation signal, saying 'Come and sleep with me', that it could even over-power the 'species signal' that said 'I belong to a different kind of finch'. And in a bizarre way, this was what seemed to be happening with the Java sparrows and the doves.

Despite the fact that the doves were so much bigger, their fluffed-out, rounded shape appeared to be an irresistible signal to the small birds. Even when they were not asleep, the doves were much more rounded in body-outline, and when they added fluffing to their already plump shape, they presented a super-normal stimulus to the smaller birds. If roundedness meant 'Come sleep with me', then the doves' super-roundedness meant COME SLEEP WITH ME! And the little sparrows were compelled to obey this signal even if it meant ignoring the fact that they were clumping with a totally alien species.

The small finches of the family to which the Java sparrows belong are highly sociable birds and often roost in dense clumps, piling into a roosting hole together, or sitting in a long row on a branch. The most favoured position is in the centre of the clump, where it is warmest, and whoever happens to be the unlucky bird at the end of a row will eventually become dissatisfied and try to improve its placing. It does this by hopping along the backs of the others and then pushing itself down into the middle of the row. After a little pushing and squeaking, peace then reigns again. This is apparently what was happening when the Java sparrow was playing leapfrog over the dove's back. The dove was so big that the sparrow must have looked upon it as a 'row' of sleeping companions, with itself at the end of the 'row'. Leaping on the back of the dove, it tried to find the middle of the row, but with-out success. The dove's broad back refused to part in two and let the sparrow in. After futile attempts, leapfrogging back and forth, the persistence of the sparrow led it to try an assault from below. This ingenuity was rewarded by finding a place between the bigger bird's legs. At last the ingenious clumper was there — in the favoured central position — and could settle down for the night.

These unexpected observations started me asking questions about the whole range of possible 'feather signals' that one bird could send to another, and I began to explore the evolution of the many strange feather exaggerations that exist in the bird world, from crests and ruffs to 'beards' and throat-plumes. It dawned on me that, since the postures of the feathers were basically concerned with temperature control—sleek when active, fluffed when cold or resting, ruffled when sun-bathing—there was a way in which the many feather displays of birds could be explained, in evolutionary terms. When birds display, they are usually in a state of great excitement—courting, fighting, pairing, defending—and I remembered the phrase 'I went hot and cold all over', used to describe a state of human shock. If birds were in a tense condition during moments of sexual or aggressive drama, then they, too, would be undergoing strange sensations of heat and cold, as their autonomic systems suffered temporary upheaval. They could not break out in a cold sweat, go red in the face with pent-up anger, or blush with embarrassment, but they could do the avian equivalent. That equivalent would be the sudden raising and lowering of their feathers, as their temperature control went haywire under the stress of the moment. In a simple form this would lead to sudden puffing out or sleeking of the feathers, but in more advanced cases, where evolutionary specialization had begun, it could mean that only part of the plumage would react in this way. In this manner, it was possible to envisage the development of increasingly bizarre forms of feather display, with huge erectile crests evolving, and all the many other glorious elaborations of plumage that have enchanted human artists for hundreds of years.

I wrote a long paper on 'autonomic signals' and began to look deeper into the whole question of the origin of courtship displays, bringing more and more species of birds and fish into my aviaries and aquaria. Pheasants and cardinals, bullheads and cichlids, sunfish and swordtails, were all added to my growing menagerie. I wanted to be able to generalize when making statements and, despite his misgivings at the way I was spreading my range of

interests, Niko continued to give me encouragement and did
nothing to stop me turning the zoology department into a minor
zoo. Alister Hardy, the head of the department, was also sympathetic and seemed delighted that the place was coming alive
with animals. He dropped in to my basement aquarium-room
one day and said that we had an important visitor coming to see
us and as I had the biggest collection of fish he would like to make
my laboratory a feature of the guided tour he was planning.

I was rather horrified at this suggestion because the room was in
such a mess. I had been spending so much time up on the roof
with my birds that some of the tanks were badly neglected. I
asked whether the aviaries might be more suitable for the mysterious visitor, but Alister explained that our guest's father was a
marine biologist and fish were therefore at the top of his list.

'Who is his father?' I asked. 'Do I know him?'

'Ah, yes, well ... ' Alister was obviously hesitant about reveal-
ing the guest's identity. 'It's rather hush-hush, you see. Security,
and all that. But since you ask, his father is the Emperor of Japan.'

Although it was some years since the war had ended, it appeared
that the Foreign Office was still concerned about the safety of the
Emperor's son, Prince Akihito, who was making the first foreign
visit by Japanese royalty following the cessation of hostilities. The
country was full of ex-prisoners-of-war whose memories of
Japanese camp brutalities remained all too vivid. It was known
that at least three such victims were now working in the science
departments at Oxford and there were fears of an anti-Japanese
demonstration, or possibly something worse.

I did my best to clean up the aquarium room, filling empty
tanks with fresh water and planting new vegetation, but time
was against me and when the prince arrived in the department I
still had one large tank that was empty except for a thick layer of
stinking filthy mud. I thought if I stood in front of this tank it
might go unnoticed.

The door swung open and Alister Hardy ushered in the prince,
a small, composed figure who seemed somewhat bemused at
being brought down into the dank dungeons of the department.

Clustered around him was his protective entourage and a bevy of interpreters. Close behind came a phalanx of university officials and hard on their heels was a group of slender, elegant young men with tightly rolled umbrellas, representing the Foreign Office. Behind them came a rearguard of huge, broad-shouldered men with straight backs, big feet and ominously bulging jackets. Wave upon wave, this variegated crowd edged and squeezed itself into my cluttered laboratory in which almost all available space was already taken up by nearly a hundred aquarium tanks. There was scarcely room for a dozen people to stand between the tanks with comfort and to my alarm I realized that altogether there were between forty and fifty of them. The crush slowly increased until I found myself, nose to nose with the prince, pressed tightly up against one of the tanks. There was no hope of moving along the rows of tanks to show him the many different kinds of fish they housed. It was clear that all I could do was gently rotate myself so that I could talk about the one tank that was within our reach. I indicated my intention with my hand and the prince and I edged our way round to face its glass front. The interpreters strained forward for the exchange of golden words and a hush fell over the packed mass of bodies. Only the bubbling of the dozens of aerators could be heard. I peered intently into the tank and the prince peered intently alongside me.

It was inevitable, of course, that this was the one tank out of my whole collection that was empty. It was the one with nothing in it except a thick layer of black and brown, stinking mud. I stared at it stupidly, wondering how on earth I could present it as representing the nerve-centre of Oxford research. I was obviously expected to make some sort of speech about the mighty strides being made by Oxford science, so that my words of wisdom could be relayed back to the Royal Palace in Tokyo. I cleared my throat but no words came. My mind was going as blank as the horrible tank. Eventually there was a high-pitched, nasal exchange between the prince and his interpreters, one of whom thrust his head in by my cramped elbow and intoned:

'Prince Akihito asks hhot is hhappening in hhis tonk.'

'In this tank,' I heard myself reply, in lofty tones, 'we are maturing the substratum.' My words were duly translated with great urgency and emphasis. The prince nodded wisely and breathed out a nasal noise of respectful wonder. There was then a further exchange of rapid Japanese, followed by thwarted attempts at ritual bowing, and the prince turned to face the door. This was a signal for a mass retreat and the whole sardine-tin of crushed bodies went into reverse, peeling off up the stairs in layer after layer, until I was left completely alone, still gazing at my empty tank and wondering what else I could have said. It occurred to me later that the Japanese probably thought the incident was a deliberate piece of devious concealment on our part, to prevent them from discovering our latest research discoveries. Perhaps not, but it was the only consoling thought I could offer myself.

Alister Hardy took it all happily in his stride. A brilliant marine biologist by training, but a Victorian naturalist at heart, he had an endearing weakness for anything colourful or bizarre. The first time I took tea at his house he regaled me with a long and complex story about a stuffed mermaid that brought ill fortune to anyone who possessed it. Owner after owner had inexplicable misfortunes while it was in their hands. 'And now,' he beamed, 'it is in my hands!' And with a melodramatic flourish he produced the odious object from where he had hidden it behind a chair. It was a dark shiny brown in colour and had the face of a desiccated, drought-starved child. Its brittle, mummified body tapered off into a twisted fishy tail. It was the kind of shrivelled cadaver that made one think instantly of witches' covens, black masses, and hideous sacrificial rites. Alister was clearly enjoying the impact the thing made, and pretended for some time that he believed it really was a mermaid, before he eventually admitted that X-rays had revealed it to be the front half of a mummified monkey joined on to the rear half of some large fish.

Alister's fascination with anything to do with the sea led him in later years to consider the possibility that mankind was, in truth, a kind of 'mermaid' species, in the sense that we had gained

1 In 1978, after an absence of thirty years, I paid a nostalgic return
  visit to the family lake in Wiltshire, where my obsession with
  natural history first began.

2 I was always impressed by the way Ramona leapt to the protection
  of any persecuted or despised animal, like this old crow. This
  particular bird surprised her by suddenly starting to talk.

3 My mentor, Niko Tinbergen, in his natural habitat. The maestro of ethology was always more at home among the sand-dunes than in the laboratory.

4 The wreckage of the satirical Fink, Fink and Smith Psycho-hydraulic Machine, photographed by Niko Tinbergen on the morning after its demonstration to the 2nd International Ethological Conference. *Top right*: Me (alias Dr Fink) hiding behind a false moustache. *Bottom left*: David Blest (alias Lavatory Smith).

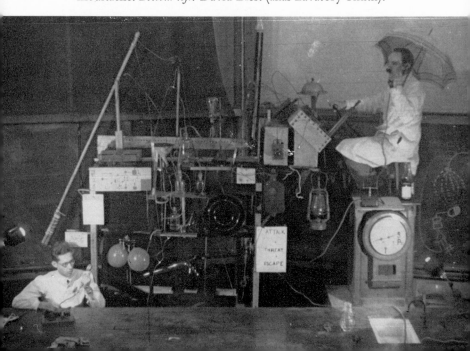

many of our modern characteristics as a result of having passed through a semi-aquatic stage, somewhere between five and ten million years ago. Such an evolutionary transition, coming between our early arboreal phase and our later, ground-living, hunting phase, would help to explain our naked skin, our sub-cutaneous fat layers, our remnant hair patterns, our large, flat hands with sensitive fingers and many other unique human anatomical features. When he published this theory, following a talk to a sub-aqua club, it produced immediate controversy and earned him a stern rebuke from his old friend, the great anatomist Le Gros Clark, who rang him up and pleaded with him to abandon the idea, exclaiming: 'Alister, Alister, think of your reputation!' This only slightly subdued his enthusiasm, because, try as he might, he could think of no good argument against his theory. His great quality was (and is— for in his mid-eighties he still has the fresh, open mind of a twenty-year-old) an ability to relish the outlandish that marks the brain of a true explorer. The scientist in him brings caution to bear at a certain point, but not too soon— not before he has had time to savour and consider some new thought and give it the chance to breathe a little. All too often today, research scientists clamp down too soon with an iron self-censorship that stifles rebellious ideas at birth. The result is safe, respectable and often rather boring research that fails to explore new directions, and sometimes does little more than prove the obvious. Rebel spirits like Louis Leakey and Alister Hardy are sadly becoming a rare and vanishing species in the scientific world, and it is the poorer for this change.

But Alister's plunge into the world of aquatic man was still some way off in the future. At the time of my first tea-party with him he was more obsessed with certain insect problems. For some reason he had been arguing with the famous entomologist, E. B. Ford (Henry to his friends), about the height at which moths flew in the night air. Only Alister would have conceived the practical solution to this problem and then have actually carried it out. He managed to persuade the fastidious Henry to ascend with him at night, in the small basket of a barrage balloon, armed with butter-

D

fly nets. The two eminent scientists were seen disappearing into the dark heavens, sweeping wildly with their nets at increasing heights and scoring their success at each air level until finally their argument – whatever it was – had been settled.

Henry himself was another of the Oxford zoology department's great eccentrics who, like Alister, would have been more at home in the Victorian era. A geneticist of world repute, his lectures had become something of an Oxford legend, largely because of his refusal to recognize the presence of female undergraduates. His attitude towards women would make today's male chauvinist pigs seem like rabid feminists. His crisis came during the war years, when more and more young men were called up and the proportion of female students at Oxford rose dramatically. No matter how many women were present at his lectures, he steadfastly ignored them, beginning each talk with the word 'Gentlemen ... ' Eventually the masculine element was so depleted that he was horror-struck to discover his audience consisting entirely of women, with the exception of a single lonely male. Taking a deep breath, he began his lecture with the word: 'Gentleman ... ' At last, even that solitary male disappeared from the scene and he was faced with the ultimate horror – an audience composed solely of women. Scanning the lecture hall and blinking his forlorn, bespectacled eyes, he announced in ringing tones: 'As no one has turned up for my lecture today, it is cancelled', and swept out.

He was the master of the cutting remark and was once overheard to say of his old friend and teacher, Julian Huxley: 'The trouble with dear Julian is that he confuses the weight of a volume with its avoirdupois.' He disapproved of any form of popularization of his science and frowned upon that part of Julian's complex character that drove him to seek a wider audience for biological discoveries and ideas. Julian himself would probably have chuckled over the insult, had anyone dared to tell him of it. He was well aware that his popularizing had made him enemies, but he had no regrets on that score. And personally I was entirely on his side. I had particular admiration for the fact that Julian had been the first professional biologist who had dared to break scientific etiquette by launching himself into the modern mass media. Films, radio, television, paperbacks, magazines were all enlisted to help spread the evolutionary ideas he promoted so passionately. He started the children's zoo at Regent's Park, which has been copied all over the world, and had the newsreel cameras there to record the day he opened it. He was a founder member of the B.B.C. Brains Trust and even persuaded his brother Aldous to join in on occasion. He was prepared to write an article for *Penthouse* with the same eagerness that he would approach a learned journal. And he pioneered natural history filming, bringing in a young John Grierson (later to become the doyen of documentary film-makers) as his cameraman. His film of the life history of the gannet won him the film world's top award, and he once said to me: 'You know, I am the only Fellow of the Royal Society ever to win a Hollywood Oscar.' When I asked him if I could see it, he brushed my request aside, muttering: 'I don't know where it is. Filthy, ugly thing, it's upstairs somewhere.' But even if the aesthetic quality of the statuette displeased him, the gaining of the award certainly did not, and he was particularly delighted that Walt Disney was inspired by his early film work to produce, some years later, a long series of 'true life adventure' films, which reached possibly the widest audience ever in the history of popular natural history.

I had sent Julian copies of my early papers and he was quick to visit me at Oxford to learn of the new work that was being done on the subject of animal courtship, one of his favourite topics. Back in 1914 he had written an immensely influential paper on 'The Courtship Habits of the Great Crested Grebe' in which he had introduced the idea of 'ritualization'—the process by which animal movements became transformed into 'symbolic' ceremonies. Konrad Lorenz rated it as a landmark in the history of modern ethology and looked upon Huxley as one of the founding fathers of the movement. A few years later I managed to get the two great men together for a lunch at the London Zoo restaurant. In my naïve way I was expecting to spark off a soaring conversation that I would recall with pleasure in the years to come. But I should have remembered my experience with Dylan Thomas and the way he had remained jokily unsoaring. Konrad and Julian spent the first part of the lunch swapping limericks—or so I gathered. I am not sure, because I was called away urgently to take a phone call and returned just in time to hear Julian, head to head with Konrad, intoning: ' … and on her behind, for the sake of the blind, the same thing was written in braille', at which point they both fell about laughing and I was reminded once again of the essentially childlike quality of creative minds.

By contrast, the letters I received from Julian in response to the papers I sent him were always intensely serious and bursting with ideas, and he encouraged me in particular to try and sort out a general theory of animal courtship. He felt the subject needed updating and I was at work on this when Niko asked me if I would do him a favour. He had been invited to attend a luxurious conference in Paris, organized by Pierre Grassé, but wanted me to go in his place. 'There is going to be lavish wining and dining,' he groaned, 'and I couldn't face that.' His frugal eating habits were my good fortune and I assured him that it was he who was doing me the favour. 'You will have to read a paper, of course,' he added as an afterthought, 'but you have your new stuff on courtship ceremonies—that will do well.' And off he went to tell Grassé of the change in personnel.

What I did not realize at the time I agreed was that the conference was a small and very select one, and the twenty delegates were all giants in their field. Grassé had obtained a huge grant of money for the occasion from the Fondation Singer-Polignac (Singer Sewing Machines had married Polignac Brandy) and the delegates were to be housed with their wives in one of the best hotels in Paris. They would confer in a palatial *salon*, and would then be taken on a long gastronomic tour of the whole of France, visiting only the greatest of the French restaurants, with a special banquet prepared at each one. This was definitely not a gathering for junior research workers such as myself. When Niko showed

me the details I realized that Grassé would have to explain
apologetically to him that his invitation was not transferable. But
for some reason Grassé accepted, presumably because he did not
wish to offend Niko, and Ramona and I set off for the conference
of our lives. Nothing before or since it has ever come close.

From the moment we arrived in Paris to the moment we left,
two weeks later, we were in a permanent state of gastronomic
overkill. There were more banquets than speeches—twenty-eight
of the former to twenty of the latter. It reached a point where a
meal of baked beans on toast would have been a relief. I think the
opulence of it would have killed Niko, and he was wise to have
refused.

Only a few individuals had been chosen from each of the parti-
cipating countries and it was daunting to discover that Great
Britain was represented by only two: the august, imposing figure
of J. B. S. Haldane and myself. Haldane was amused that Niko
Tinbergen had sent a junior in his place and he and his young,
second wife, the spiky, shrill-voiced geneticist Helen Spurway,
befriended Ramona and me from the start. Haldane, for some
reason, was at his most outrageous and rebellious, and we provided
the perfect audience for his antics. There were times when I had to
smile weakly at our astonished French hosts and imply in my
smile that not all British scientists were as difficult or eccentric as
the Haldanes.

The trouble began when Haldane insisted on giving his speech
in the host tongue. It was a matter of old world courtesy, he
explained to me, always to speak in the language of your hosts.
Grassé tried to dissuade him, having already suffered from his
excruciating French, and pointed out politely that there was
simultaneous translation available over headphones, for each of
the delegates. Haldane would have none of it. As he started to
speak, the French delegates looked at one another in pained awe,
arched their shoulders briefly in that most delicate of French
shrugs, and promptly donned the headphones that gave the
English translation. Haldane was not amused, but battled bravely
on in French. At one point, in order to explain different theories

of causality, he stunned his hosts by rapidly crumpling up every piece of paper in reach, piling them up on the table and setting fire to them. The flames and smoke were reflected a dozen times in the huge mirrored walls of the rococo *salon* and the vast chandeliers jangled in the sudden upsurge of heated air. Grassé was sweating visibly as Haldane declaimed in French: 'You may say the paper burns because it is combustible, or you may say the paper burns because I lit it with a match, or you may say ... ' but nobody was listening. We were all transfixed by his sheer wildness in those overpoweringly formal surroundings.

Afterwards he and Helen insisted on taking Ramona and me out to see the 'real Paris'. I complained that we had been invited to a private dinner party that evening by one of the French delegates, but Haldane assured us there was plenty of time and swept us off to look for a typical bistro, away from Grassé's formalities. Trailing dutifully along behind him, we came to a busy crossing with Parisian kamikaze drivers hurtling three abreast in both directions.

'As a good ethologist,' boomed Haldane, 'you should know how to get across this street. It is all a matter of making the appropriate display. Most people try to stop oncoming traffic with a frontal display, like this,' and he raised a palm towards the speeding cars as if trying to repel them. 'Wrong!' he thundered. 'That merely foreshortens your display and makes your arm look smaller. What is needed is a *lateral* display, like this,' and he thrust one arm stiffly out in front of him and the other stiffly behind him, at right angles to the traffic. 'Now I look much bigger to them, like an aggressive fish displaying side-on.' And without the slightest hesitation he walked straight out into the road. To our surprise it worked. The drivers screeched and swirled around him, but his determined, stiff-armed walk got him through. We were less courageous and it took us ages to make the same crossing, while Haldane waited triumphantly on the other side. He passed the time by cocking his leg against a lamp-post, imitating the territorial scent-marking of a dominant dog. When I enquired why he had decided to mime a pee on the lamp-post, his explanation was that the post in question happened to be in front of one of Paris's main police stations, and he did not like police. (Several years later, Helen was in trouble in London when she deliberately trod on the tail of a police dog, claiming that England had become a police state. Shortly after, she and Haldane left for India where they made their final home together.)

Finding a suitably grubby bistro, Haldane ordered bottles of wine and I taxed him about his extravagant behaviour since we had arrived in Paris. I could not help feeling that it was partly an act, as if he were consciously parodying himself. He agreed that this might indeed be so.

'You see, my friend the actor Michael Redgrave, whenever he has to portray an old professor figure [Haldane was portly, with a large bald head ringed with white hair, a bristly white moustache and the appearance of having slept in his elderly but expensive suit for several days] he always pays me a visit and sits there watching me – the way I look, the way I dress, the way I move. Then he goes off and does this excellent impersonation of me. It is possible that I myself then tend to imitate his imitation. By the way, did you know that Redgrave has a parrot called Onan?' I admitted that I did not. 'Yes, he calls it Onan because it scatters its seed on the ground,' and Haldane chortled gently into his red wine. 'Snails!' he shouted, 'we must have snails,' and ordered us a dozen each.

It was the first time I had eaten snails and I was none too happy about the idea. My gaucheness delighted Haldane and he poured more wine. Despite their unappetizing appearance, I found the molluscs, or at least their garlic dressing, quite delicious. 'More snails!' bellowed Haldane. I tried to refuse, but was promptly served with a second dozen. They really were magnificent. '*Encore* – more snails!' yelled Haldane, now well into another bottle of wine. I had been plied with too many glasses to refuse and bravely downed a third dozen.

'I enjoyed your paper on your queer fish,' said Haldane. 'Not bad for a first paper.'

'My what fish?' There was an army of small snails floating

about in a sea of red wine inside my stomach. I was no longer
concentrating.

'Your homosexual sticklebacks,' he replied.

'Ah yes, sticklebacks,' I murmured.

He was thoughtful for a while, then boomed out: 'But homosexuality must be a sin!'

'What on earth are you talking about?' I had lost him altogether.
What was this nonsense about sin?

'Yes, yes,' his insisted, 'homosexuality must be a sin, otherwise
why should the pit of hell be bottomless?' It was funny-time
again. I seemed to be destined to act as the straight man for great
brains.

Ramona was getting agitated. It was nearly time for our formal
dinner and I was clearly in bad shape. She managed to drag me
away from the protesting Haldanes and we took a jarring taxi-
ride to our host's apartment. The dinner was formal as only the
French can be formal. Course after course was elaborately served,
interspersed with stiffly polite conversation. Half-way through I
knew I was never going to make it to the end, but I hung on
doggedly and that was my mistake. By the time I could bear it no
longer I was so near to being sick that there was no hope of
reaching the lavatory in time. My host, leading the way down an
interminable corridor, was wearing an immaculate blue blazer.
He seemed to be walking in slow motion. I felt three dozen
snails about to explode from inside me and quickly clapped my
hand to my mouth. But the pressure was too great. Between my
straining fingers, machine-gun bursts of snails fanned out and
festooned that creaseless blue cloth. I plunged past the startled
man and disappeared in a heaving wreck into the sanctuary of
the lavatory. Looking up after a few consummatory moments, I
saw the retreating figure of my elegant host disappearing back in
the direction of the dining *salon*. He was obviously unaware of
the state of his snail-clad back. I tried to shout a warning, but all
that came out was a cracked moan. I envisaged him sitting down,
amidst the gilt and the Buhl and the silver and the crystal, and
taking up again his polite conversations, as if nothing had hap-

pened, while at the same time he slowly squelched a sea of snails on to the satin back-rest of his ornate dinner chair.

Later, when a servant ushered me into an anteroom to recuperate, I heard gales of laughter sweeping in from the direction of the dining room. Ramona was entertaining them with the tale of my three dozen snails. In the end I think I quite made the evening for them, giving them a chance to unbend a little more than usual. Somehow the blazer catastrophe must have gone unnoticed. The next day we sent a huge bunch of flowers and a box of chocolates to our unfortunate hosts, to make amends, and I swore never again to undertake a solo attempt at decimating the world's snail population.

I was just about recovered in time to listen to the bee-dance talk by Karl von Frisch. It was a beautiful experience. Von Frisch was a shy, gentle man with the serenity of a peasant farmer. His white hair rose stiffly from his head and his leathery face was deeply tanned from long hours in the sun. His smart suit hung on his body as if it were a stranger to him and was anxious to return to the wardrobe where it clearly spent most of its life. He proceeded to tell us, in soft tones, of the latest developments in his research into the language of the honey-bee, research so elegant that even the most worldly and cynical of those present were moved by it. Casting a sidelong glance at Haldane, I was shaken to see that he was weeping. There was no expression on his face, but tears were streaming down his old cheeks. He leapt up at the end of the speech and pronounced that von Frisch's work was '*un des chefs-d'oeuvre de l'esprit humain*'. He then proceeded, with his advanced knowledge of mathematics, to demonstrate that von Frisch had discovered even more than he claimed. Unfortunately von Frisch spoke only German and Honey-bee, and it took some time for the interpreter to explain the intricacies of Haldane's comments in his native tongue. The problem was increased by the fact that von Frisch was rather deaf, so that the interpreter had to bend forward and shout at his chest, where his hearing-aid was secured. The German professor was clearly distracted by the curious intimacy of this jabbering, suppliant figure bowed down in front of him and found the details hard to follow. His brief reply was oddly mistranslated into English as: 'I am an anti-mathematical genius, but I thank Professor Haldane for his compliments.'

A French wasp expert then took the floor, heaped more praise on the embarrassed German's head and followed with a long and complicated question. The interpreter lunged towards von Frisch's chest again, but the old man waved him back, unclipped his hearing-aid, pulled out a length of wire and handed the receiver-box to him. When the interpreter came to translate the reply into French, he discovered to his horror that the French wasp man was also deaf and that he, too, was wearing a similar hearing-aid. The Frenchman had to come forward and unhook his receiver in the same way as von Frisch. The three of them stood close together, facing the audience, like a close-harmony trio, with the interpreter in the middle, holding one hearing-aid in each hand. As the discussion between the two entomologists went back and forth, matters became so complex that diagrams were needed on the blackboard. Connected together by wires, the trio became hopelessly tangled as first one, then the other, moved to draw on the board and then turn back to the audience. The interpreter was half-strangled by now and was no longer sure which receiver was German and which French. The two scientists, now as deeply enmeshed in debate as the interpreter was in wires, were becoming so excited by their exchange of ideas, that they seemed oblivious of the fact that the entire room was so engrossed in their electronic maypole dance, that the finer points of their discussion were going unheeded.

A final flourish at the blackboard was too much for the wiring, and the climax of the performance came with the tearing out of the ear-pieces and a joyous round of applause.

When it arrived at Konrad Lorenz's turn to deliver his speech he seemed unduly subdued. There appeared to be some kind of ancient feud between him and Haldane, and because the Haldanes were going on the gastronomic tour of France following the week of talks, Konrad and his wife Gretl declined the feasting and left early for Germany. Perhaps he was also inhibited by the presence of Danny Lehrman, a vast, twenty-stone American who had recently published a strong attack on Lorenz's ethological theories. When they had first met, in the foyer of the conference hotel, Konrad had slapped Danny on the back and roared cheerfully: 'Now that I know we are both fat men, it is impossible for us to be enemies!' Their social exchanges remained good-humoured and there was a great deal of energetic friendliness on both sides, but beneath the surface there was a deep rift in their approach to animal behaviour. Lehrman loved Lorenz's observations but hated the instinct theories which he constructed from them. He tried to sum up his feelings when, at the end of his own speech, he said: 'It would be most unfortunate if this criticism ... should be taken as a total rejection of the great contributions which the ethologists have been making to the study of animal behaviour.' Konrad was equally diplomatic, but privately did not take kindly to the Lehrman assault on his theoretical standpoint. Undeniably one of the world's greatest naturalists, he also wanted to be considered as a great thinker, and Lehrman's concessions plainly failed to pacify him. I was made vividly aware of this when his anger was transformed into a jest at Lehrman's expense. Driving me through Paris between speeches, Konrad spotted the huge bulk of Danny Lehrman slowly crossing the road some distance ahead. 'Let's see how fast he can run,' he chortled, and slammed down the accelerator, aiming the powerful car straight at the lumbering figure ahead. Danny took flight just in time to avoid being mown down and spun round furiously to be confronted with Konrad's laughing head protruding from the driving window, cheerfully shouting a friendly greeting. 'That should facilitate discussion,' roared Konrad, inexplicably, as he drove happily away, leaving a dumbfounded Lehrman staring after us.

Despite Konrad's feelings about him, Danny Lehrman was a delightful personality and, on the tour of France that followed, we became close friends. He was far from being a dour, laboratory-bound psychologist. To my surprise he turned out to be an avid bird-watcher and a P. G. Wodehouse addict. He could recite, verbatim, whole Wodehouse stories, relishing every lunatic detail. He had come to terms with his enormous weight and was never offended when it became the inevitable source of humour. The highlight of a later visit he made to see us in Oxford was the moment when, on entering our small Singer sports car, his feet went straight through the floor, so that although he appeared to be standing inside the car, his feet were resting on the road beneath. Unwisely, we took him punting on the river and, of course, the punt sank. But his own laughter was always as loud as ours. Ramona adored him and they became great crow-watchers together, arguing over every black speck in the sky, as to whether it was a jackdaw, a crow, or a rook, with Ramona perversely insisting that every large black bird had to be one of her beloved crows, and Danny pretending to take her seriously and lecturing her earnestly on corvid silhouettes.

When the Paris speech-making was finally over, it was time for the great tour. Pierre Grassé had hired a professional guide who had obviously been warned that this was going to be a difficult party to handle. As the poor man nervously herded us in a trembling glasshouse of a coach, he eyed us with deep suspicion and terrible anticipation of ghastly events to come. His companion, the so-called driver, who had the appearance of an out-of-work apache dancer, appeared to have lost the use of his arms from an over-indulgence of gesticulation at passing motorists. His feet, however, were remarkably powerful and beat a deafening tattoo on the brake and accelerator, as if he were enjoying a vigorous work-out on an exercise bicycle. The vague sense of insecurity this gave to our motley, international group brought us closer together, as if we were the victims of some air-disaster or hijacking, and the trip began in a general atmosphere of brittle chivalry and artificially cheerful back-chat. But as the effects of starting before dawn began to make themselves felt, a heavy-eyed slumber overtook the more elderly occupants of the bus, so that from the outside it resembled a huge, badly aerated tank full of giant dying goldfish.

It was the apache driver's job to touch down twice a day at

carefully selected restaurants, once for a three-hour lunch and once for a three-hour dinner, then finally to decant us into a hotel for a night of recovery. Interspersed between these major events were many brief cultural stops to listen to Grassé reading short sermons from his guide-book on the architecture and history of assorted Romanesque churches, ancient tombs, caves and châteaux. On the ramparts of the tallest and largest of the châteaux, I found myself ordained to be present at the uttering of the dying words of the world's greatest bee-keeper, for von Frisch, apparently tiring of it all, heaved himself up on to the topmost stone and, tottering on the brink at a dizzy height, let out a shuddering cry of 'BEEEEEES!' Just as he seemed to be about to hurl himself to the ground far below, he paused and pointed at a crack in the wall. I peered over and there, sure enough, was a nest of bees. Smiling all over his leather-bound face, the grand old man dismounted from the ramparts and sauntered triumphantly off, leaving me feeling rather foolish and thankful that I had not tried to grapple him back to safety.

The dinner at Poitiers, on our first night out from Paris, was suitably magnificent, marred only by a mysterious incident in which Haldane tried to throw his fish on the floor, turned purple and stormed about the place demanding satisfaction. This appealed enormously to Danny Lehrman because it was like a Wodehouse story coming to life for him and he tried to explain it to me on several occasions, but since it involved an excellent pâté, the now nearly demented guide, a train journey and a box of live newts, I gave up and pretended to myself that the whole thing was a hallucination caused by coach-lag.

The following morning we visited the cathedral and the guide, so Helen Spurway claimed, tried to dispense with one half of the Haldane act, by ordering the mad chauffeur to drive on without her. After a long sprint in the true Bannister tradition, she found the bus parked a mile or so away near yet another Romanesque church, which we were giving the treatment. Whining his apologies and insisting it was all a mistake, the frightened guide plunged into a nearby shop and bought her a box of chocolates, which only deepened her suspicions. Inside the church, meanwhile, Grassé was holding forth on half-columns, blind arcades and groin-vaults, listened to intently by his faithful secretary Madame Fontan, while the rest of the group clustered around a notice on the door which listed all the movies being shown locally, in order, according to their moral merit. Top of the list were the ones to which you could take your whole family. Next came the ones that you should only go to if, by so doing, you prevented your-self from committing worse sins. Next came ones that, if you had to go, you should certainly scold the owner of the cinema for showing. Finally, in red ink, or blood, were blazened the terrible names of the films which the church was sure would send you to hell, once your ravaged eyes had been assaulted by them. This little notice provided an excellent guide to film-going, we were told, because from it you could select at a glance the best and most lurid films in town. The cinemas at the bottom of the list, we gathered, were always packed.

The next few days we spent based at the Hotel Cro-Magnon on the very site where, as someone inaccurately put it, our forebears had fought bare. We were in the centre of ancient *grotte* country, surrounded by prehistoric scratchings, painted caves, postcards, guides and (according to Lehrman) short-toed tree-creepers. Lehrman was never without his binoculars and was for ever wandering off and being shooed back to the fold by the sweating guide, who looked like a small sheepdog trying to outflank an errant hippopotamus.

We stumbled through cave after cave, some huge, others narrow and frightening. In one of the latter, as we were squeezing our way out, there was a pitiful scream from Lehrman, who appeared to be stuck. When it was pointed out to him that he had got in, so he should be able to get out, he retorted plaintively that it had been so damp inside that he had swollen considerably, and suggested that the authorities would have to consider blasting. There was more trouble at the next cave where a scratching on the wall was officially identified as a rhinoceros.

'That,' screeched Helen Spurway, 'is NOT a rhinoceros.' The

local guides, not tuned in as we were to Helen's wavelength, took this as a major affront. Lulled into arrogant self-assurance by the continuous awe and amazement of their more usual clients, they were livid. They thought at first that they had misunderstood, but no, this foreign devil really did have the audacity to question the authenticity of this, THE rhinoceros of FRANCE! It was hours later that we emerged panting from that dank hole in the ground. Interminable argument had eventually been settled by arranging for a special trip to the cave that night for the Haldanes alone. We never heard what actually happened, except that they walked there and back in the pouring rain, and the subject was never referred to again.

If you put alcohol with their sugar, von Frisch had told us earlier, bees don't want to dance, and we saw what he meant. Day after day we imbibed the best that French bottles could hold, and more and more we felt like stranded whales as our bus lurched round mountain roads in a manner calculated to turn white the hair of any aeronautical acrobat. We drooled at the valleys far beneath us, giggled inanely at landslides, and tittered at near head-on collisions. But thankfully we survived long enough to see Lascaux. What an extraordinary sight. Even Helen had to admit that it was too good to be a fake. The cultural indigestion of the tour suddenly evaporated. The all-too-frequent, cynical jokiness vanished. As we stood gazing at the painted walls of that magnificent cave we behaved for the first time as though we really were in church. For me, personally, it was the greatest aesthetic experience of my life, and I only wished I could stay on there alone for hours, staring at the exquisitely portrayed Stone Age animals on the curving, floodlit walls. As far as I was concerned, the Sistine Chapel simply wasn't in the same class.

Looking closer at the painted animals, the huge bulls, one eighteen feet long, the elaborately antlered stags, the stiff-maned prehistoric horses and ponies, the cattle and the bison, I was reduced to total silence. Their freshness was astounding, as if they had been painted only yesterday, instead of many thousands of years ago. The secret lay in a combination of three lucky chances.

Firstly, the walls of the cave had already been covered in a crisp white layer of calcite crystal deposit, before the ancient artists had gone to work. It was as if nature had specially prepared the wall surfaces for them. Some time after the cave had been painted, the entrance had become accidentally blocked – the second lucky chance. There had been no deterioration of the surfaces over the millennia that followed, and no defacement by vandals in more modern times. Thirdly, although the entrance had been blocked enough to prevent easy human entry, it had not been sealed off completely, providing a preservative ventilation of the cave air.

The cave had been discovered only a few years earlier, by a schoolboy whose dog had disappeared down a mysterious hole. The young man who was showing us around now was that same boy, elevated to the role of official guide. Still marvelling at the crispness of the lines and the brightness of the colours, we emerged again into the harshness of the summer sun of central France, strangely quietened and pensive. What we had seen was not merely the hunting record of a Stone Age tribe, it was the surviving proof of the antiquity of the intense aesthetic urge of the human species. I made two vows: to undertake a long-term investigation into the origins of the artistic impulse, and to return one day to view the walls of Lascaux, alone and unhurried.

I kept both my vows. Eight years later, in 1962, I published a book on *The Biology of Art*, and a few weeks after its publication I revisited the Lascaux cave. Sadly, I regretted the keeping of the second vow. At first I thought my memory was playing tricks with me – that over the years my imagination had 'improved' the cave frescoes, sharpening their lines and brightening their colours far beyond reality. What I saw on that second visit was what the now countless thousands of excited visitors were seeing each season, since the fame of the cave had spread around the world. And it was not what I remembered seeing back in 1954, a few short years after the cave had first been opened to the public. The pictures were now dull and strangely scummy, as if I was viewing them through dirty water. People still marvelled at them, seeing them for the first time, but for me this second visit was a deeply depressing experience. I prided myself on being a good observer and I was upset to think that I could exaggerate and romanticize what I had seen as a younger man. Lascaux was still a wonder, but not quite the glory I had remembered.

The following year, 1963, I read a newspaper article on Lascaux with a mixture of relief and horror. The famous cave had been closed to the public because the painted surfaces were rapidly deteriorating. My relief came from the discovery that my memory had not, after all, been playing tricks with me. I had remembered the magnificence of the murals accurately – the objectivity of my observational powers was reinstated. But the news of the decay of the pictures also filled me with horror. It had been caused by the breathing of the thousands of tourists that flooded the cave each year. The human animal perspires at a rate of about $1\frac{1}{2}$ ounces of water an hour and breathes out 20 quarts of carbonic acid gas, which can attack the white, calcite crystal surface of the cave walls, on which the prehistoric pigments rest. The pigments themselves were iron and manganese oxides mixed with animal fat. The human moisture and gases were rapidly disintegrating the precious frescoes and, in a space of twenty years of exposure to modern humanity, the great works of art that had been perfectly preserved for twenty thousand years previously, were being obliterated. Worse was happening. By 1963 there were no fewer that seven hundred small patches of a green alga called *Pamelococcus* covering parts of the paintings, and the upheaval in the cave atmosphere had also meant that new layers of opaque calcium carbonate were being laid down on top of some of the exquisitely portrayed animals. Together, these changes seemed to spell disaster for Lascaux and French scientists were hard at work trying to solve the problems. But they could hope to do little more that halt the deterioration. There was no chance that they could restore the frescoes to that original brilliance I had witnessed on my first entry into the cave. If attending the Paris conference had done nothing else for me, I would still have been grateful for the opportunity it gave me to experience one of the marvels of the world of art, during the few brief years when it was still at its most marvellous.

After our gallant band left Lascaux, it set off through the savage valleys of the Dordogne and then up and up to the medieval stronghold of Domme. There the mayor of the town was ready to meet us and another vast, interminable banquet began. It was interspersed with speeches from the mayor, who said how glad he was to see so many nationalities together in peace at Domme. But he then went on to hurl curses and abuse at the English. It appeared we had done something terrible to a compatriot of his and Ramona and I were beginning to feel quite uncomfortable until he explained that the victim in question was Joan of Arc. He was completely serious in his attack, saying he could never forget what we had done and when Haldane rose to reply I was convinced that he was, in some eloquent way, going to pacify the old man. Instead he went to great length to explain that at the time the English had burnt Joan of Arc, all his ancestors were in Scotland and hated the English as much as the French did. That narrowed the enemy down to Ramona and me. As soon as the meal was over, the old mayor made a bee-line for Ramona, grabbed her by the arm and marched her off to show her his battlements where, according to his lurid descriptions, the worst atrocities had been committed by her distant ancestors. As they disappeared from view inside some dark turret, Haldane remarked that he now reinterpreted the mayor's verbal onslaught as a wily device to provide an excuse to get Ramona off on her own, and he may have been right, as it was some time before we saw them again.

After several more days of sampling the tall châteaux and *haute cuisine* of France, the coach was finally lurching its way back to Paris. We had at last become conditioned to the driver's romantic style of navigating the narrow country roads and everyone was forced to admit that Grassé had done us proud. It had been an epic journey and we felt wonderfully relaxed and at peace with the world. The Haldanes felt so relaxed that, to the unconcealed mirth of the rest of the group, they started kissing and cuddling like a pair of teenagers. It went on so long that the rows of eminent professors sitting behind the Haldanes' position were persuaded to prostrate themselves so that Madame Fontan could record their courting activities with her cine camera. She concentrated mainly on the changing directions of the deep furrows on the top of Haldane's bald head, which held us all transfixed, as a newly discovered courtship reaction for the human species. Haldane, in a benign mood, ended the day with a speech of appreciation in which he apologized for the fact that his wife's voice made a noise 'not unlike that produced by a brick being pressed on a circular saw', but pointed out that she did have her good qualities, which indeed she did. Not least of them was a tireless energy and an ability to take as good as she gave.

We encountered the Haldanes only on rare occasions after that memorable conference. The last I saw of Jack Haldane was a few years ago on British television when, in a final extraordinary appearance, he spoke his own obituary. After many years in India, he had returned to a London hospital to die. He sat in his hospital bed, explained that he had terminal cancer which was causing him some discomfort, and then proceeded to give a brief and modest summary of his various scientific discoveries and achievements, finishing with a characteristic short downward jerk of his head that he always used when ending a social encounter, and bade us a calm farewell. A few days later he was dead and the film was shown on television the following evening. One of the great eccentrics of British science had departed.

Back in Oxford, after the French interlude, I applied myself to an increasing variety of behaviour problems and busily wrote paper after paper for the scientific journals. After I had obtained my doctorate I was given a research assistantship and brought more and more species of birds into my ever-growing number of aviaries. The roof of the department was now festooned with them. I abandoned my fish studies and concentrated entirely on the birds. After a year or so I was beginning to get restless again and wanted to move on to mammals, but there simply weren't the space or the facilities to keep them in conditions natural enough to satisfy me. Talking it over with Niko, the suggestion came up that perhaps there might be a research opening for behaviour studies of mammals at the London Zoo. The director of the zoo, Leo Harrison Matthews, was an old exploring companion of Alister Hardy's—they had been to the Antarctic together as young men on board H.M.S. *Discovery*, and a quick phone call from Alister secured an interview for me at Regent's Park.

Leo Harrison Matthews was another 'old school' naturalist, a man who had travelled the globe in true Darwinian fashion. In his search for zoological material, he had endured enough hardships and enjoyed enough adventures to fill a Hollywood epic. He had been attacked and bled by vampire bats in South America, had a bad tooth removed by a ship's cook with a chisel, and fed off fried elephant seal's trunk (sage in one nostril, onion in the other) in the frozen wastes of the South Polar region. And on and on. I could have listened to him for hours. But when it came to the question of a research appointment at the London Zoo, things looked bleak. There simply was no money to spare.

Just as I was leaving, he had a last-minute thought and asked me to hold on a minute while he rummaged through some papers on his desk.

'Have you ever done any filming?' he asked. I explained that I had made two films, one of which had won an amateur award and been shown on television.

'Really?' he said, sounding pleasantly surprised. 'Well, cast an eye over this, then,' and handed me a document headed 'Proposals for establishing a joint Zoological Society/Granada TV and Film Unit.' It seemed that Sidney Bernstein, head of Granada TV, and Solly Zuckerman, now Secretary of the Zoological Society, had hatched a plan to set up a special unit at the zoo to make natural history television programmes, in opposition to the B.B.C. The B.B.C. was about to be shaken to its foundations by the upstart arrival on the scene of the recently formed Independent Television companies and a whole new era was dawning for British television. The B.B.C.'s complacent monopoly was about to be swept up into a harsh competitive situation, with alternative channels battling for the viewers' attentions. There was a great deal of outraged clucking in the Corporation hen-coops but, as we know in retrospect, nothing could have been better for the B.B.C. in the long run.

One of the areas in which the B.B.C. staff already prided themselves was that of natural history coverage. They had George Cansdale in the studio and David Attenborough in the field. David, in particular, had a special relationship with the zoo, late in 1955 when I went there for my first interview. He was engaged on an excellent series of 'Zoo Quests' in which he filmed the catching and bringing back alive of exciting new inmates for the London Zoo. Many of the zoo labels had the B.B.C.'s name on them, as a direct result of his beautifully filmed exploits. The B.B.C. had got wind of the attempted I.T.V. invasion of their territory and some lively negotiating was going on behind the scenes. But Sidney Bernstein had gone one better than his old established rivals. Unlike them, he was prepared to finance a full working unit inside the zoo, staffed by Granada employees, but operating under the aegis of the Zoological Society. As its head, he wanted a professional research zoologist, rather than a trained presenter or actor. He was insistent on this, demanding that the productions of the unit should be scientifically authentic, and a credit to the august and learned Zoological Society. Some of his colleagues considered this to be a somewhat idealistic approach. Could a professional zoologist be found at short notice who was capable of fronting his own weekly TV show within a matter of a few months? They thought it unlikely. And so, to be honest, did I. There was no video tape in those days and the thought of going on the air with my own TV show, live, with animals I had not yet studied properly myself, and which could do anything at any moment, and probably would, terrified me.

I expressed my doubts to Leo Harrison Matthews, but he suggested I go away and think it over. Ramona's reaction was unexpected. Instead of criticizing me for abandoning my promising research projects at Oxford and launching myself into 'show biz', she was thrilled by the idea. It dawned on me that her life as a

housewife in the Oxford suburbs was not only unfulfilling, but
was also right on the doorstep of her earlier, more glamorous
years as a history student. To be in Oxford, but not part of the
academic scene, had been disturbing her more than she had been
prepared to admit. But now, with the hustle of London beckoning, she was aglow with excitement. That decided me. In February
1956 I went for a formal interview at Granada and a few days later
was hauled off to a small TV studio for a screen test. Harry Watt,
an Australian film director now working for Granada, was the
producer in charge and he seemed to be satisfied with what I
considered to be a bungling performance. In early March I
learned that I had been given the post and was about to become
the head of the Zoo TV and Film Unit. The problem was time.
I.T.V. had first gone on the air in September 1955, but that was
only in the London district. Other regions were following
rapidly and Granada, which serviced the north, was due to take
the air only seven months later, which meant early May 1956. It
was now March 14th and they wanted me there in twelve days'
time, so that I would have a clear month before my first
programme was shown. Academic research does not operate at such
lightning speeds. Had I been coming from Fleet Street I would
have taken it as normal, but from my perch on the dreaming spires
of Oxford, it seemed an impossible schedule.

First, there was the difficulty of disposing of my vast menagerie
of animals at the zoology department. Then there was the problem
of writing up the results of my latest research project. I knew
that if I left it until later, there would be no hope for it. Also,
there was the matter of selling a house, finding a new home, and
moving – all in the space of twelve days. Working day and night
I somehow managed to write a fifty-page paper on my finches. I
was still tapping away at my typewriter as the removal men
began to strip the house. My desk was the last object to go
through the door. In London we were lucky to find a tiny basement flat less than a hundred yards from the zoo gate. On April
3rd, we started work at the zoo and a month later, on May 3rd,
Granada TV went on the air with its first programme. My own

debut was five days later and it was incredible to think that a mere forty-three days earlier I had still been in the tranquil world of my Oxford laboratory. The new world I had entered was far from tranquil – it was a screaming chaos by comparison. There were moments when I ached to crawl back into my academic retreat. But Ramona had joyfully thrown off her ill-fitting suburban shell, and was so deliriously happy that that alone made it all worthwhile. Granada had bent a golden rule and permitted a husband and wife to work alongside one another. They had given Ramona the position of Zoo Unit Researcher and this move brought us closer together than ever before. With the hazards ahead, this was just as well ...

5

HIJACKING A TELEVISION STUDIO IS NOT EASY, but it can be done. And I can vouch for the fact that on one occasion, at least, it *has* been done. The incident arose from my purist demand that TV should come to the animals, instead of the animals being taken to the TV. In the past, all animal studio shows had involved the wretched animals being bundled into bags and baskets and trundled off in noisy, vibrating cars or taxis, to be dragged out suddenly into the blinding lights of a B.B.C. building miles from Regent's Park. This meant that only the tamest of pets, or the most docile of creatures, could be shown. It also meant that all they were ever seen doing was sitting blinking in dumb shock at the frighteningly strange scene. Attempts to be more ambitious in B.B.C. studios had several times led to disaster. One of George Cansdale's giant fruit-bats had responded to the welcome warmth of the studio lights by promptly spreading its wings and taking off, leaving George naked, as it were, with his head craned upwards and a fixed grin on his face. Recapture among the thousands of lights, cables and metal grids that make up the roof of a TV studio was impossible and for weeks afterwards the giant bat would swoop down through B.B.C. plays, newscasts and weather reports, adding repeated screams from lady performers which were not in any script. The charming creature had a wonderful time, flitting in and out of a wide variety of productions before it was finally trapped by a lure of over-ripe bananas. The viewers missed him.

None of this was for me. I insisted, with a vigour that made several Granada executives wonder whether a tame actor might, after all, have been safer than a wild zoologist, that I was taking

NO zoo animals to ANY studio outside Regent's Park. Granada would have to bring their cameras to the zoo and make the programmes there. But what if it rained? Where would all the technical paraphernalia go? There had to be a base. In that case, I said, Granada would have to BUILD a special television studio inside the zoo, where the animals could be kept for several days before the show went on the air. That would mean they were then fully accustomed to their new surroundings and would behave more naturally.

'I want to see animals BEHAVE on television—not just sit there like unanimated glove puppets!' I was quite surprised at how forceful I had become—but it was the forcefulness of panic.

'Be reasonable,' they said. 'How can we build you a studio in four weeks? It simply can't be done.' But I was adamant.

At this point a brilliantly resourceful man entered the scene. Like me, Denis Forman had been quietly enjoying his research when Sidney Bernstein had inveigled him away to the richer pastures of the television world. Denis's research had been into the history of cinema and being a good administrator he had risen to become the head of the British Film Institute. But Sidney soon changed all that and now Denis, suffering heavily from the birth pangs of I.T.V., was deep in crises of every kind known to show business. He and Harry Watt were the joint producers for the Zoo Unit, among other things, and my purist rebellion on matters of animal welfare brought Denis hotfoot to the zoo.

I expected a battle, but was taken aback when he agreed totally with what I was saying. It meant a new kind of animal programme and Granada prided itself on pioneering new ideas. So, yes, of course, you must have a TV studio in the zoo. And away he went at emergency speed in a large black car to try and persuade Jack Hawkins that TV was not the enemy of the cinema.

Only after he had left did I realize that, despite agreeing with me, he had made no suggestion as to how a studio could be erected in a matter of a few days. I thought I had been conned and sank into a mood of sombre pessimism.

But Denis was far from idle. Like a military commander, he

surveyed possible strategies. Since no Granada studio existed and there was not time to build one, it was a case of rent, borrow or buy. But who on earth would have a *portable* TV studio? Such things simply did not exist. But yes they did – at least one did. Each year a portable studio was transported to Wimbledon for interviews with sweatily triumphant tennis stars, fresh from the holy turf of the centre court. The studio was erected well in advance and would soon be needed, but it might give us a breathing space. A few hasty phone calls revealed that the studio, in collapsed sections, was already on its way to Wimbledon, on huge lorries. I am not sure how Denis managed to divert those lorries to London Zoo, and I am still uncertain how Wimbledon managed with its tennis star interviews, but a few days after Denis's visit to the zoo, a TV studio started to spring from the ground in a large back yard between the zoo's animal hospital and the bird house. It stayed there for many months, despite repeated protests from its rightful owners, until, after long arguments on design, a new and splendidly permanent studio was constructed alongside it. It was in the original, hijacked studio, however, that I first tasted the agonies of presenting live animals on live TV. It was in there that I ceased to be a researcher and became an 'anchor man' for apes, ants and armadillos.

Our very first television presentation was thrown into total confusion by, of all people, Nikita Khruschev. The Russian leader was about to make a courtesy visit to England and, looking for some colourfully Russian gesture of friendship, decided to present the then very young Princess Anne with a Russian bear. News of this unsuitable gift broke just three days before we were due to go on the air with a carefully rehearsed sequence of tolerably amenable zoo inmates. I was taking no chances on my first show. It was to be a weekly half-hour series called *Zootime*, but time was the only thing we had little of. I wanted to leave the Russian bear to a later show, when I was a little more competent at my job, but the news was so big that there was no choice. Nikki, the bear, *had* to be in the first programme. It was a scoop.

I gave in and was relieved to discover that Nikki was, in reality, only a tiny bear cub. Easy, I thought, until I saw the scars on the hands of the Head Keeper who was in the process of being hustled in secret to Buckingham Palace to show the little princess her new toy. The cub *looked* enchanting, but its throaty, snarling roars gave the game away. This was clearly a monster in teddy bear clothing. As I peered into the back of the car waiting to speed to the Palace, I saw the Head Keeper start to writhe and twist as if going into terminal convulsions. It was merely the bear cub objecting to its confinement and heaving its small, but intensely muscular body this way and that, to break free of the tight grip of the keeper's experienced hands.

'Looks cute, doesn't he?' he panted, still lurching about as if having a fit. 'But he's not. Brown bears – little bastards. Bloody great jaws, take your thumb off! And everyone says OOOH! how lovely, let me cuddle him. Be the last thing they cuddled for a while, that's for sure. GET-ARHT-OF-IT!!' He broke off his short lecture on bearmanship with an anguished shout, as the wild-eyed cub saw its chance and clamped its heavy jaws on to his forearm. 'Can't take your eyes off him for a second,' he muttered, as he was whisked away to the Palace lawns. The Queen, who is no fool with animals, quickly sized up the situation and made sure that Princess Anne was kept at a safe distance. As the Head Keeper struggled to control the small, writhing ball of fury on the great lawns, he overheard her say of Khruschev, with unusual bluntness: 'What a silly man, to give a little girl a pet like that.' And she wisely and promptly handed over the bear cub to the London Zoo for permanent safe keeping.

Princess Anne's fortunate loss was my unfortunate gain. The day of the first edition of *Zootime* loomed upon me and I had a sneaking feeling that I was about to bleed for my art. Sneaking feelings are often wrong, but not this one. While the dumpy cub entranced two million viewers and helped launch *Zootime* into a long-running series (lasting more than 500 weeks), it was, as predicted by the Head Keeper, sinking its powerful teeth as deeply into my forearm as its straining jaw muscles could manage.

It was then that I learnt my first Zoo Lesson: Never mind the
killers, it's the cuddlies that get you.

As soon as the programme came off the air and we were told
that it had been a success, we all went off to celebrate in the
keepers' club next to the beaver-pond. We received a warm
welcome from the keeper staff, partly because we added an exotic
new element to the social life of the old-established 'zoo village',
and partly because we held the promise of endless gratuities for
help with future TV programmes. We were well aware of this,
but warmth was warmth and, after our ordeal, we had no wish to
question its source. We badly needed the friendliness that the club
provided and collapsed into its beery atmosphere with gratitude.

The director of *Zootime* was trying his best to congratulate
everyone concerned, while he was still visibly in a state of shock.
Like me, he had been rushed through the preparatory stages by
Granada, to be ready for the company's launching date and, like
me again, this had been his first experience of live television.
Although he was mouthing at me the comforting words due to a
patient who has survived high-risk surgery, and was scattering
extravagant praise in all directions ('Mr Croucher, darling, your
cockatoo was *ri*veting!'), it was clear that he was far from happy.

His name was William Gaskill and he was later to become one
of the leading avant-garde stage directors of London, based at the
Royal Court Theatre in Sloane Square. If Granada had run a
nationwide competition to find the most unsuitable director for
an animal television programme, Bill Gaskill would have been a
runaway winner. His great love had always been the theatre, and
what he was doing directing bears and cockatoos was as big a
mystery to him as it was to the rest of the zoo.

He was at pains to make this point to his Granada overlords on
several occasions, but was always politely returned to the zoo
with the comment that it was necessary for him to gain the
'widest possible experience of all branches of television' before
being placed in his chosen slot as a director of major TV play
productions. With this future reward dangled enticingly in front
of him, he trudged hopefully on with *Zootime* week after week

until he finally gave up and decamped to risk financial insecurity in pursuit of his true love.

Before he departed he taught me a great deal about projecting myself to an audience. This was something that had been sadly lacking in academic life. Throughout the world, university lectures are delivered hour upon hour by individuals who, although brilliantly trained in their special subjects, are never given so much as a passing hint in the subtle art of holding the interest of their listeners. A few are naturally gifted speakers, but many, far too many, are not. And university education is the poorer for it.

I was under the illusion that I had picked up a reasonable speaking style over the years, but Bill was far from satisfied.

'You must stop lecturing to a piece of machinery,' he said. 'That is not a camera you are talking to, it is a family of people sitting in their home. If you had dropped in on them to have a chat about zoo animals, you wouldn't speak to them like that, would you? Relax, give them a smile, unstiffen yourself.' I did my best, but under the stress of dealing with unruly animals, it was not always easy. He kept on at me, never allowing me to forget my weaknesses and little by little I warmed to this strange new medium. I created an image of an imaginary family in my mind and converted the dark, unblinking TV camera into their listening faces. Gradually I transformed the lens of the camera into a single person and learned to talk to it as though it were an old friend. It made me feel rather foolish at first, but after a few weeks I was able to ignore all the other people in the studio watching me and chatted intimately to the camera as though 'he' and I were the only two people involved. With Bill's invaluable help I was slowly changing from a lecturer into a television performer.

Bill, too, was starting to find some reward in his unexpected role. He was learning to anticipate the kind of movements that animals of various species were likely to make, so that he could select his shots to the best advantage. His theatre-born, pseudo-effete pose concealed a tough North Country background that drove him hard. Nothing was too much trouble for him. If some-

thing had to be built, he would build it himself if necessary. The
zoo staff found it hard to pigeon-hole him. At the zoo, there
were people in smart suits who sat behind desks or wandered
around the grounds giving instructions, and people in uniform
who did the manual labour and looked after the animals. There
was a sharp division between the two. Just as they had got used to
Bill waving his hands about with directorial authority, they
would come face to face with him in the television yard, clad in
old jeans, hacking out a huge hamster burrow from foam concrete. They found this confusing at first, but soon came to accept
the TV Unit as an oddity in their midst, where ordinary zoo rules
and orthodox status displays did not apply.

In essence we were like a small repertory company, with a
different 'play' to put on each week and, like the typical members
of such a company, we all turned our hands to whatever new
problem arose, regardless of our official capacity. One form of
versatility was, however, denied to Ramona. As she was young
and good-looking it was automatically assumed by the press that
we would be appearing together as a husband and wife 'animal
team' on television, following in the footsteps of Armand and
Michaela Denis, the safari experts, and Hans and Lotte Hass, the
sub-ocean film-makers. The *Daily Telegraph* commented:
'Women are penetrating fresh worlds of activity every day – and
so is glamour. Michaela Denis, who has explored the jungles of
the world, and Lotte Hass, under-sea explorer, have a new rival ... '
But it was not to be. I would have been delighted to have Ramona
join me on the screen, but Granada policy decreed otherwise. To
have put up a third married couple in the limited list of 'Nature
Jockeys' would have looked too much like trying to copy the old
established formats. To Granada, such a criticism would have been
anathema, so there was a strict instruction that Ramona was to
stay behind the scenes. I grumbled about this decision, fearing she
might resent it, but she accepted her role cheerfully, and busied
herself exploring the zoo for new candidates for our weekly
Zootimes.

In addition to producing a weekly live show for television we were also actively filming behaviour items for another, more ambitious programme called *The World of Animals*. This was where I hoped to be able to present some of the latest ethological discoveries to a wider audience. But progress was slow. It was clear that we were never going to be able to keep up the pace of two weekly shows and, after a few attempts, we shelved the more serious programme until a bigger film crew could be established at the zoo. This was eventually done, but in the meantime *Zootime* was the focus of our attention and we became more and more ambitious in our efforts to show animals actually doing something, instead of just sitting there looking pretty. Being a live show, with no second chances, this policy often led to disaster.

Inevitably the animals did things we did not expect them to do, with embarrassing results. As a rule, we had two cameras inside the zoo TV studio, now known to viewers as 'my Den at London Zoo', and a third camera somewhere outside to cover species too big to be moved. One day, camera three was all set to travel along the fronts of the outside cages of the Lion House, to show off the impressive collection of Big Cats housed there. All had gone well at rehearsal earlier in the day, but when it came to transmission time, their mood changed. For some inexplicable reason, the first male lion at which we pointed the camera took one look at the strange apparatus hovering outside the bars of its enclosure and promptly decided that it must represent some kind of threat to leonine masculinity. The lion's way of answering this threat was to rush over to his mate and mount her. Since *Zootime* was intended primarily for younger viewers and was transmitted at tea-time, I was at a loss to know how to word my commentary at this point and suggested casually that we might now move on to look at some of the other inmates of the Lion House. As we left the copulating pair, with the great male roaring and twitching to a violent climax, a second male lion, pacing angrily up and down, came into view. I began to give the viewers some of his personal details—his age, name, and weight—when to my audible anguish he, too, leapt on his startled female, who had been enjoying a quiet snooze in the afternoon sun. Grabbing her by the neck, he too launched into a vigorous mating act, snarling and grimacing in feline ecstasy. I burbled on with an inane commentary about the number of pounds of meat each lion was fed every day, while the (no doubt entranced) youth of Britain learned a new meaning for the word 'lionized'. Gratefully we then moved on to less sexually aggressive tigers and leopards, but in the final enclosure, sure enough, there were more lions and yet another explicit sexual act. This male, however, added something of his own, to round off the item. After completing his climactic roar and getting a savage swipe in the face from his female as he dismounted her, he strolled over to the front bars of his cage, slowly rotated himself, and then urinated with great force straight at the camera. Male lions have a special way of urinating, using a powerful, horizontal jet aimed backwards at some landmark in their territory, so that their personal scent is deposited on it. One of Granada's cameras was now firmly inside this particular male's territory and, as far as he was concerned, was reduced to a mere tree-stump.

Later, the Lion House keepers told me that one of the male lions had developed a particularly devastating refinement, if that is the word, of his urinating technique. When he discovered that the spray created by his jet of liquid hitting one of the cage bars could reach his adoring public, crowded to watch him from the other side, he introduced a special multi-squirt to help pass the boredom of the zoo day. As the front rows of the crowd leapt back screaming after his first dousing of them, others quickly took their place to see what was happening. They then took the full brunt of his second squirt, which he had saved up for them, so that they, too, retreated yelling and cursing. On a good day, he might even catch a third wave, by carefully staggering his ejection of pungent liquid. It was just about the only assault device left to the Lord of the Jungle, in his sadly reduced circumstances, and he made full use of it.

More trouble was in store for us when our outside camera was coasting down the front of the Birds of Prey Aviaries. There, to enliven the sleepy birds, we had arranged for them to be given special pieces of fresh meat to tear apart with their powerful

5–6 The Grassé conference in Paris, 1954. On the far side of the table, third from right, with his head on his hand, is Professor J. B. S. Haldane. Next to him sits his wife Helen. Seventh from right sits the impressive bulk of the American professor, Danny Lehrman. Ramona is in the distance behind him and I am on his left. Outside on the steps (*below*) the eccentric Professor Haldane is holding hands with his young wife in the centre of the front row. In the back row: Danny Lehrman (*second left*), Konrad Lorenz (*third left*), myself (*fifth left*); front row: Karl von Frisch (*left*) and Pierre Grassé (*right*).

7 My television debut was complicated by the unexpected arrival of a celebrity bear cub called Nikki, presented to Princess Anne by the Russian leader Khruschev. The cub's bite was worse than his bark.

8 Giant tortoises and microphones do not mix. If the huge reptiles decide to leave while you are on the air, it is difficult to persuade them to change their minds.

talons. The close-ups were suitably awe-inspiring. What we had not reckoned on was that one of the eagles was a finicky eater and insisted on downing a fully furred, complete mouse. No naked slabs of pre-chopped meat for him. Seeing him grab the dead, white mouse in his claws and knowing how many of my viewers owned beloved pet mice, I quickly changed my commentary so that the director had to cut back to a picture of myself sitting talking inside the zoo studio. I chatted on about eagles for a minute or so, until I was fairly sure that the little mouse would have vanished down the eagle's gullet. Then, mentioning the beautiful eyes of these great birds and the way in which their magnificent vision had involved a shift of the eye position from the sides of the face to the front, as in humans, I suggested we might take a closer look at the face of the eagle we had just been watching 'having its tea'. As I looked back to the TV monitor screen in the studio I was horrified to see, in beautifully focused close-up, the bulging face of the bird with the long tail, hind feet, and little white rump of the mouse, still protruding from its beak. With a blink and a few sickening gulps, the eagle started to swallow, the rear end of the mouse slowly sliding down its throat and out of view, until only the long, mousy tail was left hanging from its mouth like a reptilian tongue. Then, with a few more gulps, this too began the gentle slide to oblivion.

As I had used the words 'having its tea' I had set up an inevitable comparison between the action of the bird and that of my tea-time viewers at home. A million tea-time cakes and biscuits stuck in a million throats right across the country and angry phone-callers jammed the zoo's switchboard. Several of the phone-callers, it seemed, had been physically ill at the sight, and had thrown up all over their tea-cups. It was the occasion on which I learnt my second Zoo Lesson: Fur in the mouth makes people feel sick.

This particular problem has always faced the zoo's reptile keepers. So many of their animals insist on fully furred prey and will die of starvation rather than settle for anything less. This means that, for many people, a visit to the Reptile House has an

E

added horror. Not only are there those dreadful, supposedly slimy creatures, which their children insist on seeing, but on top of that there is the sight of the corpses of white rats and white mice strewn about the cages, any one of which may suddenly be engulfed in gaping serpentine jaws. When we decided to present a whole edition of *Zootime* from behind the scenes in the Reptile House, I went to the length of opening the programme by announcing what we were about to do and suggesting that the scenes we were about to transmit were, in my opinion, unsuitable for adult viewing. The younger viewers, naturally enough, were delighted by this and several wrote to me to suggest that in addition to the usual 'X' certificate, for adults only, there should be a 'Z' certificate for children only.

As it turned out, the mouse problem was to be the least of our worries in the Reptile House presentation. There were other, more dangerous, hazards ahead. The show started badly, when a giant tortoise escaped. You may imagine that an escaped tortoise is about as troublesome as a legless bag-snatcher and as easy to catch, but it is not that simple. A fully grown giant tortoise can weigh anything up to a quarter of a ton, and if he decides to vacate the scene it is more than one man can do to stop him. Captive giants usually lack the necessary determination to take off in this way, however, and we had prepared a low, wooden pen to enclose a few of them behind my speaking position, which we thought would be sufficient to keep them in place until we were ready to display them to the waiting millions.

There was one fact we had overlooked: television lighting appreciably increases the temperature, even in a hot Reptile House at the zoo. Reptiles, especially tortoises, respond quickly to a temperature increase by becoming much more active than usual. So it was for one of our penned-in giants. Gearing himself into unaccustomed mobility, he lunged forward at his wooden barrier at the very moment I was saying: 'Hallo, and welcome once again to *Zootime*, coming to you from the heart of London Zoo. Today we are inside the Urggh ... ' I broke off suddenly as I felt something huge and massively heavy pressing against the backs of my legs. Looking down I saw the vast bulk of the giant tortoise lumbering over the defeated and flattened wooden barrier which had been torn loose, nails and all, from its companion planks.

Trying to smile, I continued my introduction, knowing that all that could be seen at that moment was my face, in close-up. What was invisible was my legs, slowly doing the splits to let through the broadest shell in the animal world. Stumping steadfastly onwards, the giant met the distraught figure of the 'floor manager', the man who gave me all the vital timing signals from the director in the control van outside the building. The floor manager firmly placed the heel of one shoe against the front edge of the giant's carapace and tried to force him to a halt. All that happened was that the struggling man slowly slid backwards and disappeared between the two cameras that were facing me. The giant plunged sedately on and jammed tight between the two camera supports.

Now neither camera could move and this was the point at which I had to walk across to my left to introduce a charmingly professional python – about the only animal that day which did not cause us havoc. I started to move across hopefully, but caught sight of the TV monitor which was showing me what the viewers could see at home. Its screen was a blank except for an unusually boring wall. I was trapped. Moving back to the only spot where I could be seen, I suggested that we take a look at the crocodiles outside. While talking about them, I signalled wildly for the python to be brought across to me, where it could be seen. While this was being done, the floor manager somehow contrived to get the giant tortoise past the cameras and, opening the door to the outside area of the Reptile House, shooed the giant through it. We breathed again, but now the TV monitor had been knocked out of my line of vision and I could no longer see the crocodiles about which I was supposed to be giving a running commentary. Covering the microphone as best I could I hissed at the floor manager: 'The monitor, the monitor!'

That led to the next unhappy incident. It so happens that the

word 'monitor' is not only used by TV technicians to denote
what the rest of us would call a 'television set', but is also the
popular name given to a type of giant lizard. One of these
monitor-lizards was due to appear later in the programme and
was being held, with some difficulty, by another keeper, over to
my left. Hearing me call for the monitor, he naturally assumed
that, in the chaos of the moment, I had decided to bring his item
forward in the programme sequence. He responded helpfully by
closing in on my left flank with his monitor just as the python
keeper closed in from the right. As the director cut back to me
from the crocodile scene, the two huge reptiles came face to face
and both disliked intensely what they saw. Struggling between
their writhing forms I suggested that perhaps we might take just
one more peep at the crocodiles. The director, thoroughly
confused by now, took me at my word and switched again to the
crocodile pool, or what should have been the crocodile pool.
What none of us knew was that, outside, the escaped giant
tortoise had by now clumped its way round to where the third
camera was positioned and was slowly thrusting it backwards to
a point where all it could show us was yet another blank wall.

Had I been more experienced I would have explained the whole
sorry story to the viewers, who would no doubt have enjoyed
the situation immensely. But I was still at the stage where I did
not like to admit that things were going awry. So I soldiered
bravely on by suggesting that we look at something a little
smaller – a charming frog from South America. This would give
the monitor-lizard keeper and the python keeper time to calm
their charges down. The frog keeper came forward and placed
the exotic-looking frog on a little platform I had moved hurriedly
into position. The frog, which I noticed had an exceptionally
large mouth, eyed the scene for a second and then made the leap
of the century, vanishing instantly from view. Beautifully fielded
by the frog keeper he was caught in mid-air, but objected so
strongly to this cricket-ball treatment, that he promptly clamped
his remarkably strong jaws on to the man's thumb. Luckily we
were still in the days of black-and-white television because in

the next close-up, blood was clearly oozing from the seized thumb and the keeper was in considerable pain. I had no idea that a frog could inflict such a bite, but I had to take attention away from the keeper's plight and suppress my interest in his thumb, so I snatched up a salamander from a nearby container and began talking rapidly about that instead. The keeper, imagining, like me, that we were now in close-up on the salamander, started to try and shake the frog free, flicking his hand vigorously, as if trying to remove from it a piece of sticky paper. Unfortunately his actions were all too visible to the viewing millions, and the next day we received angry complaints about the brutal way we had treated that 'charming little frog'. Not a word, of course, about the poor man's brutalized thumb. I wished then that we did have colour television, so that they could have seen the blood properly and understood.

We were not yet out of trouble. The climax to the Reptile House programme was to be a demonstration involving a cobra. This was the one truly dangerous item we were going to attempt. Most snake-charmers who work with live cobras render them harmless before showing them in public. This is done in a number of ways. Some of them cut out the fangs, others block the fangs with wax, or stitch the mouth of the wretched snake tightly shut. But the London Zoo would never dream of harming a cobra in any of these ways. So we were going to be dealing with a live and fully venomous snake – one of the deadliest in the world. If you are struck by one, you take half an hour to die and it is one of the most painful deaths known. We had prepared everything with great care. Nothing could go wrong. Reg Lanworn, the Overseer of Reptiles at the zoo, was one of the most experienced snake handlers alive. So it was almost in jest that I had given the camera crew a short lecture before we went on the air, asking them to keep well away if they saw a hooded snake approaching them unexpectedly.

Everyone knows the classic image of an Eastern snake-charmer in turban and loin-cloth, squatting on the ground, playing a flute to his cobra as it rears up out of a small wicker basket. As the snake-charmer swings from side to side playing his instrument, the great snake sways back and forth in time with him, its sinister, spectacled hood widely spread. This was the scene we wished to re-create, though without the fancy costume.

The scientific object of the exercise was to demonstrate, once and for all, that, despite the flute-playing performance and the cobra's apparent musical interest, snakes are in reality totally deaf. It is not the music to which they respond, but the swaying movement of the flute. To prove this, we were planning to show the full flute ritual first, using a snake-charmer's flute I had managed to acquire from an Indian shop in the West End, and then to repeat the performance, but without the music. If all went well, the cobra would sway just as much to the silent flute as to the played one.

You may perhaps have wondered why cobras rearing up from wicker baskets do not simply slither away and disappear. The answer is that their tail-ends are tightly bound with tape to the bottom of the baskets. This does not hurt them, but secures them and prevents their escape. Reg Lanworn had prepared his cobra in this manner and placed the round lid on top of the basket. All was ready. When we came to the cobra climax of the programme, I briefly explained the danger involved, to impress the viewers, and Reg carefully lifted the lid. The cobra responded magnificently, rearing up and facing us with its glassy stare, its long, forked tongue flickering. I began playing my flute and swaying from side to side in the approved manner. The snake followed suit. Then I repeated the movements in total silence and, to our great relief, the snake obligingly swayed once more. We had proved our point. At least something in the programme had gone as planned, I thought. But I was premature—the snake still had to be calmed back into the basket and the lid re-placed.

As Reg Lanworn reached forward with a snake-rod, to encourage the cobra to withdraw, the lid poised in his other hand, the serpent slowly turned away from us and lowered itself on to the table top. Then, to our utter dismay, it slowly began to slither out of the basket, across the table and down towards the floor of the Reptile House. Reaching ground level it made off with unseemly haste, heading straight for camera number two. The cameraman, thank heaven, had taken my little lecture seriously and instead of helpfully trying to field the snake, began to shin up his camera pedestal until he was more or less on top of his machine. It is the only time I have ever seen a television camera operated from above.

The cobra slithered gracefully across the base of the camera and disappeared into the darkness of the Reptile House, with two assistant keepers in hot pursuit. Trying to keep as calm as possible, I thanked Reg for a fascinating display and covered our confusion by suggesting that as a farewell to the Reptile House, we might perhaps have a last look at the giant tortoises. While I was saying this, another keeper rushed across to remove the front of the wooden pen in which all but the escapee were still sitting, quietly munching large lettuces. With the front of the pen in place, we could see nothing, and I knew it had been only lightly nailed down before the programme had started. That was why it was possible for the liveliest of the giants to knock the front panel down and take off on its disastrous stroll. What I did not know was that, following the escape, the panel had been replaced much more firmly than before. Now, the tortoise keeper was lying behind me on the floor, hiding from view, and sweating to prize it loose. It refused to budge. I sensed something was wrong and filled in with a few well-chosen words about the conservation of giant tortoises in the wild state. Eventually I was given a frantic wind-up for the end of the show, just as I heard a terrifying creaking and a crash, as the panel finally gave up the struggle. Unfortunately the keeper had no time to get out of the way, as the camera moved in on him for the final scene. All he could do was to fling himself flat on the ground behind the group of tortoises and hope that they would hide him. But big as they were, his buttocks still showed clearly in amongst their shelly humps. As the credit titles rolled slowly up over humps and buttocks, I wondered what exactly people would make of this bizarre

combination of reptilian and human protrusions. But I was even
more intrigued by the mystery of the cobra's escape.

When we gratefully at last came off the air, I looked at Reg
Lanworn and he shook his head. He was as mystified as I was. As
soon as we had made sure that the cobra had been safely re-
captured, we went to look at the wicker basket. There, neatly
bound inside it was the shed tail-skin of the snake. The one detail
we had overlooked was that the cobra was about to shed its skin,
and the tightness of the binding had been just enough to start the
process off prematurely. It was a freak chance, but then it had
been a day of freak chances and one more at this stage hardly
surprised us.

Curiously, we never received any complaints about the many
mishaps that occurred during our *Zootime* programmes, so long
as we were the ones who suffered. Providing the animals were
unharmed, it seemed to add spice to the series. Meeting some
Zootime viewers in the grounds one day, I asked whether they
noticed how often things went wrong and whether they minded.
On the contrary, they explained, it was the chance that I would
be eaten, or at least bitten, before the half-hour was over, which
gave the programmes their special charm. They knew they were
watching a live programme, rather than some carefully edited,
canned film.

From that point, I gave up worrying about mishaps, and even
began to play on them. I no longer pretended they were not
happening. Instead I explained the unpredictability of animals in
strange places, and tried to use the occasional escapes and errors as
means of explaining the behaviour of the animals concerned.
There was a charming owl that gave me just such an opportunity.
It was sitting on my wrist with great composure one moment
and the next it was flying straight up into the air and out of sight.
In the early days of *Zootime* we used a boom-microphone,
instead of the later 'neck-mikes' that replaced it. A boom-mike
is suspended from the end of a long, counter-balanced pole at
the other end of which sits the boom-operator. As I was not
moving about while talking about the owl, the operator had

momentarily relaxed his attention and did not see the sudden take-off of the owl. The owl, having spotted the pole above its head had decided that it looked like a much more comfortable perch than my wrist. Flitting up through the air it landed firmly on my end of the pole and in settling there immediately un-balanced the boom-mike, which dropped heavily downwards just as I looked up to see where the owl had flown. The large microphone hit me squarely in the eye.

As far as the viewers were concerned, all they had seen was a man with an owl on his wrist – the owl disappear upwards out of view – and a large black metal object descend and hit the man as he looked upwards. Jacques Tati could not have timed it better. But instead of trying to gloss over what had happened, I turned it to my advantage by explaining a special feature of the owl that had made such an accident possible. Any other bird, flying up from a standing start, would have made a beating noise with its wings which would have alerted the boom-operator. But owls hunt stealthily by night and swishing wing-beats would be useless for sneaking up on their prey. During the course of evolution, they have developed the remarkable ability of almost completely silent flight. I made the owl flap its wings again to prove my point. So an accident was converted into a useful demonstration of an important aspect of owl behaviour.

There were many such incidents and I often learned new facts of animal life myself, while actually on the air. I had always been fascinated by bird-eating spiders – huge hairy arachnids which apparently do include small birds in their wild diet from time to time. They are always cropping up in spy movies and horror films, crawling in slow sinister fashion towards the exposed flesh of our hero or heroine, who sweat manfully or scream in panic according to gender and the demands of the script. The implication is that these giant, poisonous spiders are malevolent creatures who will sting you to death as soon as touch you. Yet another myth that needed exploding. No wild animal goes out of its way to attack human beings, unless there is a very good reason for doing so. The risk of retaliation is far too great. Snakes and spiders only attack if they feel that they themselves are under attack, and must defend themselves. Step on them or lie on them and, of course, they will react, but leave them alone and they will leave you alone. I set out to demonstrate this fact, using Belinda, a tame bird-eating spider from the zoo's collection.

Belinda's powerful jaws were capable of delivering a savagely poisonous bite, but her venom was normally only employed to subdue her prey. Head Keeper Ashby, the zoo's spider man, assured me that she was docile enough if handled gently. So she was brought to the 'Den' and placed on my desk-top during a *Zootime* programme. I placed my hand flat on the surface of the desk in front of her and waited for her to crawl over it, which she did with great professionalism in stately movements of her fat furry legs. I wanted to show that this could be repeated, so, using a small sable artist's-brush, I gently turned her round for the encore. But she had done her act and now refused to budge, sitting quietly sunning herself in the appealing warmth of the television lights. Not to be thwarted I prodded her plump abdomen softly with the tip of the brush. Still no movement. I prodded a little harder. Her reaction took me by surprise. Instead of moving forward as I wanted, she suddenly started jiggling her back legs against the hairs on her body. The jointed legs were jerking up and down so fast that she looked like a clockwork toy. I became so engrossed in what I thought must be some kind of visual display, that I failed to realize the truth, namely that she was tearing her hair out and throwing it in my face. Feeling the very fine hairs touch my skin, I brushed them away, but I was too late.

'Those are urticating hairs,' explained the Head Keeper, who was looking slightly alarmed. 'Really?' I said, rather lamely, trying to recall the meaning of the word 'urticating'. I should have remembered from my botanical days that *urtica* is the Latin name for a nettle. He then went on to explain that when a bird-eating spider is mildly disturbed, its first line of defence is to scratch up a cloud of stinging hairs that cause intense skin irritation to any animal which comes close and threatens it. He showed me a bald patch on Belinda's back, where she had torn her hair out on previous annoying occasions. She needed her jaw-poison for more pressing, feeding engagements, but a few back-hairs she could easily do without, hence this spiderly striptease.

After the programme was over I soon remembered the meaning of the word urticating, as my face and neck turned bright red with an itchy rash. It was a hard way to learn, but it was a lesson equally hard to forget.

Scorpions gave me a different kind of problem, but one that was also memorable. I had reasoned that, since a scorpion's sting is in its tail, all one needed to do to incapacitate the animal was to pick it up *by* its tail. It could hardly prod its venomous spike into your flesh if you were holding it by the bulbous root of that same spike. Simple. Or so I thought.

A group of scorpions were duly placed in a shallow container and *Zootime* was on the air again. They were not particularly happy about being exposed in the open and started rushing around looking for a non-existent stone under which to crawl. Bumping into one another, they began flexing their curled tails in the air and flicking them menacingly this way and that. My bravado was beginning to evaporate and I felt a mounting dread inside me that had an unfortunate side-effect: it made my palms start to sweat. My fingers became so slippery that, when I finally reached down to grasp hold of a swishing scorpion-tail between finger and thumb, it immediately slid from my grasp. The scorpion was not amused. In fact, it became visibly more angry and swivelled round to face me, thrusting its tail-spike up into the air.

I tried again to grab it and failed once more. The studio had gone unusually quiet. I had made the fatal mistake of promising the viewers that something was going to happen. The correct script-line for such an occasion was not: 'I am going to show you how ... '; it was: 'This is almost impossible, but let's see if ... ' But I was still learning. Right now I had placed myself in a cul-de-sac at the end of a one-way-street. There was no evading the issue. Wiping my hands on the sides of my trousers, I slowly lowered my thumb and forefinger behind the body of the largest and most spectacular of the scorpions. I thought he would be the easiest to grasp hold of, but in reality all I was doing was picking the most deadly one present, with the biggest poison gland.

This time I was lucky. My grip held firm and I was able to raise the leg-waving animal from the ground and hold it up in the air for a dramatic close-up. But I had been focusing so intently in my mind on the scorpion's sting-in-the-tail, that I had overlooked the fact that, at this size, it also had a powerful pair of crab-like pincers. With the agility of a trapeze artist, the scorpion was now swinging its head-end up towards my fingertips, its pincers snapping savagely in the air as it tried to counter my grip with one of its own. I barely had time to drop it before it made contact.

Afterwards, I asked the keeper what would have happened if it had managed to grab me. 'That,' he replied with quiet amusement, 'could have aptly been described as a vicious circle. You would have been unable to let go of him and he would have refused to let go of you. I think he might have won, though, because once he had an anchorage on your fingers, he would have had much more power in his tail.' It was a sobering thought.

'Have you finished with the scorpions now?' he enquired. 'I'd like to get them back to their cages.' I thanked him and, taking a box from the shelf behind him, he proceeded to pick up each of the scorpions with the casual grace of a greengrocer transferring plums into a housewife's shopping-bag. It was a perfect piece of zoo oneupmanship. The secret, of course, was that his hand moved so fast that the scorpions had no time to react. They were taken up and whisked through the air and released before they could begin to attack. All the same, it made me feel suitably foolish and reminded me once again how much I had to learn about hundreds of different zoo inmates. When I had been at Oxford studying small birds, it had taken me months to learn how to catch a tiny finch in an aviary with a sudden flick of the hand, so that it was unharmed and suffered the minimum of disturbance. Each kind of animal required a special style of handling and no one man could become an expert in all areas. Every head keeper had his own highly skilled way of dealing with his particular charges and my respect for their expertise grew daily.

Only where the zoo lacked a certain type of animal was it necessary to call in outside help. This arose in the case of bats, which were not one of London Zoo's specialities. When I decided to devote a programme to these remarkable creatures we therefore went in search of an expert batman and found him in the person of Andrew Watson.

Andrew arrived at the zoo in a small car with the registration number BAT 13, and a huge fruit-bat hanging upside down in the centre of the rear window. It swung there like a furry mascot, almost ignored by following drivers until it unexpectedly spread its wings and yawned. Andrew reported that his rear-view mirror often reflected curiously swerving vehicles immediately behind him in traffic jams. He claimed that it helped to reduce the boredom of London driving.

Alighting from his car, he carefully unhooked the fruit bat, undid his waistcoat and hung the animal from his tie. He then buttoned up again, leaving his lower button undone so that the bat's head could protrude slightly if it felt like sniffing the afternoon air. He explained that this was the most efficient way to keep his pet warm and that it was the best possible manner in which to transport such an animal.

We set off for the TV Den with Andrew carrying a sinister box that contained the star of the show, a live vampire. Vampire bats had always held a special fascination for me and I wanted to explode yet another ancient myth—namely that they sucked blood. I hoped to demonstrate that, although they do indeed feed on blood, they do not suck it—they lap it like a cat. Their teeth are so sharp that they are capable of slashing the flesh of a sleeping mammal so delicately that it feels nothing. While it continues to slumber, the vampire then sits next to the wound it has made and laps up the escaping blood with its long tongue. The zoo's director, Leo Harrison Matthews, had once unwisely left his feet uncovered when camping in a tent in a South American forest. Vampires had visited his naked toes as he slept, sliced them open and lapped greedily at his blood without him knowing a thing about it—until the morning, when he found the neatly made incisions.

Although the loss of blood is not serious to someone who has been vampirized in this way, and Leo has not developed unduly elongated incisors as a result of his experience (as Hollywood movies would have us believe), there are two serious dangers involved. First, the saliva of the bat contains a special chemical which prevents coagulation of the blood, and keeps the wound flowing conveniently at feeding time. This slows down the normal healing process and can easily lead to infection of the cuts. Second, and more worryingly, wild vampires can carry a number of diseases including rabies. If you find yourself on the menu of a disease-carrying vampire then the consequences can indeed be terrible and possibly even fatal.

Andrew's primary concern, however, being a bat fanatic, was for the safety of his vampire. On no account was the creature to be allowed to escape, in case it came to any harm. Its sinister reputation might easily lead to panic reactions and sudden death—for the bat. Strict security regulations were put into force in the zoo TV studio that day. It was as though Garbo herself was on the set. There were to be absolutely no visitors and the camera crew were carefully briefed. We could not even rehearse, because the climax was to be the feeding of the vampire with fresh blood and Andrew wanted it to have a good appetite.

All went well during the early part of the show, with Andrew waiting patiently in the wings for his turn to appear, his pet fruit-bat tucked snugly beneath his waistcoat. It occasionally poked out its pop-eyed head to survey the world, looking curiously obscene in the process, as if Andrew had forgotten to 'adjust his clothing when leaving'. When it was time to show the fruit bat to the television camera and Andrew's front was shown in close-up, this effect was considerably enhanced and the bat's head looked even more like a rococo, furry phallus. Andrew himself was cheerfully oblivious of this and proceeded to stuff chunks of banana up his waistcoat with disarming abandon, finally ripping open his waistcoat buttons and flashing his giant bat to the waiting millions. It was a bravura performance.

Then it was time for the entry of the vampire. Both Andrew and I were on neck-mikes – small microphones hung like nooses around our necks, with long cables trailing off to some distant sockets. While he had been wielding his fruit bat, his cable had become entangled in nearby furniture and Andrew was on a shorter length than is ideal for demonstrating vampires, but he was now in the full flood of his wild enthusiasm for his animals and I did not like to interrupt him. The vampire was carefully brought out of its box and placed on my desk, near to a shallow glass dish full of fresh blood that Andrew had obtained from a friendly neighbourhood slaughterhouse. The bat sniffed appreciatively and hopped across to the dish. I was amazed by its curious gait. Other bats scuttle and shuffle along the ground when walking, but not the vampire. It moved in a highly efficient quadrupedal way, skipping about like some sort of long-legged wind-up toy.

I realized that this skilful ground-level locomotion was its answer to the problem of creeping up on unsuspecting, sleeping mammals. It could stalk them quietly after alighting near by and could then rapidly hop back out of the way if they stirred. Indeed, it was capable of hopping backwards as fast as forwards, and this was to be our undoing.

After it had dutifully lapped up a large meal of blood with its long, muscular tongue, it stood up and clearly felt much revived. Without warning, it began to skip vigorously about on the desk top and Andrew, for the first time, looked alarmed. He decided it was high time to end the item and moved in to catch the bat. This was no easy feat, as the vampire, if badly caught, was going to be all too ready to bite the hand that had fed it. Andrew failed at his first attempt and the vampire decided it was time to leave. Instead of flitting off with a beat of its wings, in true Dracula style, it chose to hop away, off the edge of the desk and across the floor of the studio, through a mass of cables and the rapidly retreating legs of the floor manager.

Andrew was horrified. The bat might be hurt! Completely for-
getting that he was wearing the neck-mike, he took off across the
studio in hot pursuit. About half-way across, while still clearly in
vision, his length of microphone cable ran out and he was jolted
to a sickeningly jarring halt by the loop around his neck. All the
viewers saw was the escaping bat followed rapidly in the same
direction by Andrew's anxious form. As he loomed too close in
front of the camera and went slightly out of focus, they saw his
contorted, apparently strangled head judder to a sudden standstill
and then disappear inexplicably downwards out of sight, as if he
were being dragged under by some horror-movie monster. From
below there came strange gurgling noises, as he tried to tear off
the neck-mike noose and continue his hunt for the vampire. By
now, of course, our television audience, knowing nothing about
the intricacies of neck-mikes, was totally convinced that the
vampire had somehow struck him down in agony. Many of them
fled to their telephones and called either the zoo or their local
papers. The zoo switchboard was jammed, first with viewers and
then with newspaper reporters. Was it true that a vampire was
loose in London and had already killed an eminent scientist?
Bram Stoker (the author of *Dracula*) would have loved it. Needless to say, everyone was deeply disappointed by the true facts.
Had they stayed at their television sets, they would have seen the
cameras swing round to cover the mad pursuit across the studio
of the now mikeless Andrew, who finally triumphed and cornered
the delightful bat as it hopped gaily about in a state of blood-
bloated euphoria.

After that experience I decided to try and improve the image
of bats in the public imagination. Clearly they were in need of a
P.R.O. to enhance their much-maligned reputation. I asked some
zoo visitors why they were so frightened of bats and the main
fear the women seemed to have was that a bat might swoop down
on them and become entangled in their hair. The old wives' tale
insisted that, when this happened, the only way to remove the
bat was to cut off the mass of tangled hair, an idea which filled
them with horror. To counteract this nonsense we went to the

lengths of making a film of a girl having a bat thrust into her long flowing hair. The bat was seen to crawl out again with perfect composure each time this was done. I then went on to explain that, not only could it easily get out of human hair, when artificially placed there, but it would also be highly unlikely to swoop into it in the first place. The echo-sounding system by which bats navigate in flight is so sensitive that they are hardly going to go blundering into unsuspecting females out strolling in the moonlight. Indeed, it was hard to imagine how such a strange animal myth could have arisen. I asked Ramona to check back into the history of the hair-tangling tale.

She came up with an interesting answer that forced me to modify my total rejection of the old story. It seemed that, back in the days of simple peasant dwellings, where bats often roosted in the rafters and crude ceilings of the rooms, women sitting by the evening fireside *were* sometimes faced with the scary problem of bat-tangled hair. Baby bats cling tightly to their mothers' fur and, once in a while, may lose their grip and fall to the ground below. If this happened immediately above a long-haired girl, and the baby bat fell on to her head, it would immediately respond by shuffling deep into the hairy mass on which it now found itself, clinging tighter than ever once it felt itself snugly embedded, and refusing all attempts to dislodge it. This could lead to feminine panic and tearing at the hair which could, in such rare cases, actually lead to the legendary entanglement becoming a reality. But today, of course, such a chain of events is so unlikely that unless a modern female goes to great lengths to spend many hours sitting underneath nursing bats that have hiccups, they are unlikely to suffer the dreaded fate.

We are not alone in having animal phobias. We share them with our closest living relatives, the great apes, as I found out on another *Zootime* occasion. Without realizing that I had given myself a problem, I arranged for a large python and a pair of charming orang-utans to appear in the same programme. They were completely separate items and were not due to appear in close proximity, so I thought there would be no difficulties. I knew

that tiny, wriggling snakes or large insects sometimes upset apes
if they encountered them at close quarters, but I felt that the vast,
comparatively immobile bulk of a big python, wrapped around a
keeper's body, would fail to trigger off the typical panic reaction
to a 'creepy-crawly' that apes share with so many human beings.
But I was wrong. As soon as the orangs had been brought in to the
TV Den, they spotted the giant snake and their reaction was
immediate. I have never, either before or since, seen two orangs
move at such lightning speed. Nor had their keeper, who was
taken unawares. In zoos, orang-utans all too often become lazy
and lethargic, squatting on concrete floors all day looking like
rusty Oriental statues of rather seedy Buddhas. When they do
move they seem to be swimming through treacle. Zippy they
are not. But all this changed the moment they set eyes on the
beautifully patterned coils of the tame python. With tiny,
bird-like squeaks, they flung their incredible hulks straight up
the nearest TV scaffolding and disappeared amongst the canopy
of powerful roof lights. The ape keeper used every trick known
to the Monkey House to persuade them to come down, but they
refused to budge until the snake was removed. I never tried to
mix apes and snakes again on *Zootime*.

I did, however, make a special film on the subject, using a toy,
mechanical snake and a young chimpanzee. The snake could be
wound up with a small key, so that it writhed realistically for a
few moments before coming to rest again. When we showed it
to the chimp in front of a film camera, we were able to record
the violent reaction of the juvenile ape to the snake's sinuous
movements. He screamed and fled, never taking his eyes off the
toy for one second. Only when the writhing movements had
stopped and the snake toy lay still, did the chimp risk an approach.
With all his hair standing stiffly on end, he swayed himself
hesitantly forward, barking a warning cry. Then he reached out
one foot and sent the toy flying through the air with a vicious
kick. Emboldened by this, he followed the toy to where it had
landed and dealt it a powerful blow just behind the head. When
the snake continued to lie inert and apparently dead, the ape very

carefully reached out and picked it up by the tip of its tail, dashed its head to the ground and simultaneously fled once more. He returned again and again, each time repeating some kind of attack until it seemed certain that the 'enemy' was no longer a threat. He then grabbed hold of it and began mangling it and throwing it about before finally kicking it high up into the air and abandoning it.

The remarkable thing about this response was that the chimpanzee in question had spent nearly all his life in captivity, where he had never had the chance of encountering a real snake. As a tiny baby in the wild, he would have been clinging to his mother's body and would have been protected by her from any dangers that threatened. So he had had little chance of learning about snakes during his lifetime, and the violent reactions he was now showing seemed to be entirely inborn.

I wanted to know precisely which features of the snake were triggering off his fear and, later, his savage attacks. Was it the sinuous movements or the lifelike patterning painted on the toy snake's body, or both? On another day, I showed the chimp a length of rubber tubing which I suddenly began to waggle in an undulating, snake-like way. The animal was immediately frightened by it, but not as strongly as with the toy, wind-up snake. After a short while, he overcame his fear and began to play happily with the length of tubing, as if it were just an ordinary object to be investigated. I then took it away, painted the surface of the tubing with zig-zag, snake-like patterns, and tried the test again. When I wiggled this improved snake model at the chimp, he immediately fled again, then returned and attacked the tubing with a swift blow. He then proceeded to behave towards the painted tubing in the same way as towards the toy snake, eventually throwing it roughly away and abandoning it.

So both the sinuous movements of a snake *and* its characteristic patterning played a part in identifying it as a dangerous creature to be treated with great fear and ultimate hostility. This makes sense in terms of the natural life-style of wild apes, who live in areas where venomous snakes abound and can obviously constitute a real danger. When I carried out an investigation into the animal hates of young humans, by means of a TV quiz, I found that, out of about 50,000 British children, roughly one in three of them put the snake at the top of their lists of 'most-hated animal'. These were children living in a country where there is a greater chance of being struck by lightning than of being killed by a venomous snake, and I could not help the feeling that, perhaps, in man too, there is a deep-seated, inborn fear of these reptiles, dating back to the remote past when our ancestors, like the present-day wild apes, faced a real threat of being struck down by snake venom. It would certainly make good evolutionary sense.

Another, more unexpected, chimpanzee phobia turned up when we were testing ape food preferences. Different kinds of nuts, fruits and vegetables were offered to young chimps and we recorded which objects were taken first and which were ignored. Then we added a mushroom to the list of food objects. The result was dramatic. One young male approached the harmless, edible mushroom, sniffed at it and then promptly fled, screaming and defecating across the floor of the TV Den. He then did something he had never attempted before. He flung open two sets of swing doors and rushed outside the building. Once outside he ran off as fast as his legs would carry him, still screaming wildly, as though a lion was chasing him. I caught up with him cowering in a corner and tried to coax him back into the Den, but without success. Every time we approached the swing doors, he veered away again, whimpering. It was several days before we could persuade him to return to the interior of the TV Den, and we did not dare to continue with the mushroom test, for fear of upsetting him to the point where he would refuse to enter the building ever again.

Some time later, using a more docile chimpanzee, we did however attempt to record this strange mushroom reaction on film. The response was less violent, but again there was distress after sniffing the object. In this case, the animal then attacked the mushroom, pulverizing it and then carefully sweeping each fragment away, out of range. When offered a wooden mushroom, there was no such response, but when a banana – the animal's favourite food – was smeared with mushroom, so that it smelt like the fungus, it was rejected as a suitable object for eating. So it seemed that it was the characteristic odour of the mushroom, rather than its shape, that was the vital clue, apparently telling the ape that here was something nasty, to be avoided at all costs.

Again, this makes sense. In the natural home of the chimpanzee, there are poisonous fungi as well as poisonous snakes, and a negative response to them might well be important to survival. But again there was little or no chance that the apes in question had learned this from personal experience. Once more we seemed to be dealing with an inborn phobia.

As the *Zootime* series progressed I seemed to learn something new every week. The only difficulty was that, as soon as I had discovered a new problem that warranted a serious research investigation, it was time to move on to next week's programme. I remembered that at Oxford, Niko Tinbergen had warned me against my tendency to spread myself too thinly over too many problems in too many species, but now it was I who felt the need to dig a little deeper into specific projects. But there was no let-up: week after week, the show had to go on. I began to miss my laboratory for the first time since leaving the zoology department.

By the end of the first year we had transmitted fifty-one half-hour programmes and made several films. Altogether I had been involved in devising and presenting about 300 different animal items. I was getting zoological indigestion. I was also becoming too easily recognized to be able to wander quietly around the zoo making observations. As soon as I stopped in front of an enclosure I became swamped by autograph hunters. At first this was a great ego-boost and I enjoyed it unashamedly, but after a while the appeal of it began to wane.

My original intention in coming to the zoo had been to make serious animal behaviour films which would spread the word about ethology to a wide public. But they were gradually taking second place to the increasingly popular *Zootime* series. Much as I loved doing the programme, it fell far short of the behaviour presentations I had in mind. I was seriously thinking about the need to return to academic research. The balance between the two sides to my personality – the research scientist and the popularizer – was becoming upset, and I talked the matter over with Granada. They agreed to augment the film crew at the unit and we were given extra space in the old animal sanatorium building for film studios in which we could attempt more careful, long-term studies. But they also persuaded me to keep on with the *Zootime* performances and, being a live series, it always somehow managed to demand priority.

My unhappiness about the superficiality of much of what I was doing had a curious effect. Since it was impossible to make *Zootime* more academic and gain satisfaction that way, I plunged headlong in the opposite direction. I became more of a 'ham'. It was as if I was saying to myself, all right, if we can't be more serious, then let's have some fun. *Zootime* had a new director by this time, called Mark Lawton, and together we set about livening up the proceedings. We introduced star guests and competitions and let 'show-biz' take over. There were chimpanzee tea-parties and elephant bath-times. I even presented one programme riding on the back of an elephant, until she walked under a low tree and I disappeared among the branches.

Instead of my earlier insistence on the virtues of watching animals, rather than handling them, I played for dramatic effect by becoming more intimate with them. I had my face licked by a huge male wolf, spat upon by a llama, and belched at by a camel. I had my hair groomed by a baboon, ruffled by a gibbon and messed on by a macaw. My fingers were nibbled by a mongoose, nipped by a bushbaby and pierced by a pelican. The ethologist was becoming the 'zoo-man'.

I was acting a part and almost perversely an archness was creeping in, as if I was pushing my role to a limit where I would eventually rebel against it. The extreme was reached with two highly contrived scenarios: The Great Banana Theft and The Ostrich Egg Omelette. Each had a serious zoological point to make, but the message was so overlaid with theatrical nonsense that it was virtually submerged.

The banana theft set out to demonstrate that apes have fingerprints very similar to human beings'. Various chimpanzees and orang-utans were invited to the TV Den and I then pretended that one of them had stolen some bananas from a tin on my bookcase. Incriminating banana skins were found but it was impossible to identify the culprit. The only thing to do was to call in Scotland Yard, in the person of Chief Superintendent Bob Cherryl (who had recently retired from his post as head of the Yard's fingerprint department). Bob arrived and took out his special fingerprint kit. Dusting the tin, he found a good print on it and sent it off for photographing. He then turned his attentions to taking the fingerprints of all the suspects. Because he played it straight, with a completely deadpan face, the ensuing chaos, with ink and papers flying in all directions was undeniably hilarious, but was more in keeping with slapstick circus than popular zoology. Eventually he obtained the vital prints, had them mounted, and then compared them with those from the tin. He was able to indicate sixteen details – whorls, loops, forks and breaks – in the print

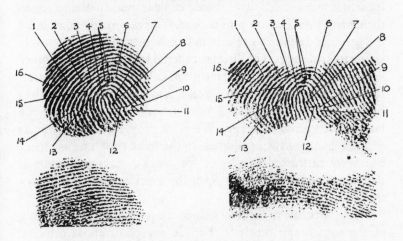

Ape fingerprints taken by Scotland Yard from the plundered banana tin (right) and from the 'guilty' orang-utan Annabelle (left)

lines of one particular orang called Annabelle, which matched up
with those on the print from the tin, and Annabelle, the fattest
and greediest of all the apes, and the number one suspect, was
finally convicted of the heinous crime.

The ostrich egg drama was even more contrived. The point I
wanted to make was that if ostriches in the wild went to a great
deal of trouble to keep potential egg-thieves away from their
nests, then this could only mean that the eggs tasted good.
Ostriches had sometimes been seen to perform the 'broken-wing
display' – an elaborate distraction device, in which the parent bird,
on seeing an enemy approaching the nest-site, would run away
from the spot, dragging one wing low, as if it were broken. Many
different kinds of birds show this remarkable behaviour as a way
of protecting their offspring. It encourages the attacker to chase
the adult bird, which appears to be an easy prey to catch because
of its crippled condition, and to forget about the nest with its all
too vulnerable eggs. Once the killer is closing in on the parent
bird, the latter then takes off at high speed, abandoning its 'act'
of being wounded.

In order to prove that this is a worthwhile strategy for the
ostrich, it was decided that I should cook and eat an ostrich egg as
the climax to a *Zootime* programme. This was made possible by
the presence in the zoo of a lone female ostrich who was busily
laying infertile eggs. The director ordered from 'props' a complete
kitchen in which I was to perform this culinary feat. My assistant,
Michael Lyster (a highly resourceful zoological technician I had
filched from Oxford) and I were to take our time over the
business of opening the egg. We were provided with hammers
and chisels and a saw, in addition to the usual cook's implements,
and were instructed to play it for laughs, making it seem as
difficult as possible to crack open the giant egg, with its heavy
shell.

When we came to the final item in the programme, the making
of the ostrich egg omelette, I made my point about ostriches
caring for their eggs carefully because they tasted so good, and
then moved into the kitchen setting. First, I called for a large

china bowl and tried to crack the ostrich egg on its rim, as one would do with an ordinary hen's egg. As the egg hit the edge of the bowl, the bowl cracked and fell to pieces. There was not even a scratch on the tough surface of the shell. First joke over. Then I tried smashing the egg down on to a plate. The plate cracked. Second joke over. Then I held the egg still, while Michael tried to saw it in half, but the saw kept on slipping. Third joke over. Now we went to work on it with the hammer and chisel. We had to be careful here. If we hit it too hard we would literally end up with egg on our faces, and none in the frying pan. The chisel slipped. It slipped again. The floor manager was signalling that time was running out. We started to panic and now, at last, we were really having trouble getting the egg open. In desperation, we switched to the hammer alone and started thumping the shell. Then we went back to the saw once more. Futile. Our growing concern was, for the first time, making the incident truly funny. Two inept men bungling an apparently simple kitchen chore was reducing a million housewives up and down the country to a state of helpless hysteria.

When we did, at last, crack the shell open with one almighty crash of the hammer, and tip the mass of gooey contents into a giant-sized frying-pan, there was, we were told later, more hysteria. In my haste, I had forgotten to put any butter into the pan and was now merrily whisking away at the equivalent of twenty-eight hen's eggs in a rapidly heating pan, with nothing between its hot metal surface and the sea of raw egg. The floor manager wrote the single word BUTTER on a large card and held it up. I let out a curse not suitable for family viewing and Michael rushed in with half a pound of butter, which I then did my best to squeeze down through the glutinous egg mass. I did this with the help of a large spatula of the type normally used for flipping over omelettes or serving up fried eggs on to a plate. There were a number of apertures pierced in this implement and through them there squirted jets of melting butter, like yellow fountains, which I dodged with little success. I was now getting the one minute (to end of programme) signal and gave up my butter-pressing act in favour of swirling the whole horrible mess around frantically in the hope that it would stop looking like the contents of a giant's spittoon before I had to eat it. Michael was hovering with a plate and a fork and, when we reached the thirty-second signal I had no choice. Spooning out a large portion of the still raw and glutinous goo, I moved in for my final close-up. Wishing the viewers goodbye, I forked up a drooping lump of mucoid, buttery jelly, that purported to be a tasty ostrich egg omelette, grinned a gelatinously drooling grin into the camera and sighed: 'Ah, deeelicious!'

Nothing delights British television viewers more than the genuine—as opposed to contrived—discomfort of a serious TV front man. We had a rapturous response to the programme, but science and zoology had somewhere flown out the window. I had enjoyed the nonsense, but the programme left a nasty taste in my mouth in more than one sense. I had finally achieved the reaction inside myself that I wanted. I had pushed myself over the top and was now only too keen to pull myself back. My mind was made up—I was going to leave Granada and return to the academic world.

The fact that it was many months before I finally handed in my resignation was due entirely to one animal—a small chimpanzee called Congo. He had originally been acquired as a *Zootime* mascot—a regular performer who appeared each week and became an old friend of the viewers. But he soon became much more than a mascot. Even for a chimpanzee—the most intelligent of all animals next to man—he was exceptionally bright. He did not live in the Monkey House, but had his own quarters in the TV Unit with a full-time attendant to look after him, as befitted his star status. I spent long hours in the privacy of the Unit observing his behaviour patterns and out of these hours of watching grew a determination to make a detailed study of chimpanzee behaviour. It was this study that kept me sane throughout all the superficialities of *Zootime*, in the months ahead.

6

'THE ONE IN THE CORNER IS A TROUBLE-MAKER. If you choose him you'll be in for a stormy passage.' The Monkey House keeper picked up a small female chimpanzee and thrust her into my arms. She was quiet and friendly. 'This is the one for you,' he insisted.

I was not so sure. I knew nothing about young chimps, but the small male in the corner seemed to have far more character than his rather docile companions. He was protesting wildly about something and while I held the little female I continued to watch him. His vigour and alertness impressed me. I moved across and sat down beside him, pretending to ignore him. To have stared too closely would have been interpreted as a threat, and I wanted to put him at his ease.

I was in a special quarantine room at the zoo, where a group of six one-year-old chimpanzees had recently completed their medical check-up, following their arrival at Regent's Park. Five of them were destined for the Monkey House. The sixth — whichever one I chose — was to come and live with us in the TV Unit, as a resident star of the *Zootime* series. Knowing how closely I would have to work with the one I selected, I refused to be hurried. When I made my final choice, it would be tantamount to adopting a child, and I risked irritating the keeper by rejecting his more experienced decision on my behalf. I put the friendly little female down and she ran across and began playing quietly with the rest of the group. Only the small, angry male remained alone and aloof. Still not looking directly at him, I reached out my hand in his direction. His hair stood on end and he began to sway his body from side to side. He seemed uncertain whether to attack me, or run from his corner and join the others. I let him calm down a little, then slid my body sideways until I was nearly touching his. He started hooting at me and was on the verge of biting me when, instead, his mood suddenly evaporated and he flung his arms around me and clung with a pathetic intensity to my jacket.

Had I realized then that he had been caught by killing his mother in the wild, and then taking the screaming, clinging baby from her body, I would have been horrified. But the time when I was to become seriously concerned about the way in which wild animals were captured and transported to zoos was some years off in the future. As a young zoologist freshly arrived at the zoo, I was still so excited by close encounters with exotic species, that I did not stop to think about the more unsavoury aspects of zoo management. Later, when I became a zoo curator, my scientific curiosity became slowly eroded by my increasing knowledge of the manner in which zoos acquired their new stock. This led me to instigate a comprehensive breeding policy, in which I struggled to set up natural breeding groups of every species in my care, so that, in theory, it would never again be necessary to plunder wild stocks. In the ideal zoo world, I argued, all the zoo inmates would be born in captivity and would themselves breed. It was the only way I could justify to myself the zoo context.

But that was a personal enlightenment yet to come. In the meantime, I was totally absorbed in the fascinating business of acting as a pseudo-parent to this bundle of shiny black fur clinging trustingly to my tweed jacket. It dawned on me that I was the one who had been adopted. I had just become an ape's mother.

I apologized to the Monkey House keeper for ignoring his advice and set off for the TV Unit with the young male chimp still clinging to me like a giant flea. He peered at the passing scene with a suspicious eye, shifting his grip from time to time as I strode along. My jacket now felt decidedly damp and the next morning it took one of its many subsequent trips to the cleaners. The smell of chimpanzee urine was to become one of the dominant odours of the weeks ahead. Any sudden panic while I was carrying him and I was flooded. Some months later I was fascinated to note a special change in his behaviour in this respect. As he grew older, something which I can only call a hygiene response matured in him. One day, instead of flooding me automatically, he gave a small grunt and twisted his body out away from me, urinating clear of my body. He was not taught to do this—it seemed to be a natural stage of chimpanzee development—an instinctive change in his juvenile behaviour. I was duly grateful, and came to recognize the warning grunt, which had a marked effect on my laundry bills.

Congo, as he was christened, was safely installed in his own, special star quarters in the TV Unit. A young keeper was detailed to tend to his needs and became his full-time companion. Ramona and I, Michael Lyster, my assistant, and Tony, the young keeper, became Congo's 'family'. He became increasingly at ease with each of us and his self-confidence grew rapidly. But he was still frightened by strangers and would run and cling to one of us if approached too closely. We discovered by accident that he had developed a set of friendship priorities. He rated each one of his 'family' on some kind of private scale. Tony, who spent most time with him, was number one, I was number two, and so on, according to the amount of intimate contact each of us had with him, day by day. This emerged when Ramona and I were having a mock-tussle in his presence. He immediately sprang to my defence. The four of us then experimented by pretending to attack one another. In each case, he defended the one he knew best. The intriguing thing about his loyalty rating was that it made no difference to him which of two people was the attacker and which the attacked. Regardless of who was to blame for starting the 'fight', he was always loyal to his favourite of the pair. His chimpanzee friendship knew no justice, only comrade support.

His sense of allegiance later led to passionate jealousies. Two of the victims of this jealousy were Charlie, a second young male chimpanzee who joined the TV Unit, and Anne, my secretary. Charlie was brought in as a stand-in for Congo, following a period when Congo had caught flu and was unable to appear on *Zootime* for a while. By this stage he had become a nationally famous television personality with a huge weekly fan-mail, and his illness made us realize that we would need a substitute if ever he was away sick again. Enter Charlie, a remarkably docile and, compared with Congo, rather dim-witted chimp. Charlie had been reared by a family of herbalists in Southend before coming to the zoo, which had somehow given him a most untypical personality for a young chimpanzee. Congo was an inquisitive, vigorous extrovert, always ready to leap forward and tear the headphones off an unwary floor-manager in the studio, or ram a hairy fist into a camera lens and block a vital shot. Charlie, by contrast, was a placid, sedentary introvert, more like an orang-utan in character, than a rampaging young chimp. He was the perfect foil for an extrovert and we decided to use him alongside Congo in some of the programmes – as a kind of 'straight man' to the star entertainer. Congo viewed this intrusion with the apprehension of a Hollywood martinet.

Before Charlie made his debut, the two young apes had been cheerful playmates. Charlie shared Congo's quarters and the two were always wrestling and chasing in a friendly way. I was delighted that Congo had a companion of his own species. Charlie was younger and smaller and I noticed with interest that if ever Congo became too boisterous and upset Charlie, he immediately eased off and made amends. There was a natural restraint in Congo's domination of the relationship. But matters changed when Charlie made his debut on *Zootime*. Congo's restraint went into a sharp decline.

At first, things ran reasonably smoothly, but the crisis arose when we decided to give Charlie a solo spot in the programme, before the 'star' made his appearance. Congo could see the entrance to the studio from the window of his room and when he caught sight of Charlie being carried in through the studio door, he flew into a towering rage, screaming and crashing about in his room in an alarming fashion. Word of this was passed to me while we were on the air and, fearing that there might be something wrong with Congo, we let Charlie stay on to take his place. For Congo, that was the last straw.

The following week, I was going to talk about chimpanzee play and I wanted to demonstrate the way in which Congo and Charlie wrestled together in a friendly way, without hurting one another. Michael was standing by, out of shot, as I introduced this item, with Congo and Charlie both clinging to his body, one under each arm. A few seconds before they were due to appear, Congo lent across Michael's body and, without his usual warning hoots and hair-bristling, attacked Charlie as hard as he could, sinking his teeth into the nearest bit of Charlie's flesh that he could find. It happened to be Charlie's upper lip. Charlie let out an ear-piercing yell that could be heard even outside the sound-proofed studio building. Still screaming, he was rushed out and taken to his room to be calmed down, while Congo, now a picture of juvenile innocence, made a solo appearance and I rapidly switched from a demonstration of social-play to a discussion on object-play, showing how quickly Congo could learn to open a series of boxes after only a single instruction from me.

It was the last time they appeared together in the studio. In their room, they had to be housed in separate sleeping-cages, and their close friendship seemed to be at a permanent end. Charlie's lip was badly bruised and swollen, but it soon healed without leaving a scar, except perhaps on Charlie's memory. Congo now once again reigned supreme in his *Zootime* role. I was frankly astonished by all this and began to wonder if I was reading more into chimpanzee behaviour than I should. Was I beginning to see them too much as human beings? Was I anthropomorphizing them? My ethological training went dead against this. But when I re-examined what had happened dispassionately, I could find no other explanation than that Congo had been expressing a passionate jealousy, with his simmering hostility towards Charlie carefully stored up in his brain and kept back for action at the most telling possible moment. My respect for the complexity of the ape brain was growing daily.

Congo's second victim, Anne, my secretary, provided further

evidence of Congo's smouldering strategies. Concerned entirely
with office duties, Anne was never part of Congo's close 'family',
but since I spent a great deal of time with her, dictating letters
and running the business side of the TV Unit, he realized that I
had a close relationship with her that somehow excluded him.
This he disapproved of, and she found it hard to make any kind
of friendly contact with him. She persevered whenever they met
during the day, but after an occasion when he tried unsuccessfully
to attack her, I advised her never to enter his private quarters.

One day there was an urgent call for me and she had to ignore
this advice. Running down the long corridor to look for me, she
went in to his room to see if I was there. It so happened that
Michael was in the process of feeding him and had gone out of
the room for a moment to get some fresh fruit from the refriger-
ator. Congo was sitting in his sleeping cage, but the door was
ajar. As soon as he saw Anne, he flung open the door, rushed
across the room, leapt on her and bit her savagely on the shoulder,
tearing open a large flap of skin.

Michael heard her scream, dropped his fruit, and hurtled back
to the chimp room. He was only a few seconds, but Congo had
already rushed back into his cage, and *closed the door* – something
he never did – and was now sitting calmly on his bed staring
innocently at the ceiling, as though nothing had happened. Seeing
the blood on Anne's shoulder, Michael went over, opened the
cage door, and gave him a sharp, punitive tap on his head. His
reaction was unique. He simply pursed his lips and ignored
Michael. Michael gave him another sharp tap, but he stubbornly
refused to recognize the rebuke.

To anyone who knew Congo as well as Michael did, this
reaction was extraordinary. On all other occasions when Congo
had to be punished for some misdeed and received a small smack
from a member of his 'family', he was always outraged and his
facial expressions clearly indicated this. It was never necessary to
give him more than a light tap – the fact that he was being
reprimanded by one of his close friends was punishment enough.
On this occasion alone, he refused to respond. As Michael put it,

9 Unlike giant tortoises, giant snakes are the most amenable and
  co-operative of zoo animals. Unfortunately, thousands of viewers
  switched off their sets the moment any snake appeared on their
  screens, such is the deep-seated fear of these exquisite creatures.

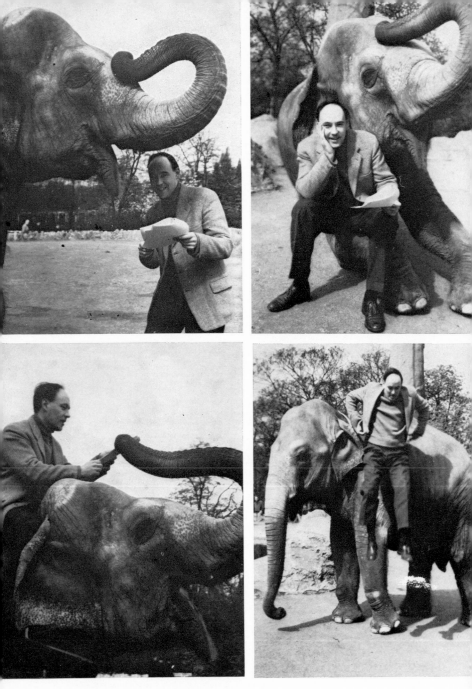

10–13 All went well at rehearsals, but when the live TV show began, the elephant from whose back I was doing the running commentary, insisted on walking under a low tree and I disappeared in a swirl of foliage.

it was almost as if he felt the attack on Anne was well worth any consequences.

The unusual features of this incident were the deliberate closing of the door and the dumb acceptance of the reprimand. It was hard for me to explain such behaviour in simple ethological terms. Strategies, deceits, the acceptance of punishment – these were patterns I knew well enough from human contexts, but had never encountered before in my studies of other animals. Clearly, the chimpanzee was going to take me into new realms of animal behaviour concepts.

I suddenly realized that here was an animal that I could study in a new way, and I determined from that moment on to make a more serious attempt to explore the workings of the ape brain. I began to work out some serious research projects that I could develop with Congo, during the quiet periods between his television appearances. Just how far *could* the chimpanzee brain go? Just how human *was* Congo? Or, to put it another way, just how ape-like were human beings? It was the start of a whole new research obsession for me.

These studies were to lead me into extraordinary situations a year or so later, when Congo was older and mentally even more advanced, but for the time being, while he was still so young, I did no more than watch and record and wait. While I did so, Congo's popularity rose to dizzy heights, through his weekly television appearances, and each week presented me with a new problem. Congo was expected to do something different in every *Zootime* and it began to tax our ingenuity. We called on the help of one of my favourite eccentrics, an artist extraordinary called Bruce Lacey. Bruce had been responsible for inventing and constructing the insane props used by the Goons in their early films. If Spike Milligan wanted a Mukkinese Battle Horn, Bruce Lacey was the man to create one. He arrived at the zoo wearing a test-pilot's outfit and carrying a stuffed swan. I was foolish enough to enquire about the swan. 'Swan Vestas,' he explained in a matter-of-fact way, striking a match on it to light his cigarette. He told me confidentially that he was rather preoccupied

F

with the construction of a robot that was going to play Lady
Macbeth, but that he could find time to help me out with some
chimpanzee intelligence-testing apparatus, if I could explain my
needs to him.

One of the things I wanted to show was the aiming ability of
chimpanzees. The act of precise aiming was a vital accomplish-
ment for early man when he first became a hunter, and I was keen
to see how well our non-hunting relatives, the apes, could manage,
given a context in which a good aim brought a desired reward.
'Simple,' said Bruce, 'I will make you a chimpanzee coconut-shy.
The apes will have to throw a ball and knock down a coconut,
which they will then be given as a reward. But we will have to
scale it down for television. And the coconut would be too
difficult for them to open. So I shall use grapes. I shall make you a
grape-shy. There will be a long slope and when the ball hits the
grape, it will roll down the slope to the feet of the successful ape.
And the ball will be hanging from a chain, so that if he misses it
will swing back to him for another try.'

And off he went to his workshop to construct the first of many
brilliantly inventive pieces of chimpanzee apparatus. The grape-
shy was an enormous success and we were astonished at the incredible accuracy displayed by Congo when aiming at his small
targets. We tried the game ourselves and found that we could do
no better than the small chimpanzee. So the ability to aim,
although rarely called upon in the natural world of the chimpanzee, was there, lying dormant, in our closest living relatives.

Strangely enough, one situation in which wild chimpanzees do
employ an aiming process was discovered some years later by a
young girl who joined the zoo film unit for a while as Ramona's
assistant. Her name was Jane Goodall and, after acting as Ramona's
film librarian for a while, she took off on what seemed to us to be
a highly risky expedition to live with a colony of wild chimpanzees in East Africa. She intended to go for only six months,
because she had become engaged to a handsome young actor in
London, but she stayed on for years, to produce the greatest

study of wild chimpanzee behaviour ever made and to become world famous. One of her many exciting discoveries was that the wild apes often fished for termites in termite hills, tearing open small holes and then breaking twigs or stems into probing tools. These they pushed deep into the cavity of the termite hill until they were festooned with clinging insects. Withdrawing them, they then passed the tools through their mouths, picking off and eating the hapless termites. The act of pushing the twigs or stems into the holes they had made, needless to say, involved a careful aiming process, even though there was no throwing involved. So eventually we did come to see a way in which Congo's aiming abilities could have been of some use to him in his wild state.

Strangely enough, one of Bruce Lacey's later chimp games did utilize a very similar action, foreshadowing Jane's discovery in nature. He made a long, sloping zig-zag panel, down which it was possible to roll a reward-grape, if Congo used a tool correctly. The tool was a thin rod. To obtain the reward-grape, he had to keep pushing the rod into one hole, then pulling it out and thrusting it into another. It was as if Bruce Lacey had read Jane Goodall's report on her termite-fishing chimps, almost a decade before she had written it, and based his apparatus on their activities in the wild.

We did not confine our exploits with Congo entirely to tests of his intelligence and manual ability. I was also fascinated by the many inborn actions that he was displaying as he grew older. He was capable of producing a whole range of facial expressions, sounds, gestures and postures, and I wanted to become fluent in chimpanzee. Most people who keep chimps seem to want to make them as human as possible, but I tried to reverse the process. The more like a chimpanzee I could become, the better Congo and I were going to get along. When I was alone with him (some people become alarmed by grunting, jibbering zoologists) I would try my best to copy each of his calls. There was the friendly OUGH-OUGH greeting noise, with the lips stretched forward in a pouting, give-us-a-kiss posture; the ARCK-ARCK noise at feeding time, with the mouth slightly open; the oooo-ooooooo whimper of distress; and the loud HOOOGH-OOOGH alarm call, used at a distance. I was intrigued to notice that the greeting call and the food noise were sometimes combined in a hybrid noise at the moment when the food tray arrived in the chimp room. It was as if the apes were capable of combining two separate signals to produce a new statement. The 'welcome' sound and the 'good food' sound combined to produce the statement: 'I welcome the good food.' Having witnessed this, I was less surprised than some people when, some years later, American psychologists discovered that chimpanzees could be trained to combine two learnt hand gestures to form a simple, sign-language 'sentence'.

I found that if I tickled Congo under the arms, he would give a staccato panting sound remarkably like human laughter, but much softer in volume. The facial expression that went with this ape laugh was one in which the mouth was wide open, but the lips were stretched out to cover the teeth. Sometimes the lower teeth might be exposed, but *never* the upper teeth. If the animal's mood changed to one of fear or rage and screaming began, then, and only then, did all the teeth, both lower and upper, come into view.

Teeth-baring in chimps is therefore rather different from that in humans and this difference can lead to some classic errors. The chimpanzee that bares all its teeth can appear to be giving a massive, Louis Armstrong style, grin. In the flesh, the ape's screaming accompaniment leaves no doubt about his disturbed mood, but on film this is far from clear and, to an inexperienced eye, the animal seems to be happily smiling at the camera. In TV advertisements and comedy films, it is possible to give the false impression that the apes are deliriously happy when they present teeth-bared faces, and the effect can be enhanced by dubbing on human laughter. And in a famous photograph of Ham, the space chimp, when he had returned to earth in his capsule, he is clearly showing the distress face, while the caption reads that his happy, smiling face tells us all how pleased he is to be back on terra firma.

A more correct interpretation of his expression would have been: 'Let me out of here, you bastards.'

This difference in facial expressions sometimes leads to odd encounters between chimp and man. For example: human smiles at ape – ape is frightened or enraged, bares its teeth – human thinks it is smiling back and laughs happily – ape sees laugh as exaggerated teeth-baring with threat noise added (the full human laugh sounds quite hostile to a chimp) and becomes even more agitated – and so on. The two species become more and more excited, one with pleasure, the other with rage or fear. The signals are the same, the meanings different.

The moral of this story is, when offering friendship to a chimpanzee, do not laugh or bare your teeth at him, but give soft, teeth-covered grunts or short, panting noises. At the same time, reach out gently with a limp hand and offer the back of it to him, like an aristocratic lady offering her hand to be kissed. If you press the back of your hand softly against the ape's lips, he will not bite it, but simply press it wetly with his mouth. This is the most common form of chimpanzee gesture-greeting and is remarkably effective at breaking the ice between your species and his. If you are not sufficiently fluent in chimp, then I cannot be responsible for the consequences. If you *are* fluent, however, you may quickly find yourself in a hairy embrace, with the ape pressing its open mouth tightly against the skin of your neck and uttering soft, gurgling noises. If you get that far, do not be alarmed by the proximity of those sharp teeth to your jugular vein. All will be well, providing you relax and accept the long-armed hugs and possibly a little delicate hair-grooming. It is a good idea, though, to groom him back, which helps to cement the friendship. Search through his fur for small particles of dried skin and remove them. Your chimp-appeal will grow by the second.

Armed with this knowledge, I was particularly pleased to see a group of chimpanzees walking down a London street one day. They were on their way to a recording studio with their agent, to make a short film. As they were strangers to me, I thought that this would be an ideal moment to test out my fluency in chimp signals. Their agent would, I imagined, be suitably impressed by my erudite approach, instead of the usual anthropomorphic nonsense. I sauntered up confidently, uttering the appropriate greeting signal of OUGH-OUGH-OUGH, proffering the back of a limp hand. Somewhat taken aback, the apes politely shook hands with me and then gazed up at their agent, as if to say: 'Who is this nut?' You can't win them all.

I was, of course, dealing with highly trained, professional chimp performers, who had been taught so many human actions that they had almost forgotten to what species they belonged. Their owner told me that they regularly watched television, and you can't get more human than that. They even flipped channels to find the noisiest Westerns.

I vowed never to let Congo become humanized to this extent, but it was not easy to restrain the desire of other people to see him as a hairy little man. Because he had become a famous television star there were many requests for him to make personal appearances, but I resisted them all, using the excuse that the zoo did not permit its animals to leave Regent's Park. Then, finally, I was talked into making one exception. The *Daily Mirror* was setting up a National Pets Club, to try and raise the standard of pet-keeping in Britain. It was a good cause, and when they announced that they were holding a special Pets Club Luncheon at the Café Royal, and Congo and I were invited, in a weak moment I gave in. It proved to be a memorable experience.

Congo had now reached a level of self-confidence that meant that any novel experience was intensely exciting. As a large, chauffeur-driven car sped us down Regent Street, he jumped up and down on the soft seat, thumping the windows at the passers-by. The uniformed chauffeur retained a stiff dignity, as if he were delivering the Queen Mother to a banquet. He had seen it all, and a young ape was not going to throw him. Unrtfounately he suddenly stopped seeing it all, because Congo reached forward and pulled the man's peaked cap down over his eyes. The phrase 'blind panic' took on a new meaning, as the huge car swerved wildly back and forth across the busy street, scattering frightened shoppers. Congo was delighted and hooted at them through the windows.

Recovering his vision and his poise, the driver deposited us with visible relief at the imposing entrance of the great restaurant. Many famous faces had entered those portals and none more confident or excited than young Congo's. Inside, the place was awash, all too literally, with pets of every description. There were film-star pets and pets of film stars; television pets and advertisement pets; and everything from humble pet mice to champion dogs from Cruft's. Punctuating the bedlam was a large gathering of celebrated humanity – pop stars and politicians, actresses and bishops. The many, small round tables were beautifully set for a splendid, long luncheon and to reduce the chaos sufficiently to make this feasible, there were rows of temporary animal enclosures arranged around a balcony above. Michael, my assistant, took Congo away for a lunch of his own, and for a moment there was comparative peace. But it was short-lived. As the meal was drawing to a close, photographers moved in and asked for the animals to join us. Congo was brought down and placed in a chair at our table, while the cameras clicked.

At this point, things moved fast. Congo was not used to white table-cloths on the tables at which he normally sat. A table-cloth was a novelty that demanded investigation. Taking hold of it in both hands he pulled it sharply towards him. When conjurers do this, all the cutlery, crockery and glassware stay put and comes to rest on the now bare table. Congo was no conjurer. Eminent bodies were suddenly festooned in knives, forks, plates, glasses, cups, saucers, ashtrays, spoons and salt cellars. Their clothes were drenched in iced water, wine and coffee. There was a great deal of leaping up, screaming and yelling. Congo was greatly impressed by this and joined in, leaping up and down on his chair and hooting loudly.

Impeccable servants rushed forward and made amends. A new cloth was brought, clothes were sponged down, tableware replaced and coffee cups refilled. Congo eyed these events with a gleam in his eye, but I frustrated him by keeping a tight grip on his collar (his only article of clothing). Held in check in this way, he was forced to change his tactics. He was sitting next to a duchess who was deep in conversation with the director of the Battersea Dogs Home. The duchess took an elegant gold cigarette case from her handbag and placed it on the table. While she was searching for her lighter, and while I momentarily took my eyes off him, he reached out, snatched the cigarette case, opened it, took out all the cigarettes, bit them neatly in two and then replaced them as best he could. I decided it was time to leave and tried to persuade Congo to accompany me before there were any more disasters. But in moving, I had loosened my grip on him and in an instant he was up on the table, drumming with his feet and clapping his hands together like a demented band leader. Then he switched to being a Russian count, hurling glasses to the floor with gay abandon.

I noticed that the duchess was having difficulty lighting her cigarette and, scooping the protesting Congo up in my arms, made for the exit as decorously as possible. Michael was waiting outside and I handed Congo over to him, to take breath, but Congo had spotted a vast St Bernard dog who was also being hustled out (having done something unspeakable that had never occurred before in the hallowed rooms of the Café Royal's Louis Suite) and had taken an immediate dislike to him. He exploited the transfer from my body to Michael's by making a sudden leap to the ground, where he set off in hot pursuit of the lumbering dog. Pausing only to bite an I.T.N. reporter who was foolish enough to approach him for an interview, and lift up a Scotsman's kilt and peer underneath, he lunged after the great dog, hooting and swaying and stamping his feet. The dog took fright and broke loose from its owner, scattering startled waiters as it made for the nearest open door, which happened to be the entrance of the ladies' room. Before we could stop him, Congo raced after the retreating hulk of fur and the door swung shut behind them. Michael and I paused on the threshold. We had never been called upon to extricate a male chimpanzee from a ladies' lavatory in an elegant restaurant before. It was unlikely that Emily Post or Amy

Vanderbilt covered this problem in their volumes on etiquette. While we debated how to proceed, screaming broke out inside the beleaguered loo and several fashionable ladies with smudged lipstick and flailing arms emerged, as if auditioning for parts in a re-make of *King Kong*. They were followed closely by a panting St Bernard with its tail between its legs, but no Congo. As the ravaged interior now seemed to be clear of humanity, I ventured inside and found Congo thoughtfully peeing into an expensive wash-basin and kissing his image in the mirror. A trembling voice from behind a locked cubicle door enquired whether it was safe to come out, but I thought a male voice in that female sanctuary might have upset her even more, so I quietly scooped up Congo and tip-toed out.

Congo himself was now all sweetness and light and nestled calmly in my arms, temporarily satiated by his social triumphs. On the return journey he even left the driver unmolested, although I noticed that this time the man was taking no chances. He was hatless.

From now on I decided that Congo would have to confine his chaos-production to the TV Unit. But this only meant that it was our own belongings that had to take the full brunt of his interminable quest for novelty. On one occasion he managed to get into my office when I was absent, undid the various bottles of coloured inks on my desk, scattered the contents over my new carpet and then, for good measure, ripped a pocket off my duffle coat and rammed it into the waste-paper basket. I only discovered how he managed this last feat when, after I had had the pocket stitched on again, he ripped it off for the second time. On this occasion I was in the room with him and found that he had evolved a game of standing on a table, flinging himself at the door where the coat was hanging, and then breaking his fall to the ground by grabbing hold of the pocket with both hands. His weight did the rest.

He also became an efficient pick-pocket and was for ever being pursued up and down corridors as he ran away with a bunch of car-keys in his mouth. Once he was ingenious enough to hide a bunch of stolen keys in a mug full of milk and then proceeded to join us helpfully in a major treasure-hunt throughout the entire unit. Only when his thirst got the better of him was his secret revealed.

The worst moment came when, after we had sorted through 68,000 postcard entries for a *Zootime* competition, selecting the correct entries to announce them on the next programme, he managed to rush in and muddle them back into the huge pile of losers. Other tortures he devised for us included 'killing' things when we were not looking. He was particularly adept at killing scripts, which he tore to pieces, screwed up into twisted balls, and stamped into any box or basket available. He had a particular hatred for my black umbrella. One day when it began to rain, I put it up as I walked through the zoo and wondered why people were laughing at me as they ran for cover. Looking up I saw that Congo had finally managed to assassinate it, and it now looked more like a decaying bat's wing than an elegant London brolly.

Clearly, he needed more exercise than he was getting, and I remembered that there was a large, empty paddock just behind the TV Unit. I decreed that he should be given a daily work-out there and that I would supervise the first visits myself. I had now introduced a sturdy collar and lead for Congo walks, and we set off like a dog-owner and a manic pooch going for a stroll. Once inside the grassy paddock, I unhooked the lead and Congo began rolling ecstatically about on the soft surface, re-inventing Greek gymnastics for himself.

Despite his apparent abandon, he was acutely aware of my position in the paddock and avoided straying too far from his 'pseudo-parent'. I was the safe base from which he explored his new world. Every so often he would launch himself on a long, galloping voyage of discovery, running in a great curve that eventually brought him back to me. Then off again, his sense of security recharged.

On subsequent visits to the paddock he became progressively more adventurous, as the terrain became more familiar. There were trees dotted about the paddock and he began to explore their lower branches. At first, he was extremely tentative and soon jumped down again and ran back to me to make body contact. In his whole life he had never climbed a tree, which was a ridiculous situation for a young chimpanzee. In the wild, he would have been an arboreal acrobat by now, fearlessly flinging himself from branch to branch, leaping and brachiating with great skill. But Congo was like a city child on his first visit to the countryside. He felt magnetically drawn to those leafy branches, but his inexperience held him back, forcing him to pluck up courage each time he clambered aloft.

Then, one day, he suddenly seemed to master the whole problem of tree-climbing, as if his ancient ape heritage had burst through and swept aside all caution. In a moment, he had scaled a huge tree and disappeared into its upper regions. I was taken completely by surprise and was horrified when I realized that he was still wearing his collar and lead. There was a loop at the free end of the lead and I had ghastly visions of Congo hanging himself if it accidentally caught on the end of a branch. I was helpless. If I gave chimpanzee alarm calls and tried to hurry him down, that might only agitate him and increase the chances of a disaster. But the longer he stayed there, the greater was the risk of a spike of the tree catching the dangling loop. All I could do was watch and wait and try to encourage him down without any fuss.

He was thoroughly enjoying himself, leaping and swinging about at high speed. My neck was aching, staring up at the small black form as it hurtled through space. After what seemed ages, he started his descent and then it happened. The lead, dragging behind him, stuck firm in the fork of a branch. He was jolted to a halt. Startled, he began to pull on it and it stuck even tighter into the fork. My worst fears were realized. But as I watched, Congo turned, calmly unhitched the lead, and proceeded on his way down the trunk and into my arms. I was never more grateful for the fact that the chimpanzee is the second most intelligent animal on the face of the earth. And on this occasion, at least, the most intelligent.

The next time I took Congo tree-climbing – definitely without a lead this time – it happened to be a day when Regent's Park was rather crowded. The paddock was on the perimeter of the zoo and overlooked the public park, where the sunshine had brought large crowds out to lie on the grass, or stroll along the paths. Often, when Congo had been exercising, one or two people had paused to watch. But on this occasion, quite a small crowd had gathered and Congo was eyeing them suspiciously. To him, it was his paddock and here was a roaming band of strange creatures apparently about to invade it. Mistakenly thinking that he would be much more excited by his new-found game of tree-climbing, I took him to a suitable tree, unhooked his lead, and lifted him on to the trunk. I turned my back for a second as I walked away to a point where I could watch his aerial gymnastics and that was where I made my vital error. He must have been waiting for just such an opportunity.

No sooner had I turned away, than he was off at full speed, making for the admiring crowd. Little knowing what was heading their way, they laughed and shouted encouragement. This terrible threatening noise only enraged the small black ball of fury all the more. He hurled himself at the railings and, before I could do a thing, he was up and over and down the other side. Once again, my heart was in my mouth, but luckily there was a double set of railings and before he could get over the second fence, I went into action. This time I did not need to hesitate. Instead of chasing after him, which would have been futile, I did just the opposite. Shouting his name like a war-chant, I retreated across the paddock, watching over my shoulder as I went.

Congo was about to clamber over the second line of railings and set about his admiring public when he caught sight of my retreating figure. With a screech, he turned and leapt at the inner fence. In a split second, he was over it and was galloping after me, whimpering and screaming.

When I was far away from the railings I flopped down in the grass and in a moment a panting form flung itself at me and clung to me, as if it were never going to let go again. Luckily, Congo, aggressive as he was becoming, was still a child and to him I was still a parent whose sudden absence could cause fear and trembling.

I was sad to have given him such a fright, but it was a good lesson for him to learn and it was certainly the lesser of two evils. Unfortunately, however, a frightened chimp always reacts in the same way and as he clung to me I suddenly felt that side of my body getting rather hot and wet, and once again I knew that my clothes would soon be leaving on one of their many trips to the cleaners.

Curiously, it was in that same paddock, several years later, that I had another nasty panic, which was almost the reverse of the one with Congo. This time it was caused by animals refusing to run away, when I expected them to do so. I had become Curator of Mammals by then, and had turned the paddock into a wolf wood. A group of wolf cubs had been brought across from Whipsnade Park, to form a new pack. When they first arrived, I often went into the paddock with them to check that all was well with their freshly built dens. There was no need to fear them because they were so young. Even when they were half-grown wolves, it was only necessary to shout out 'Shoo!' and they would scamper off to the far end of the enclosure.

Then, some months later, a keeper reported that they had been digging up the drains that had been installed under their den floors to prevent flooding from heavy rain. I telephoned one of the zoo architects and asked him to investigate the problem with me. Arriving at the gate, I had some difficulty in persuading him that it was safe to enter. The pack now looked like adult wolves, rather than mere cubs, and he found it hard to believe that they would not immediately tear us into small, edible pieces. I brushed his objections aside so loftily that he eventually agreed to come in with me and inspect the damaged drains.

As we locked the tall gates behind us, he was immensely relieved to see the pack scatter to the far end and sit there watching us alertly. We strode across to the den, entered its low space and began examining the damage. Having arrived at a solution, we struggled out again, to find that the pack had been edging its way up towards us. The architect's alarm returned.

'Don't worry,' I said lightly, 'watch this,' and I walked a few paces towards the wolves and, as if addressing a flock of birds in an orchard, waved my hand authoritatively and shouted my experienced 'Shoo!' To my astonishment, the wolves failed to retreat in the approved fashion. 'Shoo!' I shouted again, much louder this time. Instead of retreating, they began to move closer. I was horrified to see that they were forming a circle around us. It was an eerie sight. Silently, as if following some preordained plan, the circle started to close in. Trying to keep cool, I whispered to the architect to make slowly for the exit gate. I had a distinct feeling that if we ran, it would trigger off a sudden charge and we would be easily overtaken by a snarling mass of wolfdom.

The few seconds it took us to stroll to the gate seemed like an hour. The semi-circle of loping wolves padded towards us at a steadily more determined pace. Fumbling with the lock on the gate I managed to open it and we both leapt through the welcome space and slammed it hard behind us, as the eager animals bounded up and glowered at us through the bars.

'And farmers have the nerve to say that the fox enjoys being hunted,' I gasped. But the architect was not amused. What, he wanted to know, had gone wrong? It was a fair question. As I was searching for an answer, I noticed that one of the male wolves was sniffing at a female and trying to mount her. It dawned on me that, during the few months that had passed since my last visit inside the wolf wood, the young animals had become sexually mature. Although still youngsters, they were now almost fully grown and had passed over a vital threshold. They had reached the age where, in the wild, they would now be fending for themselves, hunting with the older members of the pack. With this change, their fears of a human body entering their territory had been rapidly and dramatically reduced. I had been careless to overlook this, and apologized to the architect for having given him such a bad scare. I tried to pacify him by explaining that, despite many stories to the contrary, attacks on humans by wild wolves were extremely rare and ridiculously exaggerated, but I don't think he was very impressed with this information, having recently lost all confidence in my knowledge of wolf behaviour.

But back in the days of Congo, the paddock, despite our scares and difficulties in it, remained a wonderful ape playground, and our star chimp was able to exercise there every week. Physically, he was developing beautifully and his intelligence constantly astonished us. I was particularly impressed by his manual dexterity. One day, Michael said, 'Watch this!' and, leaving his bunch of keys on the food table in Congo's room, walked away to one side and stood leaning against the far wall, next to me. Throwing us a quizzical glance, Congo picked up the bunch of keys, sorted through them, testing each one with his muscular lips until he found the one he wanted, and then, leaping down, ran across and unlocked the door to his sleeping cage, inside which Michael had placed his evening meal. I asked Michael how long it had taken him to train Congo to do this, but he explained that it had happened first by accident, when he left the keys unguarded. Congo had learnt how to do it himself.

This combination of dexterity and intelligence started me thinking, and reminded me that there was one chimpanzee experiment that I had promised myself several years earlier, if ever I had the chance to carry it out. For some reason I had pushed it to the back of my mind until now, but the key manipulation brought it to the surface again.

The idea came originally from a lucky chance. While I was working on my fish studies at Oxford, I had tried to learn a little German, so that I could read some important articles written in that language. But I found it impossibly hard going. One afternoon in the Radcliffe Science Library, I had been struggling with a German stickleback paper for several hours, making little progress, and had finally given up in despair. Feeling that I had wasted the afternoon, I paused as I was leaving and decided to salvage something out of my visit, by reading something in English. I had come to a halt next to shelves containing American psychology journals – journals I normally never bothered to look at. I plucked out a volume at random and flipped idly through the pages. It was an odd thing to do, and I hardly expected to find anything that would interest me. But I was wrong. My casual act

led me to the starting point of what was to become one of the
most fascinating research projects I ever undertook.

The journal fell open at a page on which there was a strange,
scribbly drawing, as if a child had been defacing the learned work.
Turning the page, I found more and more of these scribbles and
looked back to discover the title of the paper. It was called
'Figural preferences in the drawings of a chimpanzee'. A female
chimp called Alpha had apparently been an avid scribbler for
some years. At the famous Yerkes Laboratories where she was
housed, she would beg for a pencil and paper and then sit in a
corner totally absorbed as she made mark after mark on the white
surface. Paul Schiller, one of the Yerkes scientists, had become
interested in this odd behaviour and had presented her with
specially designed test cards on which he had already drawn
simple geometrical patterns. He discovered that the shape and
position of his patterns influenced the positions of the marks
which Alpha made. In other words, her scribbling was not
random, but was visually controlled. He also noted that her
drawing style changed as time went on. Sadly, he died before
publishing his findings. A friend of his, Karl Lashley, came
across Alpha's drawings – 200 of them – and some brief notes
about them, when looking through Schiller's effects, and thought
they were so interesting that he devoted some time to organizing
the notes and publishing them, along with a selection of the test
drawings, in this psychological journal I was now gazing at.

I read the article through twice, not quite believing it the first
time. The idea that an ape could produce visually controlled
drawings seemed far-fetched. But on the second reading I became
convinced that the evidence was sound and made a mental note
to take the study further, should I ever be in a position to do so.
At departmental tea that afternoon, I announced flippantly that
one day I was going to hold a one-chimp show of paintings at a
London art gallery, that would astonish the world, and narrow
the gap between ape and man even more. I was not serious, but
four years later that was precisely what I found myself doing.

During my early months at the zoo, I was so absorbed with

the problems of setting up a television unit, that I shelved the idea of doing any serious experimentation with Congo. But as soon as the pressure eased a little, I felt the need to get my teeth into a detailed study of some sort that would last more than the few days I could allow for preparing a typical *Zootime* item. Congo's manipulation of the keys reminded me that it was high time to get started with an extension of the Schiller investigation.

Still not convinced that anything would come of it, I began in a modest way to see if Congo would react at all to drawing materials. Instead of setting up an elaborate experimental procedure, I decided to introduce pencil and paper as additional objects in one of his play sessions.

I remember the occasion well. He was sitting on the carpet in my office, surrounded as usual by debris of all kinds – toys, the contents of the waste-paper basket, my scarf and my gloves. He was trying to ram the hat of the *Zootime* director, Mark Lawton, into the now empty waste basket. He succeeded in doing this, piled all the waste paper back in on top of it, jumped on it, and then looked over at me. I held out the pencil. His curiosity led him towards it. Gently I placed his fingers around it and rested the point on a piece of cardboard I had found. Then I let go. As I did so, he moved his arm a little and then stopped. He stared at the card. Something odd, he noticed, was coming out of the end of the pencil.

It was Congo's first line. It wandered a short way and then stopped. Would it happen again? Yes, it did, and again, and again. Still staring at the card, Congo began to draw line after line and as I watched I noticed that he was beginning to concentrate the lines in one particular region – a part of the card on which there was a small ink-blot. Even in this very first scribble, Congo's lines were not just random scratchings and, like Alpha, he carried within him the germ, no matter how primitive, of visual patterning.

This was the beginning of a long series of picture-making tests with Congo, covering a period of over two years and resulting in no fewer than 384 drawings and paintings. And it was to grow into a project that was constantly in danger of becoming a victim of its own success. Although I was as devoted to modern art as anyone, and more than most, I was soon to face the irony of being accused of attempting to ridicule the art world and, in particular, to destroy the avant garde.

But that was in the future. At first, the Congo tests began quietly and seriously, in the privacy of the TV Unit. My main concern was to establish how far one could go in describing an 'aesthetic sense' in a chimpanzee. The first thing that struck me was the intensity of Congo's concentration when making a picture. There was no need for any kind of reward to spur him on. Indeed, on one occasion when I tried to cut a drawing session short before he had finished his picture, he exploded in a screaming temper-tantrum and only calmed down when he was allowed to continue and complete his work. Judging by the strength of this reaction, he rated picture-making as highly as eating or drinking, despite the fact that his only gratification was the production of the picture itself.

For me, this made the cave art at Lascaux easier to understand. I had always been puzzled about the way in which our early ancestors, living in the technologically primitive life-style of the Old Stone Age, had found the motivation to devote so much time and energy to their elaborate art-work. But if a humble ape could display an almost obsessional interest in picture-making, then it became much easier to accept. 'Art for art's sake', it appeared, had a much longer pedigree than had previously been supposed.

I was also impressed by the remarkable visual control that Congo exercised when placing his lines on the paper. Admittedly his pictures were never more than abstract scribbles. He never reached the vital stage of producing a representational image. But the abstract patterns he created nevertheless had a recognizable, personal style. His favourite design was a radiating fan shape. As the months passed he repeated this many times until he became so familiar with it that it became a fixed visual concept for him and he was able to vary it dramatically, splitting it into two halves, or curving the bottom of it, or dividing it by a central spot. He even produced a subsidiary fan alongside the main one and, on another occasion, constructed the fan backwards, starting at the bottom of the page instead of the top.

He also made many other kinds of mark on the papers he was given, day after day, in sessions lasting about half an hour. There were zig-zags, loops, crosses, and sometimes well-formed circles. One such circle he filled with dots. Had he been a human infant, this dot-filled circle would have been the precursor of the first true image – that of a face. But he never managed to cross that vital threshold.

I was about to start him on a new phase of experimental drawings, with geometric patterns ready-made on the page, to test his sense of graphic balance, when something happened that was to divert the serious study into a public spectacle. Baltimore Betsy arrived unexpectedly on the scene.

Betsy was a seven-year-old female chimp living in the Baltimore Zoo in the United States, where she was becoming famous for her finger paintings. Paint was offered to her in small blobs and these she proceeded to smear over large cards. As with Congo, there was an inherent sense of design, but much of the attractiveness of Betsy's work was due to the accidentally produced texturing of the smeared surfaces. Compared with Congo's austere pencil drawings, Betsy's paintings were flamboyantly appealing and not unlike some of the latest offerings by the Tachiste school. What was more, they were being exhibited and sold to admiring collectors. The challenge was too much to resist.

As far as I could see, Congo's sense of pattern and design was far more developed than Betsy's and all that was needed was to switch from pencils to coloured paints, to outshine the American ape. It would make serious analysis of the details of the patterns much more difficult, but it would also, undoubtedly, produce some attractive abstract pictures.

Congo was delighted by this change. He revelled in the fact that much bigger marks could be made with little effort, as the paint flowed from his brushes on to the large coloured sheets I provided. I was determined not to go the whole way, and let him smear the paints with his fingers, because this would then obscure his pattern formations even further, but luckily he found no difficulty in manipulating the paint brushes, which he learnt to hold in a typically human grip. I presented him with one colour after another and he went on working at a particular picture until he considered it finished. Then he would stop and refuse to add anything further.

As the weeks passed, he gained in confidence and every coloured line or blob was placed exactly where he wanted it, with hardly any hesitation. He worked for much longer now, the bright colours adding an extra appeal that intensified his concentration more than ever. Nothing would interrupt him until he was satisfied with the balance of his picture. Once, I cheated him by snatching a painting away when it was only half-done, and quickly replacing it with another blank sheet. After an initial protest, he switched his attention to the new sheet and set to work on that. Next day, I offered him his half-completed picture, in which he had begun a fan pattern on one side of the paper, but had only managed to take it half-way across the page. He promptly went on to complete it. There was no doubt about it, he knew what he liked.

At this point I risked allowing him to paint on television. This was dangerous because previously he had never painted in front of an audience and I feared that the presence of the camera crew might distract him. But it worked well and he completed his first public picture. News of this must have filtered through to Baltimore Zoo, because shortly afterwards I received a letter offering to send twelve of Betsy's finger-paintings to London for a joint exhibition, after which the two-chimp show would travel to the United States for a display in Baltimore and elsewhere.

My flippant suggestion of an ape art show, made in a light-hearted moment at the Oxford zoology department four years earlier, was about to become a reality. Part of me was highly amused by this bizarre situation, but another part was apprehensive. What had started as a serious scientific investigation into the origins of the aesthetic impulse was now in danger of developing into a three-ring circus. I made murmuring noises about my research being exploited as a joke against modern artists, but the publicity was too good to miss and Granada TV set about finding a suitable gallery. Congo was, after all, a television star and his fame could now be spread from the national to the international level.

I was against holding the exhibition in a hotel, or some other unorthodox venue. I wanted it to be mounted in a proper, recognized art gallery where it would at least stand a chance of being taken seriously. But the private art galleries in London shied away from the prospect of adding an ape to their lists of celebrated exhibitors. The problem was solved by the arrival at the zoo one day of Dorothy Morland, the director of the Institute of Contemporary Arts. When the Institute had first been approached, they had been suitably sceptical, but the place had a long history of tradition-breaking and before rejecting the proposal outright, Dorothy thought she would have a look for herself. The moment she realized that, despite the television ballyhoo that now surrounded the 'painting ape', I was entirely serious in what I was doing, her scepticism evaporated. After consulting her colleagues, it was agreed that the chimpanzee exhibition would open at the I.C.A. galleries in Mayfair on September 17th, 1957 and would run there for three weeks. Both Herbert Read and Roland Penrose, who had for many years master-minded the I.C.A. and had between them been largely responsible for keeping the avant garde alive in London art circles, then visited the zoo and Congo obligingly painted pictures for them, to prove that there was no hoax involved. Both men were duly impressed and Julian Huxley was persuaded to open the show with a formal speech, stressing that this was not a frivolous stunt, but a fascinating glimpse of the 'birth of art'.

A huge gathering turned out for the private view. Many came to scoff at the I.C.A.'s latest lunacy, but those who really understood abstract art were immediately converted. They realized at a glance that this was not a case of 'a brush tied to a donkey's tail'.

The American artist William Copley flew in to London ready to ridicule the exhibition and attended the opening party wearing a bowler hat and a cerise dinner jacket, but was soon full of apology when he saw the framed pictures on the walls. He was so impressed that he insisted on buying one, but I refused on the grounds that it would make the whole project look like a commercial exploitation.

A few days later, the I.C.A. telephoned in desapir. So many people were now demanding to purchase Congo originals, that they were under a constant bombardment. Requests were becoming demands and important clients were enraged at their refusal to put the work on sale. I discussed the matter with both the zoo authorities and with Granada TV and very reluctantly we agreed, but insisted that high prices be placed on the pictures to reduce sales to the minimum.

The following afternoon I visited the gallery with a friend and saw, to my horror, that nearly every Congo painting had a red spot on it. The I.C.A. had been stampeded with buyers the moment that the news had spread that the pictures were, after all, for sale. I insisted that the selling must stop immediately. Congo's output was limited and I had promised to send the exhibition to America in a few weeks' time. I returned to the zoo and set about replenishing the stock for Baltimore. Congo painted furiously during the next week or two and managed to finish enough new pictures of high quality for the exhibition to be re-mounted and shipped abroad. But I vowed then that never again would I put any Congo originals on sale. The whole situation was getting out of hand.

The worst aspect of what was happening was that the popular press was beginning to take an interest and was either heaping ridiculous praise on Congo's small head, heralding him as a sort of hairy Leonardo, or attacking the exhibition as an insult to human dignity and the sanctity of art.

The *Daily Telegraph* reported the show as if it were displaying the work of two major human artists: 'The originality and freshness of the works of Congo and Betsy are unquestionable ... In both cases the moment of action involved in creation communi-

cates itself forcibly. Congo's robust and colourful efforts border
on the school of Other Painting or Tachism, while the fingerings
of Betsy have a more refined quality.'

The reaction was bound to come. The art world could not
remain silent. The wretched animal was not only exhibiting his
work, but being treated seriously when real human artists were
being ignored; worse, he was being deliberately over-praised to
make his human rivals look silly; worse still, he was *selling*! This
was too much to bear. The President of the Royal Academy
launched a blistering attack, and the correspondence columns of
the serious weeklies were full of outraged onslaughts. In the *New
Statesman* I read: 'May I inquire if any of your readers would care
to join with me in amassing a fund, the purpose of which shall be
the prosecution of the organizers and the critics of this exhibition
for fraud, or, if possible, for common theft? ... It is known that
paintings, like all art objects, are human products. Because
certain humans during the past twenty years have chosen to paint
like psychotics, then like infants, and finally like animals, hardly
justifies a prestige organization in selling the reflex twitching of
apes ... ' Another writer commented sourly: 'Has not this gallery
lent itself to a gesture contemptuous of modern art? ... One
might define art ... as "the essential characteristic which differs
animal from man."'

In a later issue of the *New Statesman* leading art critic David
Sylvester retorted: 'Your correspondents on Betsy and Congo
are rather Victorian, surely? Their reaction to the news that apes
can paint is distinctly reminiscent of the outcry that followed the
publication of the *Origin of Species*.' It was a relief to read these
same words amongst all the silly spluttering and high-minded
mud-slinging. I was vividly reminded of a brave riposte by
Thomas Henry Huxley, Julian's brilliant ancestor, during the
original Darwinian outcry. At an Oxford debate, almost a
hundred years earlier, Huxley had been taunted by 'Soapy Sam'
Wilberforce, the Bishop of Oxford, with the question: ' ... was
it through his grandfather or his grandmother that he claimed
descent from a monkey?' Huxley replied: 'If the question is put

to me would I rather have a miserable ape for a grandfather or a man highly endowed by nature and possessed of great means of influence and yet who employs those faculties and that influence for the mere purpose of introducing ridicule into a grave scientific discussion – I unhesitatingly affirm my preference for the ape.' Thinking of young Congo struggling earnestly, day after day, to organize his simple, abstract patterns on sheets of paper, and of the pompous, posturing scribes who were now so eager to sneer at the exhibition of his labours, I felt myself entirely in agreement with the great Huxley.

I was delighted to read that his grandson Julian so thoroughly approved of the presentation of the ape pictures, that he was prepared to commit himself in print. Writing in the *New York Times*, he commented soberly that 'These paintings are of considerable interest because they tell us something of the way in which art may have evolved ... In fact, we are witnessing the springs of art. The results show conclusively that chimpanzees do have artistic potentials which can be brought to light by providing suitable opportunities.'

The tide was beginning to turn. As the more serious journals began to comment, and the initial furore died down, it became clear that, both in the scientific world and in the serious art world itself, many people were prepared to accept my experiments as a valid investigation. They saw beyond the razzmatazz of Congo articles and Congo cartoons (there was even a Congo calypso), and realized that if the ridiculous claims of 'great simian art' and the extravagant condemnations were swept aside, an objective, balanced view of the ape drawings and paintings revealed them to be remarkable documents of animal behaviour. If human dignity was assailed by the ape achievements, then so be it. If ape and man were brought closer together by their common interest in basic aesthetics, so much the better. We could well do with a little less dignity when facing the rest of the animal world.

I sat in my office at the London Zoo muttering dire threats against the person of the President of the Royal Academy, who was continuing to mouth savage verbal attacks at both the I.C.A.

and myself, and was stubbornly refusing to listen to the more reasoned comments that were now appearing. But he was a man I despised so much (unlike the present incumbent—a brilliant figure for whom I have the greatest respect) that to be condemned by him was praise indeed. And I was encouraged by the reactions of several major artists when confronted with a Congo painting. Salvador Dali peered closely at one and then exclaimed: 'The hand of the chimpanzee is quasi-human; the hand of Jackson Pollock is totally animal!' I was surprised by the thoughtful perceptiveness of this comment. Dali had detected, without knowing anything of the details of my experiments, that the ape was trying hard to bring order to his painted lines and shapes—was attempting to organize his simple compositions. Jackson Pollock, on the other hand, was seemingly intent on destroying order.

Picasso's reaction was characteristically more earthy. Roland Penrose had bought one of the I.C.A. paintings for him and carried it off to the artist's studio in the south of France. Picasso was delighted with it and put it in a place of honour among the chaotic debris of his palatial home. Later, he was visited by a journalist who asked him what he thought of the chimpanzee painting. Picasso disappeared from the room, then suddenly reappeared, his arms swinging low, leapt at the reporter and bit him. In his own way, he seemed to be saying that the ape and he were artists in common.

My greatest joy, however, came several years later, when Roland Penrose telephoned me to say that Miro was coming to London and wanted to see the Congo paintings. I admired Miro above all other living artists, above even Dali and Picasso, and was eager to meet him, even though it would mean losing another Congo picture. It was not that I was becoming mean with them—it was simply that I had hardly any left. By that time Congo had completely stopped painting and month after month I had been besieged by 'special requests' for just one more picture from my dwindling collection. Other apes had been rushed into the art business following Congo's initial success, but nowhere was anyone obtaining well-controlled pattern-making. It was not that their animals were inferior, merely that they had not been treated as serious experimental subjects. Hundreds of patient hours had gone into the Congo experiment and the quality of his pictures reflected this. They were unique. Most of them were experimental drawings with little 'Art Appeal', and there were comparatively few of the special paintings he did for the exhibitions, even before the rush was on to own one. Now I had but a handful left, which I was desperate to keep to remind myself of the extraordinary relationship I had developed with Congo in those exciting painting years. But Miro was different. His own pictures had given me such intense pleasure that I was only too happy to hand over one last precious Congo original.

Miro was in London for a giant retrospective at the Tate Gallery, but he set aside a day for a visit to the zoo. I had arranged for him to have a grand tour, based on a request he had made to Roland that, before looking at the Congo paintings, he would like to see 'serpents, small birds and creatures of the night', which sounded exactly like the title of one of his own, exuberant pictures. He arrived immaculately dressed and looking like a diminutive Spanish banker. The tour went well, with Miro taking an almost childlike delight in having a vast python wrapped around his body, and in watching at close quarters as a rattlesnake was made to rattle. Another snake was fed in front of him. As it darted out its neck in a lightning strike at the body of the dead mouse that was offered to it, it came within inches of Miro's face and he jumped back with a gasp. But looking at his face, I realized that it was not a gasp of horror, but of pleasure at the exquisite grace of the snake's swift movement. I recalled a comment by Victor Pasmore, the British artist, who had once asked Miro the secret of his vibrant calligraphy. 'Each line,' Miro had replied, 'must cut like a knife.' And this somehow explained his admiration for the striking snake, as its body had cut like a knife through the air.

I was careful to select animals that I knew Miro would like, basing my selection on my years of study of his paintings. In the zoo's Bird House, there was a magnificent tame hornbill that he was able to perch on his wrist and feed with a grape. Around the bird's large eye there was a splash of bright colour, exactly as if it were an eye painted by Miro in one of his pictures. I could not speak Spanish to explain why I had chosen this bird, so I simply pointed at the eye. Miro nodded and understood.

At the end of the day, we walked across to our small flat near the zoo gate, where Ramona made tea for us. Through Roland Penrose, who was acting as interpreter, Miro thanked me for the tour and then began studying the Congo paintings I had arranged in front of him. He was deeply impressed by them and after he had chosen the one he wanted, got up and started searching through the scraps of paper on my desk. I asked Roland what he wanted and was stunned to learn that he was looking for a suitable piece of paper on which to make a drawing for me, in exchange for the Congo. The only blank piece he could find was a tiny, torn scrap little bigger than a postcard. I told Roland to ask him to wait a moment and sauntered across to the door. Outside I started rushing madly in all directions looking for the largest piece of white card I could find. I knew I had one somewhere, but was afraid that by the time I returned with it, I would be too late. Throwing things all over my bedroom, I eventually unearthed the sheet of card, grabbed up a collection of pens, coloured crayons and pastels, and then sauntered casually back in again. To my relief, Miro was still sipping his tea. His eyes lit up when he saw the card and the collection of drawing materials. Eagerly he started to draw and after some minutes a beautiful sketch emerged. He sat back and Ramona poured him another cup of tea. He must have enjoyed it because he then leant forward and proceeded to dedicate the picture to her. Knowing my passion for Miro's work, she could hardly suppress her amusement at this and told me afterwards that she was certain now that I would never leave her, because I could never bear to be parted from that Miro drawing.

Perhaps sensing the unspoken exchange between us, Miro then got up again and taking one of the many books on his paintings that crowded my shelves, he opened it and completed a second drawing in it which he dedicated to me. In the middle of signing it, he went across to one of my own paintings on the wall and peered intently at my signature in the bottom corner of the canvas. When I looked at the finished dedication, I noticed that when writing my name, he had carefully copied the rolling M which I always used, in place of the sharp, stabbing M with which he signed his own name. Despite the apparent simplicity of much of Miro's work, nothing, not even a letter in a dedicatory word, is treated casually. Everything is considered with the solemnity of a genius child at play.

My happy exchange of pictures with the great Miro was some years in the future. As soon as the fuss about the exhibition had died down I returned to my serious business of analysing Congo's sense of primitive aesthetics. Abandoning the glamour of paint-brushes and paints, I switched him back to plain pencil drawings on smaller white sheets of paper. I prepared long sequences of geometrically marked sheets and offered them to him day by day, until he had completed enough to enable me to determine precisely how well he could understand the principles of visual balance. The results were even better than I had hoped for and I realized that I had enough material now to write a book on the subject. I began work on *The Biology of Art*. But I was soon interrupted by the weekly demands of my television series. The inability to concentrate for any length of time on any subject was beginning to frustrate me more and more. I had devoted three years of my life to popularizing animal behaviour and taking it, every seven days, to an audience of several million. This meant that I had presented nearly 150 half-hour programmes and I was starting to feel the need for a return to a more academic way of life. The new producer assigned to the zoo TV Unit was Milton Shulman, a theatre critic and horse-racing addict turned television executive. Like Bill Gaskill before him, Milton was not at all sure what he was doing at the zoo, since he knew little about animals and wanted only to concentrate on theatrical television productions or current affairs. Although he was the terror of the West End stage, away from his acid pen he was a charming and affable character, and was totally unsuitable for the kind of row I felt churning up inside me. I wanted to make strident demands for a more penetrating approach to filming animal studies, with a scrapping of the weekly grind and a concentration on long-term projects that would make a much bigger impact. Instead, one morning during a coffee break, when he was pondering over the likely winner of the 3.30 race at Aintree, I announced rather lamely that I was resigning as head of the unit and leaving Granada to return to the zoological world. His reaction to this seemed almost admiring, and I was not surprised to learn that before long he, too, had returned to his original habitat, at a London newspaper.

Once I had severed myself from my TV Den, and my resignation had been accepted, I was alarmed to realize that I had slammed one door before opening another. I had no idea what I was going to do next and it occurred to me that I had taken a grave risk in not finding an academic post before waving goodbye to my Granada salary. Admittedly it was not princely – they had been paying me less than £25 a week, for which I had to run the zoo TV Unit and also devise and present the weekly half-hour *Zootime* programme – but it *was* a regular salary. With impulsive abandon, I had now thrown that away. The prolonged exposure on television seemed, at last, to have destroyed the final remnants of my childhood cautiousness and shy reserve. I remembered the letter my father had felt it necessary to write to my headmaster on the day I left home for boarding-school, warning him of my lack of self-confidence. Ramona felt that perhaps now I had a little too much, but she sympathized with my decision and understood it perfectly. She herself wanted to stay on at the TV Unit and did so with great success for another four years, before leaving to start writing a series of books. But for me there was now the urgent matter of finding a new position.

I visited the zoo's director, Leo Harrison Matthews, and explained my problem to him. He told me to do nothing for the moment, but to sit tight. Some changes were about to be made at the zoo and there was an opening tailor-made for me. The zoo's Veterinary Officer was doubling up as Curator of Mammals at present, but since he had moved into his splendid new Animal Hospital, his medical duties were absorbing all his time and the zoo would shortly be advertising for a new Curator. If I applied for the post, and succeeded in obtaining it, I would have much more time for research and would be relieved of all my energy-wasting television duties. It was perfect.

Early in 1959 I was duly appointed and given new quarters on top of the Reptile House. Overnight I became responsible for the largest collection of mammals in the world – nearly 300 species. Every day felt like Christmas. There was so much I wanted to do, so many improvements I wanted to make. So many naked cages I wanted to clothe with greater interest for their bored inhabitants. So many observations, so many projects. I poured such energy into my early curatorial weeks that one afternoon, in the Rodent House, I literally passed out with the stress of it all. The keeper there thought I was dying and nearly started a major panic, but after a few moments I came round and was soon up and away again chasing new problems. A few weeks later, I fainted again, this time in an Italian restaurant where I fell forward and nearly drowned in a bowl of minestrone. I thought this was hilariously funny when I came round, but Ramona was far less amused by it and pleaded with me to take things easier. Apart from these two occasions, I had never fainted before in my life (or since), and I brushed the incidents aside, ploughing even deeper furrows into my new field of work. Ramona warned me that I would soon burn myself out if I did not learn to relax more. She was right, but it took seven years to happen. During those seven crowded years I forced myself to work harder and harder and relished every moment of it. It was not that I was driven by ambition, or the urge to earn more money. Such things never entered into it. It was only one thing that drove me on – an insatiable curiosity. Quite simply, I wanted to know everything there was to know about every mammal in the world.

'But do you know how many species there *are*?' asked Ramona. To her dismay, when I realized that I was not sure of the answer, and no books in the library could tell me, I set about writing one on the subject, in addition to all my other duties. Six years later my book *The Mammals; A Guide to the Living Species* finally appeared in print and I could tell her what she wanted to know: there are 4,237 species of mammals alive today. And a large number of them were in my care at Regent's Park.

For me, it was a zoological feast. But with my new position came a daunting new responsibility. Since I was the only curator of living mammals in the entire country (there was a curator of dead ones at the Natural History Museum, but he was as alone as I was when it came to queries), I was now automatically considered to be 'The Expert' on any and every mammalian topic. At first I hid behind the fact that I was new to the job, but after a while this wore thin, and I had to become a zoological diplomat, trying to find answers that would satisfy enquirers without either giving false information or exposing my extensive ignorance. This was a balancing act that required an expertise all of its own. Expertise in the art of concealing the lack of expertise.

'You'll soon get used to it,' soothed John Yealland, the gentle, philosophical Curator of Birds. That was all very well, but he really *was* an expert on his subject. And I was still learning. But it was a fascinating education, even though it led me into some strange, not to say bizarre, situations ...

7

'I WONDER IF YOU CAN HELP ME?'

That phrase again. The heart sinks. It happens every day of a zoo-man's life. The telephone rings and a voice, serious and concerned, wonders if you can help. Of course, you want to help, but from experience you know that the request is nearly always an impossible one: 'Where can I buy a cheetah for my girl-friend?' 'You can't—it's a protected animal.' 'Don't give me that—I've promised her one and she'll leave me if I don't get her one.' 'I'm sorry, but ... ' 'They told me the London Zoo would be useless. All right, I'll ring Harrods.' Or: 'Our tame hamster is lying on his back, his eyes are closed, blood is coming from his mouth and his legs are twitching. Are there any hamster medi-cines I can get him?' Or: 'My pet monkey has just bitten the lodger and run away. My husband says I can't keep Bimbo any longer, so could you come and collect him and give him a home in the Monkey House?' 'I'm afraid we are completely full up. We can't take any more monkeys.' 'Well, could you find him a home somewhere else?' 'Where is he now?' 'On the roof of No. 23, the house next door.'

What *do* you say to such queries? The callers are always in such obvious difficulties that you really do want to help. But you have to get on with the work at the zoo, and in the end you hear yourself passing the problem on—to the police, the vets, the R.S.P.C.A., the fire-brigade, anyone you can think of, and you feel callous. You feel yourself becoming an impersonal official. A professional buck-passer. But there is no choice.

This time, let it be different. Let my specialist knowledge unravel the dilemma with a few astonishingly enlightening words.

14 Ramona's attempts at script-writing were repeatedly disrupted whenever our chimpanzee, Congo, managed to sneak into her office.

15 Congo reached international fame as a painter. What began as a serious research investigation into the origins of human art, rapidly got out of hand.

16–18 The Spanish painter Miro (*top left*) came to the zoo to acquire one of Congo's paintings and, to my astonishment, gave me one of his own in exchange. Sir Julian Huxley (*top right*) also owned a Congo painting and agreed to open the exhibition of Chimpanzee Art at London's I.C.A. gallery. Other Congo paintings ended up in the Witney Collection in New York and the Penrose Collection in London. Roland Penrose gave the one below to a delighted Picasso.

Let there be a gasp of gratitude from the ear-piece and mumbled thanks. So, here we go again, with a tone of cheerful, expert optimism:

'What exactly seems to be the problem?'

'Sergeant Johnson here, sir, River Police. We are having a spot of trouble with a whale and we wondered ... '

'A what?'

'A whale, sir.'

'Where precisely is this whale?'

'At Kew Gardens, sir.'

'At Kew Gardens.'

'Yes, sir, at Kew Gardens.'

It wasn't quite clear which one of us was stalling for time. Sergeant Johnson seemed to be expecting some instantly masterful reply, like: 'Stand by, River Police, we are sending in our Whale Squad. Curator of Mammals to Whale-catcher One, Curator of Mammals to Whale-catcher One, are you receiving me? Proceed immediately to Kew Gardens ... ' Instead, I asked rather lamely:

'What is the whale doing at Kew Gardens?'

The tone of pained resignation in the Sergeant's voice as he answered this question, made it obvious that only an idiot would not know what a whale was doing at Kew Gardens:

'It is creating a disturbance, sir.'

'I see.' And I was beginning to. Either I was talking to a raving loony, or it was an old chum of mine trying to see how long he could keep the joke going before I recognized the disguised voice.

Loony phone calls to the zoo are not uncommon. Every zoo-man gets his share. Sometimes they are boringly demented, sometimes sinister ('The snakes will all be free tonight, free, I tell you, free!'), and sometimes hilarious. There was the famous occasion when Sir Peter Chalmers-Mitchell, as head of the London Zoo, was telephoned by a distraught lady who claimed she had been attacked by a savage animal in her bed. Her chauffeur had succeeded in capturing this strange beast and she was on her way to the zoo to have it identified. Sir Peter passed this curious problem down to the duty official, who happened to be the zoo's

Public Relations Officer. He met the lady in the main hall of the zoo's offices in Regent's Park. She swept imperiously into the building in an expensive fur coat, followed attentively by a uniformed chauffeur carrying an upturned glass on one hand. Jabbing a bejewelled forefinger in the direction of the glass, she demanded to know the nature of the beast that had violated her body. The chauffeur smiled weakly and held the glass nearer.

Inside the glass, something moved. The P.R.O. peered closely at it. It was a small feather. Nothing else, just a feather floating there. When he announced this momentous discovery, the agitated lady exploded with a shrill torrent of abuse, at the climax of which she flung open her sumptuous fur to reveal a stark naked body covered in pink, lumpy spots. She then demanded to see someone with more advanced zoological qualifications.

A Head Keeper was routed out and the whole charade repeated itself: 'It's only a feather' ... stream of abuse ... fur coat flung open ... naked body with spots ... demand for higher authority. The Head Keeper called the Head Overseer. Same again. There was nothing for it but to call in Sir Peter Chalmers-Mitchell himself. He was briefed on the scenario so far, and advanced with the stern but comforting calm of a Harley Street surgeon approaching a rich patient. He listened to the woman's story, peering intently into the upturned glass pressed on to the chauffeur's palm. 'How extraordinary!' he muttered, 'this is the first living specimen of a *Rhinoglabatis cuniculeformis* I have ever seen. We have never had one at the zoo before. May we keep it for the collection?'

The lady in the fur coat was delighted, cooed her gratitude, and the feather was ceremoniously handed over and carried away. After she had left, Sir Peter's only comment was: 'It was easy enough to invent a new species for her, but what is much more difficult is to understand how a woman who can afford a coat like that can come to be covered in flea-bites.'

I couldn't help wondering what Sir Peter would have done with a whale at Kew Gardens. Perhaps he would have asked whether it was black and white, and if it wasn't, would have announced soothingly that 'In that case, it is harmless', and put the phone down. But my whale caller didn't sound like a loony, and I was beginning to suspect a hoax by a friend. The crazy image of a whale at Kew Gardens had the strong flavour of a Spike Milligan sketch, but I knew that Spike, although always hilarious when on-screen, is usually intensely serious off-screen, especially where animals are concerned. No, it couldn't be Spike. David Attenborough perhaps? David, who is always serious on-screen, is frequently hilarious off-screen—just the opposite of Spike—and I had several times been fooled by bizarre telephone messages in strange voices which eventually exploded into David's familiar laughter. But this whale conversation was too involved and long-winded. David, I was sure, could not keep the charade going for more than a few seconds and this caller was now droning on about whether the Zoological Society had any way of assisting the River Police in their enquiries into the incident at Kew. So I was stumped.

The only thing to do was to take standard defensive action. I asked for the caller's phone number and said I would ring back as soon as I had taken advice. After a few minutes had passed, I dialled the number. It was indeed the River Police and I asked for Sergeant Johnson.

'No one of that name here, sir, sorry.'

'Thanks. Sorry to trouble you. Must have been a mistake.'

So much for a surrealist visit to Kew. Hoaxer or loony, that was that. I had a busy day ahead, and the matter went out of my mind.

I was leaving my office at the end of a long afternoon, when the phone started ringing. I dearly wanted to abandon it and get home, but you never know at the zoo ... it could be an emergency.

'Sergeant Johnson here, I'd like to speak to the Curator of Mammals.'

'Speaking.'

'I'm sorry to trouble you, sir, but you did say you'd call back. It's about that whale ... '

'I did return your call, but the switchboard at the River Police said they had never heard of you and I assumed naturally that ... '

'Damn that Barnett. He's new here ... only just started on the switchboard and doesn't know all our names yet. I'm sorry to press you on this, but we have a report that quite a crowd is gathering, where the whale is, and we really are worried about it. Could you come over to the Thames and we'll take you up-river to have a look at the problem. There may be something you can do for the poor beast. It's thrashing about in the water ... and it's pretty filthy water as you know ... and it seems to be a big one and ... '

The truth suddenly dawned on me. This was no hoaxer ... it was all too elaborate. There really was a whale in the Thames.

'But you said the whale was at Kew Gardens. I'm afraid I found that hard to ... '

'Yes, of course, I'm sorry. We work on the river all the time so we automatically assume we are talking about something in the river. When we say "at the Houses of Parliament" we mean "in the river at the point where it passes the Houses of Parliament", and when we say "at Kew Gardens" we mean in the river at the point where it passes the Gardens.'

'Even so, no whale has ever been up the Thames before. They would never make such a mistake. There have been a few cases of a dolphin or a porpoise, but a full-blown whale, never.'

'Well, there's one there now and it's lashing about with its tail and people are complaining that it ought to be helped – guided back to the sea or something. Can you come?'

'I'll be there.'

I had been on some strange quests since coming to the zoo, but nothing like this. I had scoured the East End of London in search of a baby elephant that an Indian phone-caller had offered to sell me, only to find that the address given was a bombed site and totally derelict. I had rushed north to Potter's Bar once, alerted to a strange mammal that was leaping about in what else at Potter's Bar but a potting shed. It was real, but no more than a terrified common fieldmouse. I had once taken a call for the Curator of

Birds about a noisy water rail in a wash-room in Hounslow. That one I had jibbed at— a water rail in a wash-room was just too much— but on that occasion I was wrong. There really was a panic-stricken bird in the wash-room, which the Curator of Birds finally rescued, and it was a genuine water rail (*Rallus aquaticus*, to give it its proper name). But a whale in the Thames at Kew Gardens, that was something else.

At the time, Ramona and I were still living in our small flat just outside the zoo gates, at Primrose Hill. We had a family of French friends staying the night and I knew that Ramona was struggling to prove to them that the British care as much about food as the French. I was expected to assist in making the dinner a memorable one, but not in the way that was now forced on me. Hurrying through the zoo grounds I was trying to work out a convincing way of excusing myself from the Great Meal. Helping the police in their enquiries concerning a delinquent whale did not seem to have the ring of acceptability about it, and I couldn't remember the French word for 'whale'. And our guests spoke little English. Seeing the zoo's anatomist wending his way home past the Birds of Prey Aviaries, I yelled out: 'What's the French for "whale"?' only to find myself explaining the whole Kew Whale fracas. The anatomist was thrilled.

'I am terribly short of whale genitals,' he shouted after me, in that vulturine way anatomists have, 'do try and save them for me.'

'I'm going to try and save them for the whale, if I can,' I shouted back.

Then I bumped into a young student of mine, Lyall Watson, who asked if he could come along with me to help. That reminded me that I should have alerted the whale specialists at the Natural History Museum. If the poor brute died, it would become their concern. I went back, phoned the museum and just caught a whale man as he was departing for a quiet evening at home. He agreed to be there and rather gave the impression that he considered the whale to be museum property already.

After these delays it was late when I arrived at the flat and the

French family were already in their seats at the dinner table patiently waiting for the curtain to rise on the theatre of food. There is something awe-inspiring about the way the French apply themselves to the business of sitting down at a dinner table. It is an almost sacred ceremony that brooks no interference or disturbance. Ramona was mildly frantic and greatly relieved to see me.

'The wine,' she said, 'see to the wine ... ' I explained the crisis as best I could.

'But how can I tell them you are going off hunting a whale in the Thames?' she asked. 'They'll never believe me. They'll think you are trying to insult them.'

'Do your best. Tell them it's an occupational hazard – and too crazy to be invented.'

Luckily Ramona's French is fluent and I heard her say something like 'Desmond cannot eat with us tonight because he has to catch a live whale at the botanical gardens.'

The French family spent some time explaining to one another what this might mean, accompanied by many French shrugs and gesticulations. While they were debating the eccentricities of the English, I slipped quietly away, collected Lyall Watson and drove as quickly as possible to the river.

When we located the police launch, the museum man was already pacing up and down impatiently on the quayside. He seemed irritated by our presence and as the boat chugged upstream enquired whether it was really necessary for us to be there. The whale, he insisted, was the business of the museum and the zoo was not involved. He was becoming so possessive about the poor creature that he inevitably aroused a twinge of competitiveness. I knew the chances of saving the whale were slender, but I felt I had to do whatever I could, and I rather resented the idea that the zoo was interfering in museum affairs, especially as it was I who had alerted them to the whale's existence in London. I was reasonably sure that the whale was sick, if not actually dying. No healthy whale would make the mistake of confusing the filthy waters of the Thames with the open sea, but until it had breathed its last, it was outside the museum's domain and I could not resist making this point.

'If it is dead, it's yours, but if it twitches it's mine,' I said, striking a blow for the zoo.

The comment was taken more seriously than I intended, and the museum man demanded to know what I proposed to do with it if it was still alive. I explained that if it appeared healthy and had merely lost its way, then we would have to enlist the aid of as many boats as possible and guide it or drive it back into the open sea. If, on the other hand, it was sick, then we would have to tow it up the Regent's Canal and moor it alongside the zoo's veterinary hospital where it could be given expert medical assistance.

I was indulging in fantasy, of course. There was little hope that either manoeuvre would work in reality, but I couldn't resist the temptation of putting them forward, solemnly and with feeling. The River Police, I noticed, were rather impressed by my decisiveness, and the awful truth dawned on me that, in reality, I had no idea what to do if, in a few minutes, I was faced with a fully grown whale, alive and thrashing, in the confined space of a river.

The museum man was agitatedly explaining that I must realize that all stranded whales are legally the property of the Natural History Museum and that it was only a matter of time before the animal succumbed and he would be able to claim it. Technically, all such whales were 'Queen's Fish' and belonged to the Queen, but Her Majesty, not being a great collector of dead whales, had transferred this ancient right to the museum, so that they could make use of them as valuable anatomical specimens. Thinking of the zoo's anatomist and his lust for whale genitals, I enquired whether the museum man was after any particular bits of the whale. I had a nasty vision of the two scientists duelling with scalpels alongside a beached whale's carcass. But he was only after its brains. With any luck, if it was a big enough whale, this would keep the two scavengers at a safe hacking-distance from one another.

Already I was beginning to accept the idea of a dead whale

and, as we came round the next bend in the river, I saw in a moment that I was right to do so. The giant tail-fluke of a huge whale jutted forlornly from the murky, swirling surface of the Thames. The wretched animal was tragically no longer 'creating a disturbance'. My dilemma was solved in the saddest of ways.

The museum man was demanding wellington boots, so that he could secure the whale with a rope. I overheard one policeman say to the other: 'Give him the leaky pair.' They had been on my side. Like me, they had romantically wanted to save the great beast.

There was a squelching sound as the museum man leapt from the boat and sank slowly into the stinking mud, with tiny gurgles coming from inside his boots. Slipping and sliding, he managed to tie the rope around the vast tail-fin and then struggled back on board. The boat set off downstream, and as it did so the sombre grey shape of a thirty-foot whale swung round behind it and flopped along just beneath the surface. The sheer bulk of it was so impressive that we felt more like undertakers in a bizarre funeral procession than zoologists transporting an interesting specimen. People watched this strange journey with silent, puzzled faces, and one almost expected the men to remove their hats as the cortège passed them.

We were brought back to earth with the problem of beaching the animal. The River Police, mischievously perhaps, selected a mud-bank immediately opposite a riverside pub. As the great form of the whale was heaved ashore, the mud-bank grew thick with beer-drinkers, tankards in hand, who surrounded the perspiring museum man and made helpful comments, while he did his best to persuade them not to touch it. He insisted on remaining at his post by the whale's head and we left him there prowling round the carcass, standing guard over it and trying to shoo people away. It seemed as if he imagined everyone was out to steal his whale, though how or why anyone would do so was a mystery.

At the mooring we thanked the policemen for their help. Like us, they were depressed at the outcome, but explained that it made a welcome change from fishing out the bodies of naked blondes and the more usual kind of Thames victims.

Later that night, the phone rang. It was the zoo's anatomist enquiring about the fate of the whale, and asking where it was beached. I told him the location. At dawn he was already there with his bucket and scalpels, when the museum man arrived. It is not clear what passed between them, but the atmosphere was apparently tense, the museum man having stayed up almost all night protecting his whale, only to find, after a few snatched hours of sleep, that a rival scavenger had beaten him to it. A good anatomist has to be quick off the mark. They worked away for hours in silence, each hacking at the zone that interested them, like vultures picking at a cadaver. What I never did find out was who finally undertook the awesome job of burying the unwanted bulk of the whale's body. The rule is that the first man to touch a stranded whale is responsible for burying it. The museum man had touched it the day before, but the zoo's anatomist had been the first to cut into it. Somehow I suspect that the zoo won. The museum had, after all, claimed the animal and with it, presumably, the responsibilities of disposal.

Despite the entertainment of its surrealist overtones, the whale affair left me feeling deflated. To be present at the death of any very large animal is an awesome, sobering experience. The huge bulk of the body out of which life is ebbing makes the act of dying itself a greater tragedy. It should not be so. The body of a mouse is quite as marvellous as that of an elephant. But human emotions find this hard to accept. When an elephant or a rhinoceros you have known as a friend dies in front of you, it is as if a whole city of life has been snuffed out. As a young curator I found the inevitable deaths that occurred affecting me more than I cared to admit.

It was the same for the keepers – worse in fact – because they were closer, day by day, to their special charges. Like them, I had to harden myself, but it is not always easy, especially where some human stupidity has caused the death. All too often, the thoughtlessness of zoo visitors is to blame. The largest of the London

Zoo's hippos died needlessly because a child threw a rubber ball into its hopefully gaping jaws. The swallowed ball stuck fast and the great mammal was doomed.

One of the zoo bears died on the day following a Bank Holiday, when the zoo had been particularly crowded. All day it had been begging for tidbits and stuffing itself. The post-mortem revealed that it had consumed such a huge quantity of food thrown to it by kindly visitors that it had eventually suffocated from the immense pressure of its distended stomach against its lungs. It had literally eaten itself to death.

The extraordinary feature of this bear's achievement was its loss of natural control. No wild bear would have gorged itself to that point. The answer lay in the zoo animal's monotonous, utterly boring environment. The only way the bear could relieve the boredom was by encouraging an interaction with the passing humans. It discovered that it could train them to throw food simply by waving a paw at them, or sitting up on its haunches. But the snag was that they would only continue to relieve the monotony in this way if it ate the wretched stuff they hurled at it. For most bears, this did no harm, but for this particular black bear, the strategy proved fatal.

The most bizarre zoo death scene, however, was played out at the Giraffe House. One of these toweringly elegant creatures fell sick and died late at night. The driver of the small truck used to carry zoo bodies to the pathology laboratory had left long ago, so the keepers postponed the dead giraffe's removal until the morning. When the truck was summoned early next day, before the zoo was open to the public, and backed into position to receive its load, the keepers found they had an unusual problem. Rigor mortis had set in and the giraffe's splayed legs were as stiff as tree-trunks. Tipping the animal up on to four legs, the keepers struggled to align it with the back of the truck. The driver then backed his vehicle carefully between the widely spread legs. But when he drove triumphantly away, the giraffe's body remained where it had been. The legs were too widely spread to catch on the sides of the truck. The animal was far too tall to place sideways on the truck, so the only solution was to press down on the corpse from above until its legs made contact. There was no suitable weight available and one of the keepers had to volunteer to climb on the great beast's back, like a diminutive jockey. But even his weight was not enough. Another keeper joined him, riding pillion. Then another, until eventually the stiffened legs began to splay outwards and the animal's chest came to rest on the platform of the small zoo truck. Slowly, the driver moved off and crept gingerly through the zoo. It was a sight worthy of a painting by Salvador Dalí. Seen through the zoo shrubberies, as it proceeded along the narrow paths, the truck itself was almost obscured. All that was visible was a rigid giraffe gliding along like a Loch Ness Monster, with a row of dejected keepers sitting, one behind the other, on its back.

As with the whale affair, it was the surrealist quality of the giraffe's funeral procession that provided a distraction from the sadness of the occasion. But there was no such relief for me with the one death that affected me more than any other – the early demise of my chimpanzee Congo. When I had moved from the TV Unit to become Curator of Mammals, I had rewarded Congo for all his hard labours by setting him up in a special zoo cage with several appealing young female chimps, where I hoped he would breed and establish a growing ape colony. But my good intentions came to nothing.

Congo hated the move and hated even more the attractive young females. But he was growing too big to be treated as a pet any longer and would soon be sexually mature, so there was no choice. I hoped that time would change him, make him forget his human friends and develop at last into a healthy chimp's chimp. But he had been too strongly humanized and seemed incapable of making the transition. His females adored him, but he repeatedly spurned them. When they refused to be ignored, he devised the fiendish trick of begging for lighted cigarettes from thoughtless visitors. With these he proceeded to terrorize his female companions. Holding a glowing cigarette between his lips, he would chase them screaming around his enclosure, trying to burn their fur. For good measure, he took to squirting urine over his cigarette-donors, propping his penis on the front wire of his cage and aiming it like a water-pistol.

I felt deeply depressed at the thought that I had created a delinquent ape and swore never again to rear a tame chimpanzee in human surroundings. There was nothing I could do to help him. He was a mental hybrid. As the months passed he went into a decline, becoming increasingly sombre and introverted. He now simply ignored his females, acting as though he were quite alone in their midst. Before long he was dead, while they continued to grow from strength to strength and did eventually, with new males, establish a successful breeding colony. I visited him shortly before he fell ill and we stood staring at one another. I felt like the father of an autistic child, unable to communicate, unable to explain. In the privacy of our encounter my scientific objectivity evaporated. I wanted desperately to say how sorry I was, how I hated what I had unwittingly done to him, but there was no way. We spoke to one another softly in friendly chimpanzee grunts and I left. A few days later he was dead and I felt such a powerful sense of bereavement that I dared not speak of it to anyone. I was a scientist and it would have sounded foolish. Zoo animals die every week and one has to be hard. But Congo and I had shared moments of discovery that had almost bridged the gap between our two species. It was more than a man loving his dog – for Congo was an anthropoid, a truly close relative, capable of sharing so much more with a human being than any other species. I have never known a relationship like it with any other animal, before or since, and because of its unhappy conclusion, never wish to.

Originally, I had intended to extend my chimpanzee picture-making studies, working closely with more young apes, but after Congo's death I abandoned the idea completely and never returned to it. Instead I set about the business of improving the living conditions of the huge variety of mammals in my care. I wanted to make sure that each animal at the zoo was provided with an interesting environment and appropriate companions to establish breeding groups. Ideally, I wanted to see an end to the taking of more animals from the wild, to replenish zoo stocks. Every zoo should be able to breed enough from its own existing stock to keep going without further plundering of the dwindling wild populations. I set up a kind of zoological 'marriage bureau'.

Solly Zuckerman, the Secretary of the Zoological Society, had asked me to edit a new journal devoted to zoo management and research, but I had persuaded him to change this to an annually produced *International Zoo Yearbook*, so that it could contain a reference section giving complete lists of the breeding successes of the major zoos all around the world. Scanning these lists gave vital clues about where to obtain suitable mates for solitary animals that were wasting their lives in isolated zoo cages. And it made this possible without resorting to the usual animal dealers and animal catchers.

My efforts were not always blessed with success. Congo, it emerged, was not the only humanized animal in the zoo. The place was full of them, all exotic pets donated by owners who could no longer cope with them. In the past the zoo had happily accepted such animals, but I was determined to avoid this mistake in future. This was not always easy. Some pet-owners were outraged at having their beloved 'offspring' rejected, as though their son and heir was being refused a place at Eton. They would thunder over the telephone about being tax-payers and that it was the zoo's duty to help them, and were rather taken aback when I pointed out to them that the zoo was a privately run scientific society which had never been dependent on public funding. One year, I calculated that in the past twelve months I had been offered no less than eighty-five unwanted pet monkeys alone, and had only been able to accept a few of the smallest ones.

Although I managed to stem the flow of humanized pets into the zoo, I was still faced with the problem of the existing misfits, which ranged from the mighty Guy the gorilla, down to a tiny squirrel monkey. Guy was in love with his Head Keeper and, like Congo, had long since ceased to think of himself as an ape. The only reason why the keeper did not continue to enter his cage was because Guy would have hugged him so lovingly that he would never have been able to leave again. I was scared to risk an adult female gorilla with him. My successor, after I left the zoo, was more courageous and did try introducing a mate for him, but without success. Although Guy did her no harm, he virtually ignored her and refused to mate. She was packed off for a dirty weekend with a virile young male gorilla at Bristol Zoo, who quickly made her pregnant and cuckolded the mighty but pathetic Guy.

The little squirrel monkey had a different problem. Unlike Guy he was sexually active, but seemed to be under the impression he was a springhaas. The springhaas is a gigantic rodent, superficially resembling a small kangaroo, and the little monkey had been housed with one for so long that he adopted it as a wife and tried to mate with it. As the springhaas was about ten times his size, it was an extraordinary sight, reminiscent of a tiny jockey trying desperately to spur on a racehorse that has refused to budge at the start of a race.

In a nearby cage there was another unhappy, mixed marriage, between an Old World brush-tailed porcupine and a New World tree porcupine. The Old World porcupine, a male, repeatedly attempted to mate with his New World companion, a female, but it was a painful affair. She responded with her appropriate sexual posture, but unfortunately the arrangement of her spines was different from his and after some agonized gropings he had to admit defeat. I worked hard to find him a mate of his own species and finally succeeded. To my delight, they formed a normal pair and mated successfully, but his old, abnormal bond of attachment refused to wane and from time to time he still made passionate advances towards his original, New World love, despite the prickly pain she must have continued to give him.

Next door, was a tame, hand-reared marsh mongoose, living in solitary confinement. I managed to find him an exquisite female, but he promptly went into a condition of intense stress, developed a peptic ulcer like a worried businessman, and died.

Despite these setbacks I did not despair. Many of my new pairs and breeding groups were settling down well and more and more young mammals were being born at the zoo. I longed for the day when the place would be completely rid of its humanized, mentally deformed stock and would be full of well-adjusted social groups and family units. In the meantime, however, there were enough young animals to dispose of to set up valuable exchanges with other zoos in England and abroad.

I was careful not to sell this new surplus to private individuals, because of the fear that I would once again create a pool of eventually unwanted pets that thought they were people and would start the problem off all over again. In my early days as a curator I had been persuaded to break this rule once and lived to regret it. A pair of zoo wolves had produced a large litter of delightful cubs and at the time there was insufficient accommodation for them. An intelligent and charming woman approached me and asked if she could buy a pair of cubs to rear as domestic pets. I naturally refused, but she persisted. I pointed out the dangers, but she countered by saying that, growing up as a pair, they would develop normal mating behaviour and would be treated with great care and respect. Since her husband had rebelled against having them in their London home, she was prepared to go to the length of buying a house near by which had a large garden, to be devoted exclusively to her two wolves. In the garden she would build a huge compound for them. I was impressed by her seriousness and felt that perhaps, in her case, I might make an exception to my rule. But I did not want to make it easy for her, so I placed an unreasonably high price on the cubs, feeling that if she could be dissuaded by this, then it was better for her not to have them. If she was prepared to pay so much for them, then clearly she meant to treat the project as earnestly as she was claiming. She wrote out the cheque almost before I had finished speaking.

I did not feel too alarmed by what I had done. After all, it would be a pity if people who took animal-keeping as seriously as she seemed to do, were unable to pursue their interests. That would contradict the whole spirit of zoological enquiry. But I had left one vital element out of my reckoning: the reactions of her less responsible neighbours.

All went well with the young wolves of South London during their early years. The woman kept to her word, bought the wolf-garden and constructed a splendid paddock for them, completely covered with strong wire. When the pair were fully grown to magnificent adulthood, she invited me to visit them, to prove to me that she had not taken the matter lightly. Angel-eyes and Devil-eyes, as they were now called, scampered over to greet her. I felt slightly apprehensive at entering their enclosure, but there was no danger. Like domestic dogs (which are, after all, no more than wolves in shaggy clothing), Angel-eyes and Devil-eyes had managed to acquire a double-identity. To humans they were friendly companions while, to one another, they remained true wolves. The woman obviously adored them and I congratulated her on her success, heaving a sigh of relief as I left, to think that what could easily have been a folly on my part had turned out so well.

But disaster was only a few weeks away. A gang of young thugs who lived locally had found out about the wolves. The supposedly savage animals, with their vicious reputation as marauding killers, offered an immediate challenge to their man-hood. Which of them would dare to visit the wolf-paddock at dead of night and break open the wire to release the animals on an unsuspecting London? This was the one factor that both the woman and I had overlooked. The zoo itself, of course, has stringent security regulations with night-watchmen patrolling the grounds. But it had never occurred to either of us that such precautions would be necessary in a private London garden. The woman had been careful not to publicize the presence of her exotic pets and had behaved sensibly in every way, but now all her good work was undone in one stupid, daredevil night-raid by the young thugs, to add a little danger to their stagnant city lives.

Tearing the paddock door from its hinges, they must have run in panic as Devil-eyes came loping towards them in what, for him, was a friendly greeting. Angel-eyes was more cautious, sensing that something was wrong, and stayed put. But he wandered cheerfully off in search of the human companionship he had come to trust and respect.

Now there was an adult wolf roaming the streets of London and I was to blame. I had put the clock back precisely a thousand years. We were now in the 1960s and it was in the 960s that wild wolves had been exterminated in southern England. As a result of orders from King Edgar of the Saxons, at least 300 wolves a year had to be killed, until they were wiped out. In the south this was achieved by the turn of that century, but in the far north of the British Isles the great carnivores managed to hang on until the middle of the eighteenth century, in the vast untamed forests of Scotland.

For the moment, however, London had regained part of its long-lost animal heritage, and broad, lupine footprints could be detected on its terrain once more. But London was not amused by this unexpected replenishment of its natural fauna. Indigenous the wolf may be, but welcome it was not, and something approaching local panic ensued when the news broke in the newspapers. Poor Devil-eyes could not understand the fuss, as he was driven by shouting men into a blind alleyway and surrounded by sweating R.S.P.C.A. men carrying guns, nets and nooses. Learning that he had been cornered, his frantic owner dashed to the spot and pleaded desperately with the assembled officials to permit her to calm him down, give him a friendly hug and take him quietly home. They rejected all her pleas and, to be fair to them, the wretched wolf was by now so alarmed by all the commotion that he might well have been dangerous to handle.

Closing in on his leaping, snarling form, they managed to throw a dog-noose around his neck. Tightening on the end of a long pole, the noose held him fast. It would have subdued the spirit of even the most fractious of domestic dogs, but with the immense muscular power of a fully grown male wolf, Devil-eyes fought against it like a hooked marlin, heaving and writhing until he strangled himself to death. His heart-broken owner was inconsolable and, rather than risk another disaster, found a zoo home for the female wolf– who had never even bothered to move through the open door of her compound– and abandoned for ever her dream of establishing a pack of tame wolves.

Leo Harrison Matthews, the zoo's director, was sympathetic when he learned of the details of the case and why I had made an exception in that instance, but we agreed that in future there would be no such exceptions and that no zoo animals whatever would be disposed of to private persons at any time. Not that I needed any persuading, after the wolf nightmare.

Escapes from the zoo itself were, thankfully, a great rarity, but even in the best-run institutions they did occasionally occur and I had my share. The few crises I encountered, however, dwindled into insignificance when compared with the problems faced by Julian Huxley when he was the head of the wartime London Zoo, at the height of the Blitz, and which he told me about one evening at his Hampstead home.

Shortly before hostilities had broken out, Churchill had asked Huxley what he planned to do if the zoo were bombed and dangerous animals escaped into the streets of the city. 'Shoot them!' answered Huxley, wishing to put the great man's mind at rest. Churchill brooded silently over this for a moment and then astonished Huxley by exclaiming: 'What a pity!' going on to paint an epic verbal picture of the devastated streets of the great metropolis with lions and tigers roaming freely among the smouldering ruins devouring the corpses of its human victims. But despite Churchill's romantic image, Huxley made sure that the keeper staff were armed with rifles every night, after the bombs started falling, with instructions to shoot on sight any escaped animal capable of killing a human being. Londoners had enough to endure, without having to face the additional hazard of marauding lions sniffing around their air-raid shelters.

With great reluctance he had all the zoo's poisonous snakes destroyed and also the deadly black widow spiders. If they managed to get loose, they would be too difficult to find, so there was no choice. The Reptile House staff loved their animals and had tended many of them with great devotion for years. They found their enforced slaughterhouse task deeply repellent, but it had to be done. Then the zoo waited with bated breath for the devastation to begin. First the zoo was hit by incendiaries, but without too much harm. Then, late one night, a stick of high-explosive bombs dropped across Regent's Park, demolishing several of the animal houses. Huxley, who lived on the zoo premises, leapt out of bed, donned a tin hat, and sped into action. Five bombs had fallen inside the zoo and buildings were smashed and burning. Anti-aircraft guns, positioned on Primrose Hill, right outside the zoo gates, were pounding away at the Luftwaffe above, and many of the animals were panicking in the terrifying din. The water-mains had been ruptured and the firemen who arrived sucked the sealion pond dry with their hoses to put out the fires, leaving the sealions lying disconsolately on damp concrete. The zoo's ancient Camel-House had been blown to pieces by the blast from one bomb, but to Huxley's astonishment, the camels were still sitting calmly in their now completely open enclosure, quietly munching their hay. I have always thought that you would have to put a bomb under a camel to make it panic, but even the literal truth of this statement seems to be in doubt.

One end of the Zebra House had been blown away and one of its inmates, a huge Grevy zebra stallion, was seen galloping off in the direction of the main Outer-Circle road that runs around Regent's Park. Mustering his air-raid squad of tin-helmeted keepers, Julian Huxley then led them in what must have been one of the strangest races in history. With bombs falling all around, and with the big zebra in the lead, they made a mad circuit of the deserted road, waving sticks and trying desperately to keep the animal on the circular route that would bring him back once more to the zoo gates. He nearly broke away and made for Camden Town, but they managed finally to herd him back to the zoo grounds and headed him into the stores yard.

Even twenty years later, Julian remembered the incident vividly and told me that his worst moment came when the A.A. guns on the hill went off again, after the yard gate had been shut.

The zebra, unnerved by this, backed wildly and penned Julian into a corner. Every time the guns banged, the great haunches of the zebra jerked closer to where Julian was cringing, certain that, at any moment, he was going to be kicked to death. Conveying his fears to the Head Keeper after the animal had been successfully shut away for the night, he was met with the scornful reply that: 'There was nothing to fear, sir, he's a biter, not a kicker', a fact which the man clearly felt his superior should have known.

I suggested that he had been lucky, then, that the panicked animal had not turned and given him a savage bite. A puckered smile came to the elderly Huxley face.

'Ah, well,' he said, 'I think if he had turned and *seen* me, he would have taken me for a friend. You see, I was wearing striped pyjamas at the time.'

Julian's story of chasing a maddened zebra while clad in striped pyjamas, round the Outer Circle of Regent's Park, at night, in the middle of an air-raid, had lingered with me pleasantly as yet another bizarre, surrealist zoo image, until one day when my own first escape crisis occurred. Suddenly it was no longer funny. Dangerous escapes are always hilarious *after* they happen, but the sense of dread they can produce while they are in progress has to be felt to be believed.

I was enjoying a quiet lunch in the zoo restaurant with film director Harry Watt at the time of the break-out. Gwynne Vevers, the curator of the zoo's aquarium drifted casually over to our table and in the softest possible tones murmured:

'Serious escape. Don't make a fuss, just follow me out.' He had been in the Intelligence Corps during the war and I thought perhaps he was overdoing things, reliving the cloak-and-dagger days of his past. Sadly he was not, as I soon discovered.

Asking Harry to excuse me for a moment, I sauntered out of the crowded restaurant. Outside the building, Gwynne switched to a rapid walk and sped me off towards his aquarium. On top of that building there is a sort of artificial mountain, completely covering it. On the mountain peaks live herds of wild goats and at a lower level there are the dens for the zoo bears.

'Not the bears?' I asked, disbelievingly.

'I'm afraid so,' muttered Gwynne. 'The two biggest – the Russian bears.'

'Oh, hell,' I groaned. They were monsters. They made some of the other bears look like children's teddies. If they felt like it – and they were not noted for their good humour – they could kill a man in a few seconds. In a few minutes, they could dispose of a whole family. In a few hours ...

'Oh, hell,' I repeated. I had just remembered the names of the two bears. One was called Rusk and the other, dammit, was Princess Anne's bear Nikki. I had already suffered a savage bite from Nikki when he was a tiny, supposedly cuddly, cub. Multiply that cub-bite by several hundred times and that was approximately the kind of nip one might now expect the fully grown Nikki to deliver. It was a daunting thought.

Arriving at the back of the aquarium was rather like coming on to the set of a second-rate Hollywood thriller. You know the scene. Our villain is holed up in a farmhouse and scattered all around are crouching uniformed police with guns at the ready, in case he makes a break for it. Only it was uniformed keepers, not police. Snapping myself out of my escapist, movie-watching role, I unboggled my mind, cleared my throat and made taking-charge-of-the-situation noises to all and sundry. Inwardly I was aghast, but outwardly I gave them my full Jack Hawkins commander-display. What exactly is the latest situation, I wanted to know, thereby implying falsely that I knew all about the earlier situation and merely needed bringing up to date.

'After destroying the lavatory, they doubled back and ... ' the Head Keeper of bears began.

'My God, destroying *what*?'

'The lavatory, sir.'

'Was anyone using it at the time? Which lavatory are you talking about?'

'Oh, no, sir, not one of the public lavatories. It's not that bad. Yet. It was only the keepers' lavatory, the one near the bears' inside den. It's completely demolished I'm afraid, building and all.'

'Where are they now?'

'Rampaging up and down the service corridor at the back of the dens. Smashing up everything. But if they decide to come down the stairs, there's only one way out—there.' And he pointed at a black gaping hole a few feet away from us. It was the entrance to the behind-the-scenes area of the bear section. Inside was a long dark passage at the end of which the bottom steps of the flight of stairs could be seen. There was absolutely nothing to stop the giant bears clambering down those stairs at any moment, and then out into the crowded zoo. The large wooden door that could be closed on the passage at our end had deliberately been left open to keep the stairs in sight. If it were closed and the animals reached it, they could have crushed it down in a few moments and then they would have been upon us without warning. So it was better to cluster opposite that ominously open entrance, with guns trained on the bottom of the stairway and pick them off as soon as they showed themselves.

I was impressed by the zoo's armoury. It was the first time I had seen it pressed into use, but I still hoped desperately that we could avoid firing at the bears. The noise would attract a huge crowd and if we failed to kill the animals, what might then happen was beyond thinking about. If the angered bears, perhaps wounded, rushed into a crowd of zoo visitors ...

We waited. There was a distant sound of splintering wood. If only we could somehow attract the bears back into their sleeping den, perhaps it would be possible to sneak up on it and slam the door shut—the door that someone sadly failed to secure properly earlier in the day and which had given them their means of escape. But they were finding their new territory so fascinating, so full of destructive possibilities, that it would be hard to tempt them back into their private quarters. The only hope was to offer them something in there that they could not resist. Bears have a sweet tooth and we decided to try them with a jar of honey or jam. Their sleeping den had a small, barred window looking out over their large concrete enclosure, which was fronted by a deep moat. Planks were found and laid across the moat, so that a keeper could teeter across, run over to the window with the jam and smear some on the window-sill. Calling to the bears, he attracted their attention and they lumbered in, competing with one another to lick up the jam. Behind them lay the open den-door, the long dark service passage and the flight of stairs. To shut the door, someone would have to crawl silently up the stairs and along to the door without alerting them. If he failed, they would be out after him in an instant and he would be in serious danger.

Bruce Smith, the Head Keeper of bears, insisted on trying it. It was a matter of professional pride as much as anything. Two of his bears were loose and no matter who had been at fault in letting them out, he was determined that the status of his section should not suffer. It might have been easier to shoot the two animals, but that would have been a defeat in his eyes.

I agreed to the risk he wanted to take, but only if we were able to offer him some kind of protection – some back-up in case of disaster. Having no walkie-talkies available, we gathered in extra keepers from other parts of the ground as quickly as we could and formed them into a long chain. Each link in the chain could see the one on either side of him. As long as the bears continued to lick their much-loved jam, the keeper nearest the window gave the thumbs-up signal to the one behind him, he to the next and so on, right round the bear terraces and into the passage-way leading to the stairs. There the Head Keeper and the zoo's best marksman, bearing a rifle, were ready to make their move. When the raised-thumb signal reached them they started their silent climb. As they advanced, the chain stretched out behind them, so that they were always able to keep a raised thumb in view. The moment the bears left their window, the thumbs would come down, the movement rippling along the chain and reaching the Head Keeper, hopefully in time for him to beat a rapid retreat to safety, covered by the marksman. Twice this occurred and twice the advance had to be halted as the bears temporarily paused in their gluttonous licking. But both times the jam keeper was able to coax them back. They had consumed a whole pot of jam by now and were already starting on their second. Standing in the middle of the chain, I was becoming anxious. How long could the bears devour the sweet, sticky jam before deciding to go in search of a drink? But then, with a last rush, the door was slammed fast and secured and we all sagged with relief.

The Head Keeper emerged from the darkness of the service corridor and blinked at the sunlight. Looking at his strained white face I could only think how underpaid such men are, for the risks they have to take. It was not exaggerating to say that sudden death had been averted – either that of the bears or that of a human being, but the Head Keeper knew, as he brushed congratulations to one side, that his success was cancelled out by the failure in his section which had permitted the bears to escape in the first place. All he wanted now was to climb down from the peak of tension on which he had been stranded for the past hour. As an Englishman he had two traditional alternatives open to him. One was drinking large quantities of hot tea and the other was drinking even larger quantities of cold beer. As the keepers' club was still open, he chose the latter and departed with a shaky urgency in his gait, weaving his way hurriedly through the throngs of strolling visitors, who were still blissfully ignorant of the secret drama that had been played out behind the scenes.

Fortunately, as I said, such escapes are extremely rare. And when they do occur, they are usually more likely to be tragic or funny, rather than dangerous. One of the zoo's most famous escapees was a delightfully eccentric chimpanzee called Cholmondeley. Chumley, as he was pronounced, had been a pet all his life, shared his master's table, smoked twenty cigarettes a day, drank stout, and was always fully dressed. Finding himself suddenly naked, smokeless and boozeless, in the zoo's Monkey House, following his master's retirement and reluctant disposal of his beloved companion, Chumley decided to act. Clearly there had been some terrible mistake. He was not destined to end his days in this mad-house of degenerate, twitching apes. He began by going on hunger strike. No stout, no food, was his motto. The medical staff became worried, and decided to examine him. As this was in the days before anaesthetic dart-guns, he had to be coaxed into a large box for chloroforming. A pipe opened into the side of the air-tight chamber and through it Chumley could smell the gas entering, so he promptly shoved one hairy finger into the opening and sat watching the increasingly puzzled faces of the medics outside. According to their reckoning he should have been unconscious five minutes ago, but instead he was sitting there glowering at them. Ten minutes later, according to their calculations, he should have been dead, but still he sat stolidly facing them.

When they discovered his finger-trick, they realized they were up against an unusually ingenious primate, and this was brought home to them when Chumley later managed to open a skylight in the roof of his sanatorium cage and took off for Camden Town. His previous life-style had not accustomed him to long walks, so he hopped on to a No. 74 bus and was totally perplexed when the elderly woman sitting next to him suddenly dissolved into a jabbering hysteric. Panic ensued, while a puzzled Chumley pondered on the unpredictability, not to mention unreliability, of the human species to which he had been led to believe he belonged.

His escaping brilliance undimmed, he went from strength to strength until, tragically, on one last desperate bid to return to the life-style to which he had been accustomed, he was shot by the now desperate zoo officials, after attempts to wheedle him back with glasses of stout had failed. It is easy to criticize them today for that killing, but a large ape can cause terrible wounds if angered and they were becoming seriously concerned about the safety of people living near the zoo. Chumley was a fully grown chimpanzee and, although he was courtesy itself to understanding and helpful human companions, he was easily upset by the more common panic-responses he caused during his wanderings. And an upset chimp can inflict savage injuries in a fraction of a second. One of the most famous of the Yerkes Laboratory scientists was so badly mutilated by an adult chimp that he killed himself shortly after the attack. And only recently, a young Safari Park attendant lost both his hands and suffered other mutilations during a brief encounter with an angry adult chimpanzee in his care. So Chumley's killers were not over-reacting when they shot him down. He was so human it was almost like murder, and they felt it keenly, but they had little choice.

When I told Chumley's story to Heini Hediger, the director of Zurich Zoo, he capped it with an escape story in reverse. His tale involved a large male gorilla and a young girl keeper, and the resemblance to the *King Kong* script did not end there. The gorilla, as so often happens with large apes, had outgrown his cuddly phase and had become intensely lonely. As a young animal he had been handled and caressed, played with and wrestled with, hugged and patted, and now suddenly all that lovely body contact had gone. He had grown so vast that it was becoming too risky, and so he sat alone and despondent, longing for some kind of social intimacy. But none was forthcoming. People were chummy enough through the wire and the bars, but they came no closer.

Late one summer evening, the great gorilla watched the last of the visitors depart, then one by one the zoo staff. Finally, the zoo was quiet. Nobody stirred. But then there was a distant sound of light footsteps. It was a girl keeper that the gorilla knew and liked – the last to leave for the night. As she passed by the animal's cage she called out a farewell and, glancing sideways, was horrified to see that the huge bulk of the animal was strangely twisted and appeared to be ensnared by a piece of jagged wire. Hurrying round to the back of the ape house, she unlocked the service door and moved down the dark corridor. Coming to the gorilla's cage she realized that she would have to open his cage door in order to see clearly the spot where he seemed to be caught up in the wire. Her chest rose and fell becomingly a couple of times before she plucked up courage to turn the key in his lock, but she was so fond of him that she could not bear the idea of a strand of wire cutting into his flesh and she wanted to do anything she could to bring a swift end to his plight. If she could only get a clear, close view of the problem, she would know what steps to take.

Slowly she opened the door, little by little, straining to see in the gathering dusk. To her astonishment, the cage seemed to be empty. The spot where the gorilla had apparently been caught up in the wire was now vacant. In the half-dark, she clambered into the cage to see how on earth the huge animal had managed to escape.

This was the moment the gorilla had been waiting for. Ever since he had pretended to be caught in the wire mesh, he had wanted only one thing—for the girl to enter the cage to rescue him, not so that he could harm her, but so that he could hug her to him for company, to avoid another lonely, isolated night. This may seem too clever for an ape brain, but probably, once when he was younger, his keeper had rushed in to his cage to free him from a similar predicament and he had somehow been able to store the memory of that occasion inside his heavy-browed head. Now the trick was working again and here was the door of his cage opening slowly in front of him. Hiding behind the doorway, where he had swiftly moved as soon as he heard the key in the lock, he watched the girl enter his cage space. Then, in a joyous rush, he charged forward and threw his arms around her startled body.

All the zoo staff had gone. She was the only human being left there as night fell. The contented gorilla hung on to her as though his life depended on it. As soon as she realized he was friendly, her panic subsided. The door was still ajar and her keys were still in the lock. If only she could reach it, she might be able to slide quickly out into the corridor and slam it behind her. But every time she made a gentle move to free herself, he hugged her tighter to his chest. All she could do now was to wait until he fell asleep, so she feigned sleepiness herself and closed her eyes.

As soon as she heard his breathing change, she started again to slide slowly out of his arms, and edged herself, little by little, towards the doorway. But suddenly he was awake again and grabbed after her. In the confusion, as she struggled, the door was accidentally slammed shut and automatically locked itself. The force of the slam dislodged her bunch of keys from the keyhole and she heard them clink to the corridor floor outside.

Now there was nothing to do but lie still in the gorilla's vast hairy arms and wait for morning, when the zoo staff would return and release her. It was a long night.

After she was safely rescued, dishevelled and shaken, the local press eagerly took up the story and huge crowds flocked to the zoo the following weekend.

'The gorilla must have become a great attraction,' I said, as Hediger finished his story.

'No, no, it was the girl they wanted to see. People have such fantasies. The poor girl was followed everywhere. She could hardly do her work.'

It is certainly true that people often bring their fantasies to the zoo, sometimes with bizarre results. I was reminded of the strange case of the London Zoo's tiger-toucher. He was an elderly, wizened, white-haired man with a skinny, tweed-hung body, who haunted the Lion House week after week. He would wait until there was no keeper in sight and then, with great difficulty, would clamber over the protective barrier and sneak up to a barred enclosure housing tigers. Never lions or leopards, only tigers. Calling to them, he would thrust his arm into their cage and reach out with his bony hand, trying to touch one and stroke it. Fortunately, several of the zoo's tigers happened to be unusually docile and friendly and on occasion he actually managed to make contact, tickling and fondling their soft fur and whispering endearments into their twitching ears.

The Lion House keepers soon got to know about him and were for ever rushing out and dragging him away. He always protested loudly as he was escorted from the grounds, and swore he would return. And he always did. Lurking behind trees, he would dart out as soon as the coast was clear, scramble over the barrier again, and start touching and tickling any tiger in sight. He seemed to be working his way around the whole collection, first concentrating on one tiger, then another, until he had made contact with each one. Sooner or later there was obviously going to be a tragedy, and the Lion House staff had to mount a special 'tiger-toucher patrol'. But he was too cunning for them. There were always moments when they were too busy, and then out he would pop, touching, tickling and whispering as hard as he could go.

After a while, he seemed to settle on one particular tigress. She became his favourite touchee, and he ignored all the others. Now his efforts were redoubled. Despite his advanced years, he positively threw his wiry frame over the barrier, always making a bee-line for his special female. This narrowed down the keepers' problem. With only one tigress to watch, they stood a better chance of catching him. One day, as he started his run-up, a keeper leapt out at him. In his panic, the tiger-toucher hurled his old body over the metal fence and collapsed at the keeper's feet with a badly broken leg.

An ambulance rushed him off to hospital and the Lion House staff were now convinced that, at last, he must have learnt his lesson. Peace would reign again. But they underestimated their man. As soon as the tiger-toucher was fully recovered he returned, eager to renew contact with his tigress. Lurking behind the nearby trees, he was aghast to discover that she was no longer on view. He circled the whole of the Lion House, inside and out. She was nowhere to be seen. Convinced that they had deliberately taken her from him, he stormed over to the office of the Curator of Mammals (my predecessor) and demanded in ringing tones:

'What have you done with my wife?'

The Curator, whose private life was blameless, was taken aback by this extraordinary accusation of wife-stealing, and demanded a detailed explanation. Then the whole, tragic story came out. The poor man was a widower and when his wife was dying she confided to him that she was certain she was going to be reincarnated as a tiger at London Zoo. Unfortunately, she did not tell him which one she was going to be, so that he had to caress each one in turn until he found her. He knew that once he found her, she would respond in a certain, recognizable way to his advances, and then he would be sure. He had located her shortly before his accident and was once again enjoying the close proximity of his beloved wife's body, now clothed in the beautiful, orange and black, striped fur of a magnificent tigress.

Now the zoo had taken her away and he was distraught at the loss. What had they done with her? Where was she? The Curator explained gently that she was well and happy, having been moved out to join a breeding group at Whipsnade Park, the London Zoo's country home. The tiger-toucher was overjoyed at this news and took off in great haste, presumably making for the tiger enclosure at Whipsnade. There, the much larger compound was surrounded by an insurmountable safety barrier and there was no risk of the man reaching through and endangering himself. Hopefully he came to accept this new situation, and I like to imagine him sitting contentedly in the afternoon sunshine, fondly watching his dearly loved wife as she lay in the long grass surrounded by her new cubs.

The zoo has always attracted more than its fair share of eccentrics. In retrospect one always feels a great fondness for them, even if at the time they are exasperating or downright alarming. Although I remember seeing the scrawny figure of the tiger-toucher on one of his weekly lurks at Regent's Park, his story dates from the time when I was still at the TV Unit. Later, when I was myself Curator of Mammals, I encountered my own crop of human oddities and eccentricities.

I had hardly arrived at my new, curatorial desk, when I was visited by two formidable ladies in birthday-cake hats, one of whom announced in ringing tones:

'We are here to uplift the British goat.'

As they were both gripping their shiny, thug-bashing handbags in a sinisterly anticipatory fashion, I assured her that the good name of the British goat had always been uppermost in my thinking, and enquired whether I had, perhaps, in some unintentional way, belittled or betrayed that fine animal. It seemed I had.

'We have noticed with displeasure that you persist in keeping your male goats in a mixed herd with your female goats,' intoned the second lady, swiping an immaculately gloved hand at an imaginary fleck of dirt on her pleated skirt.

'Yes, that is our breeding herd of Royal Windsor goats—the

ones from which the Regimental Mascots are selected. There is a special handing-over ceremony and ... '

'Yes, yes, we know all that, but must you keep the sexes together all the time? It is creating such misunderstandings and ... and it is jeopardizing the reputation of the British goat.'

The two heavy bodies settled back in their chairs, the hatchet expressions on their faces setting like concrete. There was a faint creaking from increased pressure on their shiny handbags. They were waiting. The silence roared.

'I'm sorry. But it is a breeding herd and they live in a large paddock in a natural social grouping. Surely that is the best way for people to see ... '

'No, certainly not!'

'I don't understand. Surely ... '

'Dr Morris, have you considered having your male goats ... ' There was a pause – the concrete faces were showing slight cracks of embarrassment, and the sensible, flat-heeled shoes were shifting uneasily– 'having your male goats ... altered?'

'Altered?'

'Yes, altered.'

Suddenly it dawned on me that these two elegant ladies wanted to castrate my male goats. They were on some bizarre errand of male destruction and I began to fantasize gigantic pairs of rusty scissors concealed in their creaking handbags. Would they stop at goats? I wondered.

'But if the billy goats are ... altered, how will we be able to maintain the Royal Herd, and continue to supply the traditional Regimental Mascots?'

'Oh dear, oh dear,' they chortled, exchanging pitying looks, 'you would have to keep stud males for breeding, of course.'

'But, but, that is what we are doing now.' I was becoming totally confused.

'Yes, but you insist on keeping them with the females.'

'But why not? What harm does it do? If the males are to be allowed to remain intact, then why not leave them with the females?'

'Because it is bringing the British she-goat into disrepute.'

'Let me get this straight. What you are asking is that if the male goats are kept with the females, the males must be castrated. But if they are kept separately, away from the females, they can remain intact? Is that correct?' They sighed.

'Dr Morris, there is nothing to stop you keeping some entire males away from the herd and others, altered, with the herd. You can do both. You don't have to choose between two extremes. Just so long as the males which remain ... entire, are kept out of the paddock containing the females. They can meet for service – that is quite adequate.'

What with celibates and services, it sounded more like a religious order of goats, rather than a simple breeding herd. I was beginning to lose my patience.

'If you do not object to the maintaining of ... unaltered male goats and of the using of these breeding males for ... serving the females, then I really cannot see why you object to running them with the females at all times.' They pursed their lips with distaste.

'We all know that males stink.' The handbags were creaking ominously. 'We all know that the foul odour of the male pollutes the air and makes people turn away in disgust. The unaltered male, that is. Now, altered males are as sweet-smelling as the females, so what we propose is this. You keep the smelly breeding males away somewhere out of sight, and you keep the odour-free, altered males in with the females in your display herd. That way, people will be able to see a mixed social group without being nasally offended. Above all, it will clear the good name of the she-goat.' At last, I understood.

'I see. Your main concern is that people should not be misled into thinking that the female is smelly. Is that it?'

'Precisely.'

'Ah. Well. Thank you for explaining your problem. I will certainly take steps to investigate, and will do anything I consider necessary to unsully the reputation of the female British goat.'

They were delighted to hear this and creaked off to continue

19 As Curator of Mammals at London Zoo I converted my large office into 'a cage with a desk'. The glass-fronted cage filled almost the entire room, so that I could continue to observe animal behaviour even while on the telephone.

20 Ramona celebrating the publication of our first joint book *Men and Snakes*, arm-in-tail with one of her favourite subjects.

their never-ending struggle to separate the smells from the goats.

I missed them. But their place was soon filled by an even more formidable lady. She did not walk into my office, she prowled in. Her feet fell on the floor like padding, leonine paws. Her pale, golden hair was mane-like, and her eyes were eager for the kill.

'I need your help with my lioness. Look at these.'

She unloaded dozens of photo albums on to my desk, as if placing a zebra carcass before me for my inspection. I opened one and flipped through it. Then another. And another. They were full of hundreds of pictures of the lion-lady reclining in the arms— I should say legs—of a beautiful, fully grown lioness. She and the animal were sprawled together in every conceivable posture— side by side, she on top, lioness on top, wrestling, playing, running, swimming, resting and sleeping. Page after page after page.

'How can I help?'

'I want to publish a book about my life with her. She lives free in the African bush, but she is my friend. We have a closer relationship than has ever existed before between man and lion.'

'I can see that. But the pictures are a little repetitive. I can't quite see there being enough for a full book. An article, perhaps ... ' And I went on to explain that there were so many hundreds of new animal books each year (which there were at the time—it was an animal-book boom period) that I did not hold out too much hope for her finding a publisher. But I was sympathetic and sent her off to another contact who might be helpful. She gathered up her mountain of photo albums and strode purposefully off to her next victim.

Which just goes to show how wrong you can be. Her name was Joy Adamson and the lioness was called Elsa. Not only did she manage to make one book out of her lioness—she made a whole shelf of volumes. The first, *Born Free*, went on to become the greatest seller of any animal book ever published, ending up as a feature film and even a complete television series. As her fame spread around the world, I remember telling a friend that I would obviously make the world's worst publisher—if I couldn't even spot the potential of an international best-seller. But he re-

H

assured me when he told me that the project had, in fact, been turned down by several of the biggest publishing houses in London. So I was not alone in my folly.

Looking back, I think I should have recognized Joy Adamson's driving energy and her determined self-confidence – two of the most valuable assets for any author. She knew she had something exciting to tell and nothing was going to stop her, short of a fatal bite in the neck from her leonine chum. But I had become so upset about the idea of 'humanized' animals, and the way that hand-rearing turned them into hopeless mental hybrids (like poor Congo), that I think this must have blinded me to the obvious romantic appeal of a woman with a tame lioness.

Whatever my feelings about Elsa's confused sense of identity, I had to admit that Joy Adamson's books did a great deal of good for the lion's public image, and helped to drive one more nail into the coffin of the Big Game Hunter. It was amazing to me that those great, hairy Hemingway-cowards were still roaming about the world with their precision-turned telescopic sights, blazing away at hapless wildlife. But they were still there, stubbornly refusing to accept what the rest of us now knew, from all the new films and field-studies that were being done, namely that their 'heroic' deeds up-country where they risked their lives face to face with savage marauding beasts, were in reality about as dangerous as taking pot-shots in a slaughterhouse.

Proof of the impact of Joy Adamson's writings came by accident – the sort of accident that can reduce a good secretary to tears. What happened was this. Back in my days as head of the TV Unit I had run a competition in which children had to write in and state which was their most-loved and their most-hated animal. They also had to answer a third question for which a prize was given. The awarding of a prize provided such a strong incentive that my office was flooded with sacks of mail – somewhere in the region of 50,000 postcards. From these we were able to analyse with some accuracy the animal likes and dislikes of British children. It took teams of sorters days to work through the mountain of cards, but the results were well worth the effort. We discovered things about children's attitudes to animals that had never been guessed before. (Younger children preferred bigger animals, for instance, while older children favoured tiny animals. Girls hated spiders more than boys, but only when the girls were approaching the age of puberty. Snakes were the most hated of all animals, but dislike for them waned as children grew older, and this applied, surprisingly, to both boys and girls.) There was only one animal that appeared both in the list of 'top ten' loves *and* the list of 'top ten' hates, and that animal was the lion. Other loved animals were little hated and other hated animals were little loved, but the lion split the world of children uniquely into two halves: those who looked upon the species as the proud, lordly king of the jungle, and those who looked upon him as a nasty, savage killer.

That was the situation before *Born Free* began to make its influence felt. Nearly two years later, after the book's fame had spread, Granada Television repeated the programme containing my competition. At the zoo we were unaware that they were going to do this. Mary Haynes, my secretary, arrived at our office, expecting the usual pile of twenty or thirty letters, to find her desk almost submerged by bulging mailbags. I found her sitting there, dumb-struck, wondering what to do. We opened one of the mailbags and plunging into it drew out a fistful of postcards. One glance told us what had happened. To this second challenge, 30,000 children had responded and, somewhere in amongst that vast mass of entries, were several important, urgent letters we were expecting from foreign zoos about vital animal exchanges. It took us several days to find them, burrowing like moles into a great swamp of children's postcards.

Making the best of a bad job, we set about a second major analysis of the children's animal loves and hates, to see if preferences had changed during the past two years. There was only one significant shift: the lion was now more loved and less hated. Joy Adamson's promotion campaign on behalf of the lion had worked. She had achieved the difficult goal of not merely providing a passing entertainment, but of actually shifting public feelings towards an animal species. Elsa the lioness had become an ambassador for her kind.

She had also done something else. She had made people start to query the morality of keeping animals in captivity – in zoos and, even more so, in circuses. The essence of Elsa's story was her freedom and that was something that zoo and circus animals were sadly lacking. More and more animal books began to appear in the 1960s giving detailed reports of field-studies of animals in their natural habitat. New television films showing wildlife in natural surroundings were becoming more frequent – taking the wonders of nature into every living-room in the country. The attitude of ordinary people towards the zoo was perceptibly changing. I found myself having to defend the very idea of a zoo existing at all.

Coming under attack at a dinner party in London one night, I retaliated by asking whether anyone knew what happened to an old lion in the wilds of Africa. No one did. I explained that after a lion had passed its peak and was no longer athletic enough to chase and kill an antelope or a zebra, it was forced to turn to smaller prey or starve. As it became too slow to catch anything fleet-footed, even small creatures, it resorted to attacking those species that did not attempt to run away – things such as porcupines – with the result that it often ended its days in a slow, torturing agony, with the savagely sharp quills of porcupines embedded in its flesh, covered in festering wounds it could not heal. In the zoo, by contrast, all the inmates had the services of a modern animal hospital where they could be treated by expert veterinarians. And they never went hungry for a day in their lives. But even with this emotive argument I found it hard to convince my audience. There was something essentially prison-like about a zoo cage and animals behind bars were captives, no matter how healthy.

This was brought home to me vividly one day in the zoo restaurant. Spike Milligan's children were visiting the zoo and I was talking to them about my work. I explained that I was the Curator of Mammals.

'What's a curator?'

'It means I am in charge of all the mammals.'

'What's a mammal?'

'That's an animal that gives milk to its young.'

One of them piped up innocently:

'Now I know what you are, you're a cow-jailer!'

This was a sobering thought. I didn't much care for the title of cow-jailer. Doubts began to seep into my mind about the validity of what I was doing. Ever since I had first arrived at the zoo I had been so excited by the marvellous variety of animal species I met every day, that I had hardly ever questioned the rightness of keeping animals in captivity. As a zoologist, my intense curiosity about every aspect of animal life had led me on in a headlong rush of enquiry and investigation. Every new species I encountered for the first time provided a special thrill of discovery and I was learning so much so quickly that the momentum of my zoo progress carried me along from day to day, with never a backward glance. But nagging worries were beginning. The more I learned about the problems of animal boredom in zoo cages, the more determined I became to improve zoo conditions to the point where an animal enclosure was more of a playground than a prison cell, and where the natural environment of each species was copied as closely as possible in the space available.

We started work designing a new pavilion for small mammals and I spent days in a specially constructed research laboratory, testing new ways of providing a more complex habitat for the zoo inmates. Bars and wire would have to go. Branches, earth, grass, sand, leaves, logs would have to be added. Flying mammals must have room to fly, swimming mammals to swim, burrowing mammals to burrow, climbing mammals to climb, and so on. It was a long, slow struggle, and it was going to be expensive, but it was the only way to answer the critics.

I was sure, too, that it was important for urban populations not to become remote from contact with live animals. TV films were all very well, but meeting a live animal at close quarters was still necessary, if each new generation of town children was to discover the magic of the animal world for itself. The zoo animals had to speak for their species, year after year, reminding people of the fantastic variety of wildlife and making them more and more determined not to allow human encroachment and folly to destroy the surviving wild fauna of the world.

While this serious work was going on, the zoo continued to provide its lighter moments — bizarre and eccentric oddities that appealed to the surrealist element in my personality. There was the night when a bevy of sodden police arrived in the middle of a thunderstorm with a request that we should without delay count up the number of venomous vipers in our snake-pit. It seemed that they had taken into custody a youth who claimed he had hidden in a zoo lavatory until the grounds were deserted, when he had leapt into the pit, scooped up all the vipers into a sack and had then proceeded to let them loose in Soho. Would we please check the validity of his statement?

Counting vipers in an open enclosure, full of rocks and vegetation, at night, by flashlight, in a thunderstorm, is a nightmare task, but the keepers did their best. The results were inconclusive and we sat pondering the problem with the police, in the steamy warmth of the keepers' club. If Soho really was awash with vipers, some late-night drunks were in for a nasty shock. With any luck, I suggested, they might imagine they were having D.T.s and become converted to lemonade for life. The police were not amused.

'We'd better get back to the apron-man,' one grumbled.

'The apron-man?'

'Yes, before the snake-boy we were on to the apron-man. Cornered him in a car-park wearing his plastic apron, with the big pocket in front.'

'What did he have in his pocket?' I asked cheerfully. The policeman who had been speaking gave me a disdainful look that clearly indicated that he considered this a question only a village yokel would ask.

'His filthy paraphernalia, of course,' he replied wearily, as he squelched to the door of the club and thrust himself back into the storm. I wanted to follow him and ask what on earth that could be, but somehow I felt that the soggy snake-hunt had taxed his patience to the limit, so I let it go. Perhaps by now, if he had escaped, he had an apron full of vipers. The Soho beat, I decided, was almost as colourful as life at the zoo. If I had an animal zoo to cope with, the police in their way had to deal with a human zoo. It suddenly seemed ridiculous to me to call the city a 'concrete jungle' – it was much more like a zoo, with city-dwellers trapped in small cages, just like the animals in Regent's Park. And this was a theme I was to return to in a book I wrote some years later, called *The Human Zoo*.

In the weeks that followed, the strange episode of the snake-boy kept coming back into my mind. An idea was forming, but I could not yet crystallize it. The zoo was continuing to provide its usual stream of distractions. Brigitte Bardot was filming at the Lion House. Edmund Hillary had turned up with a yeti-scalp. An expert cobbler had arrived to measure the elephants for leather boots. And a man had rung up my office to enquire whether I was the firm of solicitors called G. Raffe, L. E. Phant and C. Lion. It was business as usual. But as I paused to make a brief anatomical check on the delicious Bardot, the snake-boy persisted in flitting in and out of my thoughts. He was back again when I joined in the conspiracy to scratch a hair loose from the yeti-scalp, so that it could be analysed microscopically at the Natural History Museum. (Disappointingly, it turned out to belong to a species of Asiatic wild mountain goat.) And he was still there when I queried the sanity of the elephant boot-cobbler, only to be re-buffed with the retort:

'How would *you* like to cross the Alps bare-footed?'

There was really no answer to that, and I went off to cogitate over my obsession with the snake-boy's wild claims. (The vipers, it had turned out, were still safely tucked away under their usual hiding-places in the snake-pit.)

That night I discussed it with Ramona. We came to the conclusion that the fascinating thing about snakes was man's incredibly irrational attitudes towards them. At various times in human history, snakes have been worshipped, feared, puzzled over, symbolized, hated, exploited, charmed, eaten, loved, exterminated, and even petted. They have been used in magic, witchcraft, religion, medicine, warfare, torture, sport, science, commerce and entertainment. Ramona had been trained as an historian and I was a zoologist – perhaps we should combine to make a study of man's long and complex relationship with snakes. Perhaps we should write a book – a history, natural and unnatural. It would be a new kind of animal volume – an all-round view of one particular form of life, with each chapter representing a different approach to its subject. We would call it *Men and Snakes*. If it worked, we would go on to make similar studies of other animals – a whole series of books.

Ramona had at this point been working for the TV Unit for seven years, writing endless scripts and organizing the Unit's increasingly bulky film library, which now ran to almost a million feet of celluloid. She welcomed the idea of tackling a bigger writing project, something she could plunge into in much greater depth. We discussed it with a publisher and the idea was immediately accepted. Ramona resigned from the Unit and began her researches. The first task she set herself was to locate the oldest known image of a snake made by human hand. It turned out to be an extraordinary cave painting in a vast, five-mile-long cavern in the south of France, at a place called Baume Latrone. The painting itself, according to books on prehistoric cave art, was also on a grand scale – the serpent being no less than nine feet nine inches from fangs to tail-tip. This we simply had to see for ourselves and that summer we set off on a prehistoric snake-hunt – a pilgrimage to the Giant Serpent of Baume Latrone.

8

'LIFE IS TOO SHORT FOR HOLIDAYS.' I was grumbling already. I used to loathe going away on holidays. I was not happy unless I had a goal—something to work towards.

'Yours will certainly be too short unless you take some,' Ramona threw back at me. 'And you have a goal, anyway—the snake hunt.'

'All I want to do is to find the Serpent of Baume Latrone and take a photograph of it to use as an illustration in the new book. That will take one day at the most. It's not enough.'

Ramona knew that I had been overworking and was determined to browbeat me into taking a rest. She had talked me into expanding the snake hunt from one week to a full month, so that we could spend a decent amount of time lying on the sun-drenched beaches of Spain, before returning to England via the snake-cave in southern France.

'First we have three weeks relaxing and sunbathing,' she insisted, '*then* we'll go caving. You'll have the serpent to look forward to and it will do you good to take a long rest.'

'Sunbathing causes skin cancer,' I snarled. I was playing dirty now. 'And when I take a long rest it will be in a coffin. Three weeks will drive me up the sea-wall!'

'You're impossible!'

I was. Looking back, I really don't know how Ramona put up with it. I was only truly happy when I was packing a week's work into every day. It was becoming something of a joke. Only a few weeks earlier I had read in *Punch*: 'Morris ... is neurotically productive. He finds it almost impossible to relax, and scurries after new projects with the intensity of a hamster foraging for food.' Philip Oakes, who wrote the article, had always been amused by my over-active life-style, but it was no joke for Ramona. She enjoyed working, but when it came to relaxing, she was a genius to my dunce.

I tried to compromise:

'Supposing we drive down through France, stopping off to look at the dome of serpents in the Rouffignac cave, then on to north-west Spain to take in the ceiling of painted bulls at Altamira, then south to Madrid to see *The Garden of Earthly Delights* by Bosch, then right down south to Granada for the Alhambra Palace, on to Malaga for Picasso's birthplace, back up to Barcelona for Gaudi's Sagrada Familia church, and *then* to the Costa Brava for your sun-drenched beaches. Then back up through France via the Serpent of Baume Latrone. How about that? Does that sound fair?'

'No.'

'Oh.'

Ramona sighed. Something told her it was a losing battle.

'Have you any idea how much driving that will mean for you? Have you any idea how many miles that is?'

'Er ... 4,357.'

'That's ridiculous.' But she had already resigned herself, and we started to make detailed plans.

The cave at Rouffignac, our first important stop, was something of an oddity. Its eight miles of passages and tunnels had been known for centuries, but modern experts had written it off as being without any cave-art on its walls. Then, as late as 1956, it was explored more thoroughly and the astonishing discovery was made that it contained no fewer than 141 depictions of prehistoric animals, including 91 mammoths. The cry went up that it was a fake and that the paintings and scratchings must have been made by the discoverers, to create a reputation for themselves. A war of rival experts began. But it was a needless war, which could easily have been avoided if only the early records had been checked. The paintings had been referred to as long ago as the sixteenth century and, in my own library today, I have an old dictionary of 1701 which clearly states that the cave 'has Chambers, Paintings, Altars, etc, where the ancient Pagans sacrificed to Venus and the Infernal Gods'. So much for the envious critics. But when we visited it, in the early 1960s, it was still surrounded by an air of notoriety, and we were not quite sure what to expect when we reached it.

In one domed chamber, on the curved roof, there was said to be a cluster of serpentine forms, and that was what I wanted to see. Imagining that it might be a rough trek underground, we prepared for it with rugged shoes and old clothes. We were somewhat taken aback to discover that the journey into the bowels of the earth was made, not with intrepid, faltering steps, but on the rotating seats of an electric train. As we arrived at each group of drawings, the train stopped and carefully concealed lighting flashed on. Ramona was delighted. She talked gaily to the guide in her superior French and decided that this was a quest that even she approved of.

The serpent dome itself was an odd affair with literally hundreds of writhing serpentine scrawls covering its curved surface. Unfortunately the prehistorians were still working on it, so I was not allowed to take any photographs. For our projected snake book, this was a bad set-back, but there was still the giant serpent of Baume Latrone, so all was not lost. And that was more important because it showed greater detail, having a recognizable head, with open jaws and fangs. The Rouffignac 'serpents' had no heads or tails, and might conceivably be symbolic or abstract meander lines that had nothing to do with snakes. All the same, there was something strangely evocative about them – all massed together in one small dome in just one spot in the eight-mile cave. They reminded us vividly of a photograph we had come across, showing a mass of dead rattlesnakes slaughtered by men who had found them clustered together in their winter den. Could prehistoric man have found such a cluster, there in the Rouffignac cave, and commemorated the event on the roof above? It was an attractive idea, but was no more than wild speculation.

We headed south for Altamira, next to Lascaux the most famous of all the prehistoric painted caves, to gaze at its famous decorated ceilings – 'The Sistine Chapel of Quaternary Art'. There, a hundred years ago, a little girl called Maria had gazed up above her head while her historian father was scratching in the floor for bones and flints. 'Look daddy, look at the painted bulls!' she had cried, as she innocently made one of the greatest discoveries in the history of human art.

There, on the curved roof, her astonished father saw twenty-five polychrome figures of animals – bison, horses, deer and wild boar – some of them almost life-size, stretching over an area of about 60 feet by 20 feet. They were depicted with great artistry and delicacy and it was hard to believe that they were ancient. But we now know that they are, indeed, 14,000 years old, and represent one of the crowning glories of the Palaeolithic artist.

I was eager to lie on the floor of the shallow Altamira chamber and gaze up at them at close quarters. Pictures in books are useful, but they give no idea of the scale of the fresco. When we finally reached the cave and saw them, something odd happened. I felt uneasy about the paintings, but could not explain why. There was something wrong with them. Something that jarred. It had not struck me in the small illustrations in my volumes on ancient art, back in my library, but here, in the 'flesh', I could not rid myself of the feeling that there was a strange inconsistency in the details of the fresco. The animals were so beautifully portrayed, with such startling realism, that the artist, or artists, had clearly known their animals intimately. They were excellent zoologists – like all human hunter-gatherers. So why was there something stilted about the animals?

Stilted! Of course, that was it. It was their feet that were wrong. Their hooves pointed downwards, as if they weren't standing on them. How odd. I couldn't make it out. The guide was droning on about the way the bison were depicted 'in all the positions natural to that beast', but I was a curator of bison, among other things, and I knew there was nothing natural about the way they were standing. If they *were* standing. And yet the shading and proportions of the body were brilliantly done. It was as if the ancient artists had *wanted* to show the feet of the animals in this way. They were so talented that it seemed ridiculous that they should make a simple error in drawing the posture of the hooves.

The guide was going on: see how some of the animals are walking, some are galloping at full speed, some are slowly stealing along … see the flowing lines of the racing boar … see how others are lying down, resting. He gave the traditional explanation of the magic involved – how the artist portrayed the animals so that he could have power over them when the time came to set off and hunt them. By 'trapping' them on his fresco, he could trap them later in reality. It all seemed reasonable enough, but I left the cool of the cave with a nagging, indefinable doubt in my mind.

It was a doubt that was not to be resolved until we returned to England. There, while we were researching our snake book, I came across a remarkable and little-known paper by a man called P. A. Leasen which provided 'A new view of … Quaternary Cave Art'. It had been overlooked because it had been published in 1939, just as war was breaking out, when people were preoccupied with more modern dilemmas. I was irritated when I read it – not because I disagreed with it, but because I had not thought of it myself. Leasen gave the solution to my worry so clearly and convincingly that it made me feel a fool to have missed it. In a nutshell, he demonstrated that all the animals depicted on the ceiling of Altamira were *dead*! All that talk about galloping, racing, walking and resting was no more than romantic rubbish, even though it had been cheerfully accepted by generations of prehistorians. He proved his point elegantly by taking dozens of photographs of domestic animals at slaughterhouses, both before and after they were killed. Photographs of them, taken from above, as they lay dead on the ground, revealed hoof postures identical with those of the Altamira paintings. The feet, bearing no weight, pointed downwards in the same characteristic way. The feet of the live, standing animals looked quite different.

So the ancient artists were even more accurate than anyone had imagined. Their powers of observation were truly remarkable, and their ability to transfer their observations with great precision to their painting surface on the cave ceiling was even more astonishing. My nagging doubts about Altamira evaporated. Now I knew why the stilted postures worried me and seemed out of key with the accuracy of the rest of the anatomy. These were not active animals – it was a field of massacre!

Of course, this changed the interpretation of the function of the fresco. Instead of helping the hunters to gain power over the animals they were going to kill tomorrow, the drawings were more likely to be commemorating the animals killed yesterday – honouring them with a token of respect. Or perhaps the ancient artists were merely recording a triumph, with no thought of magic at all? The idea of magic in early art is often over-worked. It has become almost automatic to assume that some magical process was being invoked. Somehow, I find this rather condescending, as if we consider the primitive mind incapable of pursuing a basic aesthetic impulse.

Certainly, Altamira had been a stimulating experience, and driving south to Madrid I found further excitement in coming face to face, for the first time, with what I consider to be the greatest painting in the world – *The Garden of Earthly Delights* by Hieronymus Bosch. If I had to vacate a stricken planet and could only take one painting with me, that is the one.

A trivial pleasure was the discovery that Spaniards refer to Bosch as 'El Bosco' – which somehow seems a much more triumphant name for the great artist, and one which I have privately used ever since, when thinking about him.

Our round trip through Spain continued and eventually we came to rest at Ramona's personal goal – the beaches of the tiny fishing village of Calella de Palafrugell, where we rented a small apartment with a balcony overlooking the bay. I settled down to write a paper on the green acouchi, a curious South American rodent that looks like a guinea-pig on gazelle-legs, which I had been studying at the London Zoo, while Ramona demonstrated the art of relaxation which I had yet to learn.

Her luxuriating was rudely interrupted by the arrival of a haggard, almost skeletal dog, which established itself immediately beneath the balcony on which she was trying to encourage the second-degree burns she referred to as a suntan. It gazed up at her with accusing eyes and I knew instantly that we were in for one of her protective campaigns. Abandoning her serried ranks of tanning oils, creams, foams and ointments, she plunged into the dark hole that had been described as a compact kitchen and emerged with the remains of a chicken we had eaten for lunch.

From my writing table I heard the thud as the chicken carcass hit the dirt track below. There was a short, silent pause and then a thunderous cracking and chomping sound, reminiscent of feeding time at the Lion House. In the few seconds it took me to walk across the room and look down at the ground below, the entire carcass had disappeared. Every scrap of flesh and bone had vanished. The forlorn dog sat down heavily and unsteadily, its body jerking with noiseless hiccups, and licked its huge mouth. Then it subsided rapidly into a deep sleep.

'Whoever owns that dog ought to be ... '

'Shot?'

'Well, it's disgusting. Go down and ask those fishermen whose it is. Perhaps it's lost.' I abandoned the green acouchi's sex life and turned my attention to *Canis familiaris*. Plodding down the hot, dusty track (this was in the days before the Costa Brava was serving paella-and-chips and restaurants were hanging up signs reading 'we warm the pot'), I approached an old man mending his nets. Pointing across to the large dog slumbering in the shade of our balcony I asked, in my primitive Spanish, where the owner was. The man turned down the corners of his mouth and shook his head.

'*Perro solo. Todo solo.*' He shrugged and went back to repairing his nets.

I climbed round the track and up to the apartment door, and explained to Ramona that it was a stray dog, completely alone.

'Then as long as we are here it will come under my personal protection,' she announced, 'and I will feed it up and make sure that by the time we leave, it is strong enough to fend for itself.'

She threw on a dress and made for the local butcher's shop. The siesta period was nearly over and it would soon be open. She would buy the animal some meat. Biscuits were not good enough – it needed protein.

Half an hour later she returned visibly shaken, clutching a large lump of something wrapped in paper. It emerged that there had been a spot of bother in the tiny whitewashed cell that served as the local butcher's. Before her in the queue of women had been an immaculately attired nursemaid, wearing a spotless uniform with a crisp, white apron. She also wore an air of acute superiority which had irritated the huge lady butcher. The trouble began when she described the chicken she was being sold as a pigeon that had been stretched through a mangle. The lady butcher angrily decapitated the scrawny bird with a large axe and deliberately flicked its blood across the pristine whiteness in front of her wooden chopping bench. The outraged nursemaid looked down at her blood-splashed apron and flew into a towering rage, fearlessly confronting the menacingly raised axe and screaming a torrent of abuse. She then rushed over to the freshly white-washed wall of the shop and began to wipe herself along it, transferring to its surface a long smear of blood. When at last the blood-stains remaining on her apron had been successfully concealed beneath a coating of whitewash, she turned on the butcher again and then, as Ramona put it, things began to get really nasty. Other women in the shop were screaming now and taking sides and at any moment it seemed that human blood must also flow.

'Not at all like shopping in Hampstead,' muttered Ramona, as she started cooking the meat that she had eventually managed to purchase, after peace had, with some difficulty, and the intervention of several grinning men, been restored.

Serving up her dog-dish on a large plate she set off to carry it down and round the track to the still sleeping Perro. It was dusk now and, in the half-light, I could hear her talking softly to him and encouraging him to eat. This was followed by much slurping and crunching, then silence.

She reappeared triumphant. Perro, as he was now called, had actually managed a brief tail-wag. Nothing fancy, just a few, slow, stiff beats of the air with his long, bony appendage, almost as if he had nearly forgotten how to do it. But it was a start.

In the days that followed, the stray returned regularly to his resting-place beneath the balcony and Ramona continued her patient rehabilitation campaign. After about a week, his walk was more sprightly and he was beginning to look more like a dog than a skin-covered wicker basket. He was still a remarkably ugly dog, a fact which endeared him to Ramona. Where animals were concerned, she was never swayed by a pretty face — a trait of hers which I had always admired. It appealed to my zoological dictum of all animals being equal.

I took a closer look at her Perro. He appeared to be a cross between an anaemic bloodhound and a mounted skeleton. His short, lifeless coat had the colour of a nicotine-stained finger, and the harsh Spanish sun cast dark, vertical shadows between each of his ribs. His long drooping ears appeared to be weighted with lead, making his huge head sag down so low that his jaw nearly brushed the ground as he walked along. Behind his great rib-cage, his body narrowed almost to a point, before it met his stiff hind legs and his long bony tail, which ended in a sharp, almost hairless spike. There was no denying that he was a pitiful sight, but somehow he managed to maintain a certain tragic dignity — a slow deliberation about all his actions, as if he had come to accept a permanent need to conserve energy at all costs. I had never seen a dog that moved so slowly.

The sprightliness and bounce that was slowly returning to his gait did nothing at first to speed it up. He still plodded along like a defeated prisoner, but there was less stiffness now. Towards the end of our stay he managed his first run, and to Ramona it was as satisfying a spectacle as if he had just won the Greyhound Derby at White City. On our last morning, he positively bounded up for his final meal and Ramona's happiness was complete. But short-lived, for there was a sting in the tail of his story. With his last gulp of food, he looked around him and sniffed the air. With his new vigour, his sense of masculinity had suddenly returned. Spotting a diminutive, fat-bottomed bitch poodle in the distance, he took off in a lecherous gallop, leapt on the startled powder-puff of a dog and proceeded to rape her. The poodle's diminutive, fat-bottomed owner, a middle-aged French lady tourist with a poodle-style hair-do, ran screaming from her door and raised such a din that several grizzled fishermen dropped their nets, converged on the preoccupied Perro, and kicked him brutally all the way out of the village. He bounded off down the dirt road with stones hailing after him and that was the last view we had of him. There was a nasty irony about the fact that we had made him fit enough to warrant forcible expulsion from his home territory, but at least he had had his moment. And with any luck he was strong enough now to survive and perhaps make a new niche for himself in a less hostile environment.

We had to steel ourselves now for another animal encounter and it was one we were not anticipating with any pleasure. We had decided to visit a Spanish bullfight. Both of us hated the idea of bullfighting, but felt that if we were going to attack it, we had to witness it once in our lives, so that we could argue from knowledge instead of ignorance. But we dreaded it. One of the world's greatest bullrings was in nearby Barcelona and that was where we were heading. Second-rate bullfighting, inept and messy, in some small, local ring, we decided, would be too much to bear. So we went for the best.

Architecturally, from the outside, the bullring reminded me of the Colosseum in Rome and, as we mounted the stone steps leading to the seats, I had the creepy feeling that I was about to witness Christians being thrown to the lions. The crowd around us oozed an almost visible fog of garlic. They shoved and jostled and had about them the air of savage coarseness that I associated with ancient Rome at its most decadent. To our surprise, there seemed to be as many French and German voices barking around us as Spanish. The French, in particular, seemed to have blood in their eyes. There was a sharp, cutting quality in their excitement – and a distasteful eagerness for the imminent ritual of death. I was beginning to regret our decision. I liked bulls, dammit, and suddenly wanted to be somewhere else. But it was too late, we had arrived at the top of the steps and stood now, gazing down at the great curve of the ring, with the carefully raked circle of sand surrounded by row upon row of animated death-wishers.

It was a breath-taking spectacle, awe-inspiring in the intensity of its atmosphere. Then an extraordinary thing happened. As we stood there, uncertain about which way to move to gain our seats, there was a sudden deafening roar. At first I thought it was the crowd, or some ceremonial explosion of noise, but I was wrong, because the crowd's reaction to it was a huge gasp of dismay. It was an enormous, shuddering clap of thunder. Looking up I saw a strange black cloud that had moved over the very centre of the sky above the great circle of the bullring. Then, almost immediately, huge hailstones started falling, a few at first, then a positive fusillade, peppering the rows of seated heads and bouncing off the stonework in all directions, like the cascading sparks from a fireworks display.

I have never seen a hailstorm like it, before or since. The audience leapt from their seats and fled for the exits. We were engulfed for a second time in a fog of garlic and bodily swept backwards down the steep steps and out into the road. The vast and now angry crowd was swirling this way and that, trying desperately to find shelter from the freak storm that was beating down all around it.

The bullfight was cancelled. No bulls died that day – a wish of mine that I thought could never have come true. With a great sense of relief we ran to our car and sped away from Barcelona, heading north. We have never again attempted to visit a bullfight and never will. We unashamedly continue to attack the practice from our position of ignorance, but we can at least claim to have tried to see one. If we had been deeply superstitious we would no doubt have felt that the gods had interceded to spare us the ordeal. As it was, we were just intensely grateful for the vagaries of the Spanish weather.

Pausing on the road north next day, for a meal at a roadside restaurant, with the sun blazing down on us once again, we noticed a wooden board announcing that there was a riding school near by – beginners welcome. Ramona had never ridden a horse in her life and I was only slightly acquainted with the saddle. We had both ridden elephants and camels, but horses were something of a mystery. As we had been robbed, mercifully, of one animal 'first' the day before, we decided to make up for it by risking a little Spanish horsemanship. Once again we were heading for the unexpected.

The road leading to the riding school quickly deteriorated into a lumpy dirt-track, at the end of which there was a ramshackle building flanked by decrepit stable blocks. No human form was visible as we walked from the car, disturbing a tornado of angry flies with every step. As we approached the paint-peeling door, it flew open and a startling white-and-gold apparition stood before us. Through the dense clouds of insects that swirled around us, we saw that the white and gold adorned the gaunt figure of a tall, granite-faced man carrying a whip. The dirty stubble of his chin contrasted vividly with the immaculate ornateness of his cowboy costume. For Western enthusiasts, he can best be described as Clint Eastwood dressed as Roy Rogers. As far as we could see, his clothing was the only clean thing in the whole establishment, which had clearly known better days. It soon emerged that we were the only clients and he was the entire staff.

As I was pondering the possibility of saying we had lost our way and were looking for the road to Gerona, he strode clankily across to a rotting stable-door, flung it open, plunged through the escaping cloud of flies and dragged out a wild-eyed stallion. There was so much froth on its mouth that it looked like a barber-shop customer interrupted in mid-shave.

Our towering cowboy shouted 'Yah!' and 'Wah', and various

other endearments while tugging ferociously on its bit, which encouraged it to rear up in pain and show its gnashing, yellow teeth.

'Señor,' said Clint Rogers, gruffly, indicating that I was to be the lucky rider of this gem of the stables. I hurriedly consulted my Spanish pocket dictionary, searching for the word 'beginner'.

'*Principiante*,' I called out, hoping this was the right word. I did not like the sound of it. It had the wrong ring to it—as if I was proudly claiming to be the first in the saddle. '*No experiencia!*' I cried, feeling a little safer with that, but he was not listening. He had plunged into a second stall from which now came the sound of splintering wood and Spanish curses. Maddened hooves were being smashed against walls. Ramona's face had set into a kind of undertaker's smile.

'This one must be yours,' I ventured, but before she had time to reply, Roy Eastwood reappeared, sliding along the ground behind a wildly careering mare like a demented water-skier. 'Yooohuuu-werrhr – yerrrargh,' he was shouting, in that tender way horse-lovers have when exchanging intimacies with their wayward steeds.

'Señora,' he grunted, when at last he had her under some semblance of control.

Before we could back out of the impending fiasco gracefully, he had whisked us up into the saddles and then, to our horror, vanished a third time. My black rolling-eyed stallion turned swiftly as soon as he disappeared and began sniffing the quivering rump of Ramona's brown mare.

'Flehmen!' I called to her.

'Flaming what?' she called back, being somewhat preoccupied with regaining a lost stirrup.

'No, no, *flehmen*. Look at my stallion's mouth—it's making the flehmen expression—look at its curling lip.' I knew enough about equine expressions to see that my horse fancied hers and was becoming sexually excited.

My academic interest turned to panic when I realized that he had now decided to attempt a consummation of his passion and was heaving himself up in an attempt to mount the mare. Facing away, Ramona was blissfully unaware of the fact that she was about to become a human filling in a horse sandwich.

'He's mounting!' I yelled. 'He's mounting!'

'About time, too,' she replied, without looking round.

'No, not the cowboy, the stallion – my stallion on your mare.' But luckily the mare disapproved and kicked her would-be lover heavily in the chest. Ramona jolted forward and was hanging on to the mare's mane with both hands, as our cowboy suddenly shot into view from behind the other stable block. He was riding a magnificent white horse of spectacular proportions, bedecked with ornate trappings, as if it had come from a circus ring. He reared it up on its hind legs, like the Lone Ranger, and came to a thudding halt in front of us. Staring at Ramona's curious posture, he at last realized what we had been trying to tell him all along – that he was dealing with two hopeless novices. With dejected resignation, he corrected her grip from mane to reins, fixed her stirrup and then jogged off at a suitably snail-like pace, followed obediently by our two horses who suddenly seemed, thank God, to have lost their high spirits.

We progressed quietly down country lanes and were even beginning to enjoy it, when my stallion felt a second surge of lust and rushed up behind the mare for a second mounting. This time she responded by breaking into a gallop and making off across a field of what looked like huge melons or pumpkins, hotly pursued by my infatuated stallion. I was alarmed to see that Ramona had now adopted an unorthodox horizontal posture, sticking out sideways from her horse like a performing Cossack. Squelchy fragments of trampled melon or pumpkin were splashing up over her and it was clear that she was soon going to tilt far enough over to be able to eat and ride at the same time.

The Lone Ranger was still jogging unconcernedly along the path we had left so abruptly, bored to inattentiveness. Just as Ramona was about to invert herself, he sensed all was not well, spun round and charged to the rescue. As soon as he had sorted things out, we set off again with Ramona taking up the rear and peace descended on our motley group once more. But not for long.

Rounding a bend we came upon a scene which my eyes saw, but my brain refused to accept. There in front of us was a fortress manned by uniformed men armed with rifles. As we jogged towards it, they opened fire on us. Our cowboy's horse responded by standing to attention on its hind legs and then taking off at a gallop. Our own horses naturally followed suit and we were off again in a mad cross-country scramble, but this time with an accompaniment of a fusillade of rifle-shots. It had to be a bad dream. It couldn't really be happening. The dreamlike state was amplified by an outbreak of yelps and shrieks from trees behind us. We spun round in our saddles in time to see sixty or seventy Red Indians in full war-paint, riding straight at us from the other direction. We were trapped now by the rifle-shots on our left and the whooping, tomahawk-waving and spear-brandishing Indians on our right, bearing down on us at hair-raising speed.

Ramona, I noticed, had reverted to her mane-hugging posture, riding her mare like a baby baboon clinging to its mother's fur. If we didn't stop soon, she would be doing her Cossack tilt again. Then, from inside another clump of trees came the noise of yet another alien sound, this time a shrieking loud-speaker, babbling incoherent abuse, as if some displaced British Rail station announcer had blown his fuse and gone into uncontrollable hysterics.

Our Lone Ranger, fired by the horsemanship of the now encircling Red Indians, was showing off horribly, rearing his horse up in the air and swerving this way and that in a dazzling display that brought frantic film technicians in jeans and sweat-shirts running out of the trees, wildly waving their arms and cursing in several languages simultaneously. At this, our leader mysteriously changed his tactics and, riding hurriedly towards us, herded us back the way we had come. As we left the now totally confused scene behind us, with men in diverse costumes running in all directions arguing and shouting to one another in foreign tongues, we knew with a numbing certainty that we had just made our first and last appearance in an epic Western movie.

Knowing something about film budgets, on a more modest
scale, I shuddered to think what our accidental invasion of the
fortress-storming scene must have cost in wasted time, wages and
celluloid. Our Lone Ranger seemed unimpressed.

'*Cine!*' he grunted, as we rode slowly home, and he spat dis-
dainfully into the dust. I think he was trying to hide his envy. His
cowboy costume gave him away. For him, it had been a moment
of glory, and it occurred to me that he had probably known
exactly what he was doing to the fancy film-men who had
invaded his fly-blown domain. Perhaps he had even hoped they
would give him a part in the film, to stop him disrupting their
work with his dude tourists. Or perhaps he merely wanted to
show them that they were disrupting *his* world.

Whatever the truth, it certainly provided us with a memorable
ride and one which, as far as Ramona was concerned, was enough
to last her a lifetime.

The moment had come for us to wend our way up to France
in search of the Serpent of Baume Latrone—my final quest on
our month-long journey. We knew that the cave was 8½ miles
north of the beautiful city of Nimes and we had set aside one day
for it. After our experience at Rouffignac, where we had arrived
in rugged clothes for an arduous underground trek, only to find
a special train-tour laid on, we decided this time to treat the
second snake-hunt in a more cavalier fashion, wearing our
ordinary, colourful beach clothing and not bothering to make any
special preparations. After a pleasant night in Nimes, we casually
set off for the north, cruising gently along the dry country roads
('pootling along', Ramona called it) until we came to the River
Gardon. Here we asked the way, imagining an easy-going,
thirty-minute visit with an expert guide, concealed lighting,
booklets and postcards on sale at the cave entrance and perhaps
even an underground electric train.

We were rather shaken to find that nobody knew where it was.
There were hundreds of caves along the steep slopes of the dried-
up river-bed and absolutely no one was selling postcards. After
driving for miles on sinuous and precipitous dirt tracks, we

arrived at the village of Le Baume, only to discover that there were almost as many Le Baumes as there were caves.

Several Le Baumes later we had still found nothing. Then, completely lost, we ended up at the little village of Rossan. We questioned two old men sitting in the hot shade of the village square. To our amazement they replied casually:

'Oh yes, you are in the right place. The cave is just up that track over there. But you'll need a guide.'

'Where *is* the guide?' we enquired.

'Ah, yes, well ... there isn't one,' they decided, after a brief private exchange.

Then they called over a shy little fourteen-year-old girl and told her *she* would have to take us. She agreed after a while and led me over to the village shop. I should have realized what I was in for when she started buying candles. But by now I could already picture myself crouching with my camera in front of the giant serpent— man's first detailed portrayal of a snake anywhere in the world.

Anticipating the electric-train routine, Ramona was wearing high-heeled gold sandals, along with her pink-and-blue beach clothes. She took one look at the jagged track over the hill and retired to the car to read a book. At this the little girl became visibly alarmed. It was soon clear that she was not going off into a dark cave with a strange man even if he *was* weighed down with cameras, batteries and flash-guns and holding a fistful of candles.

Eventually, with Ramona protesting vigorously, the three of us set off. About half an hour later, after a non-stop climb up a flint-strewn, thistle-ridden track in the boiling afternoon sun, the little nymphet chirped out:

'Only three more mountains, monsieur.'

An hour later, we came to a vertical cliff. It fell straight down into the dried-up valley of the River Gardon and the little girl announced proudly that the cave was below us. Only a few hundred feet down, I think she said.

Several prayers later, we slithered into the cool hole in the cliff wall. At this point the girl informed us joyfully that the cave was composed largely of wet sticky mud and that it was dangerous to enter without spiked boots. That did it. Ramona sat down in a final sort of way in the entrance and lit a cigarette. She told the little girl to take me in to the cave and I gathered she said something about shouting if she was in trouble. Anyway it reassured the girl and off we went.

Crawling a few hundred yards in the press-up position in wet slippery mud wearing beach garments and sandals is less fun than it sounds. The trouble was that the tunnels of the cave were often only two or three feet high and I was desperately trying to save my clothes from total ruin. After a while my arms gave up and I just slithered along.

The cave began to branch into an intricate network of increasingly narrow passages. The chirpiness of my tiny guide persisted, but a little shakily, I thought. We made several plunges down side tunnels and then she decided that perhaps we were in the wrong part of the cave altogether. We turned back and after a while it became clear that we were lost. Her brother, she explained, knew the place well. He could have guided me to the serpent, but she, well, she had only been there a few times. Then the candles blew out.

From somewhere a current of air was suddenly blasting through the cave, making it impossible to keep a match alight to rekindle the candle flame. For some reason I started whistling to myself, but it sounded so ridiculous that I abandoned it and began a systematic search, memorizing each direction in turn until, like a hamster in a strange burrow, I had the feel of the shape of the warren of tunnels in which we were stranded. Then at last we came to a lumpy corner in one tunnel that I recognized and, rather unsteadily, blindly retraced our steps which, to our great relief, brought us safely back to a recumbent Ramona.

'What was it like?' she asked.

'What was what like?'

'The serpent, of course,' she said. 'I hope you took close-ups of its head?'

At this, the small girl and I set off again into another gaping black hole. This time we struggled for what seemed like miles down into the earth, sometimes through tiny apertures, sometimes along great slanting cracks, and eventually we straightened up in a vast chamber full of enormous stalagmites and stalactites. It made me feel like a parasite in a cow's stomach.

'*Voici le serpent!*' shrieked the little girl, slithering over to a place were a weird stalagmite had joined up with a stalactite in a wiggly serpentine column. In the candlelight she traced the snake-like curves with her muddy, eager fingers.

My heart sank. And my sandals sank with it, beneath the squelching mud. So this was what she had been trying to find. She was so pleased that I had to agree it was indeed beautiful before breaking the news to her that what I wanted was not a design by nature, but by primitive man. Did she know any drawings on the walls? Yes, she did, but she could not remember exactly where they were. We set off in one direction after another. At one point we reached a terrifying, sheer drop down a wall of dripping slime. Only men with ropes went down there, she said firmly. We moved on. Like a rabbit she kept diving into small side tunnels, leaving me with a candle and a glazed expression. Each time she returned slightly more crestfallen.

Then, with a shout of joy, she chirped for the second time:

'*Voici le serpent, monsieur!*'

She had gone through a minute hole and insisted that I pass all my photographic equipment through and then squeeze in myself.

'*Le serpent!*' she proclaimed, pointing proudly at the curved wall. I could hardly believe what I saw. There I was, half a mile under the earth, with a fourteen-year-old-girl, crouching in a small womb-like cavity, staring at a group of the most obscene drawings I had ever set eyes on.

'And here, monsieur,' she pointed out, 'is a drawing of a woman and here, with her, is a man, and between them, see, see the great serpent rearing up.' Freud would have loved it.

'I'm so sorry, but these are not prehistoric,' I said, holding my candle near an inscription which read something like 'Jean Dupois, 1943'.

We were looking, it seemed, at a rather exclusive wartime lavatory wall, presumably used by resistance fighters in hiding from the Nazis. Just for fun, I tried to take a photograph, but the flash equipment, smothered in mud, had succumbed to the rough treatment of the past two hours and nothing happened.

As we gloomily retraced our path to the cave entrance it occurred to me that those crude drawings would probably survive all other modern pictures. In 20,000 years' time, someone will find them again and judge our epoch by them, as we judge prehistoric man by Lascaux. One could just imagine the learned, academic theories that would be woven around them: phallic worship by a cult of priest-kings living underground in sacred sanctuaries, etc., etc. This thought cheered me up in a cynical sort of way, as the three of us trudged silently back to the village.

I was rather silent, too, as we drove dejectedly off on our way back to Paris and London. The quest had been a failure. That night, at Orange, I saw a map of the district on the wall and glanced idly at it. There was the village of Rossan, where my hopes of coming face to face with the Serpent of Baume Latrone had risen so high. And there, to my amazement, a little further down the gorge of the River Gardon, was an asterisk and the words 'Grotte de Le Baume'. So the cave I had slithered around in all day wasn't even the right one. The old men at Rossan had heard the word 'Grotte' and had automatically assumed that *their* cave was the one I wanted. And all the time the Serpent of Baume Latrone was a few miles down the river.

Next morning we sped back south again to the new – the real – Le Baume. This was going to be it. I had the camera's flash working again and I was ready for action.

At the end of a suicidal, winding mountain track, with a surface obviously prepared specially to test new motor-tyres to destruction, we found the gorge of the River Gardon again. We started the long climb down and about half-way came across a policeman sitting outside a rough cottage.

'Is this really the site of the cave of Baume Latrone?'

'But of course, monsieur.'

'The one with the famous serpent drawing?'

'Yes monsieur, but ... '

'Wonderful, at last I can take my photograph.'

'No, monsieur.'

'But why not?'

'You can't get to it, monsieur, it is on the other side of the river and there is no bridge.'

'But the river is dry; *sec, sec!*' I kept saying.

'Further up, yes, dry like dust,' he agreed, 'but here, dry like wine.' I was in no mood for witty French policemen.

'Then I will hire a boat.'

'No, monsieur. No boats.'

Ignoring his warning, we set grimly off down the slope, until we reached the bottom of the gorge. There we sat crouched on a rock gazing at the huge trout swinging and twisting in the powerful current and there, several hundred feet up in the cliff-wall opposite gaped the huge black hole of *the* cave, in which was *the* serpent.

'David Attenborough,' I observed, 'would wade across or make a rope bridge, or something.' Ramona smiled. It had always been a family joke that David was intrepid and I was trepid. I knew exactly what she was thinking.

'You're not dressed for the part,' she said, stretching out on the rock.

That did it. I started to cut a strong twig from an inoffensive little bush. And with this – to measure water depth – I walked fully clothed and – I like to think – with a certain aplomb, into the churning waters of the River Gardon.

Ramona's muffled mirth at this bizarre act changed to concern when I began to sink lower and lower in the water. She sat up and frowned.

'I'm ... all ... right,' I shouted, 'don't ... worry.'

'I'm not,' she yelled back. 'It's just that I don't want the matches in your breast pocket to get wet—you know I've lost my lighter.'

'Typical! Typical of women to think about their minor comforts when their menfolk are risking life and limb.'

'Snake!' she bellowed.

'No need to be rude.'

'Snake, snake,' she repeated.

'You and your blessed cigarettes.'

'Behind you, snake,' she cried again, pointing wildly.

Spinning round I was riveted by the sight of a beautiful snake swimming frantically through the strong current, straight towards me. It must have been feeding on trout fry in some quiet corner and my river-walk had probably disturbed it. Now the snake and I were both in mid-stream, fighting together against the pull of the water. It dawned on me that I was, so to speak, the only piece of dry land available for a serpentine landing, and I took a closer look at its head. If its jaws widened out appreciably as they met its neck, then it was venomous. They did. I took off like a hippo in the mating season.

Dragging myself out on the other side, it occurred to me that seeing a snake in the water was a good omen. If there were serpents in the river, this was obviously a good place for primitive man to paint one on a cave wall. Encouraged, I squelched my way manfully up the cliff face. With a last wave to Ramona, I turned and entered the great cave of Baume Latrone.

I knew from the books that the serpent painting was 280 yards from the entrance and so I started boldly pacing out the distance: One—squelch—Two—squelch—Three—squelch ... This time I had no candles and no companion, but I had been able to acquire a pencil-slim pocket torch that produced a dim spot of light about three inches across. As it grew darker, I flicked it on and advanced more cautiously: 83—squelch—84—squelch—85 ... Then I realized that the cave was branching out and it occurred to me that I might go on turning one way and then another until finally, and permanently, I would be lost. The books had referred to it as

'The gigantic cave system of Baume Latrone' and 'A complex of corridors connecting with other, nearby caves'. I could end my days there.

I spun round, but the friendly light of the entrance had vanished. I was suddenly more alone than I had ever been in my life. I could only make out the shape of the cave by waving the torch quickly from side to side and watching the way the spot of light travelled back and forth on the walls. I decided to take each branch of the cave in turn, starting systematically from the right hand one and working my way around.

At the 173rd squelch there was a sudden rustling sound in front of me. I froze and rapidly tried to work out the current distribution of the surviving wolves of Europe. I knew there were still a few holding out in the Pyrenees. And bears too. Bears! Yes, that was it, there *were* still bears in France somewhere – but where? I couldn't remember. (I checked when I got home and found that the last brown bear had been seen in France in 1937 – but it is surprising what a dark cave and a rustling sound can do to the imagination.)

Happily the sound stopped and my waving beam of light failed to pick up any pairs of glinting eyes. Stumbling on, I was alarmed again by a sudden wooosh over my head, as startled bats flashed past along the winding passage. I wandered back and forth through that cave for over an hour, examining the walls closely, but nowhere could I find the slightest trace of a painted serpent, or anything else.

Finally, in despair, I abandoned the search. Determined now to find out exactly why I had failed, we drove to Nimes in search of the local museum. There, we were shown into the prehistoric section and saw, occupying the whole end-wall of the vast room, a life-sized replica of the Serpent of Baume Latrone – all nine feet nine inches of it. It was an exact tracing, we were told, carefully copied from the wall of the cave. Displayed near it were photographs of all the caves of the region. I found the museum attendant and pointed to the entrance into which I had squeezed a few hours earlier.

'I have searched everywhere in this cave for prehistoric draw-ings,' I explained.

'*Ah non, monsieur, tout effacés par les vandales!*'

'Erased by vandals? That's not possible – the drawings in that cave were 20 to 30,000 years old.' The man shrugged.

'*Oui, oui, monsieur,*' he persisted, '*complètement effacés par les enfants.*'

So this was the end of the quest. A painting which had survived for thousands of years, destroyed in just a few minutes. Now only the replica remained. I left feeling deeply depressed. No wonder I had had such difficulty.

Back in London, a week later, however, there was a slight ray of hope. In a book shop in the West End I discovered, quite by chance, that at the very time I was clambering about in the caves, a new book had been published on the subject – a detailed guide to the cave art of France and Northern Spain, with maps of the caverns and instructions on how to get there. If only it had been published a month earlier!

There, on page 145 was a map of the cave of Baume Latrone. I recognized it instantly, but it was not the second cave, it was the first one – the one the little girl had taken us to. And to my intense frustration I saw that the site of the serpent drawing was only just beyond the point where we stopped when we came to the vertical wall of slippery mud, dropping away in front of us. I must have been standing only a few feet away from it.

But does it still exist? Yes, according to the authors, it is still, and I quote, 'clearly visible'. So who is right? Did I confuse the attendant at Nimes museum, with my talk about the second cave, or was the erasure so recent that the authors of the book did not know about it? There is just enough doubt left to make it worthwhile returning one day, armed with a coil of rope, spiked boots and a powerful lamp. I should have done it years ago, to satisfy my curiosity, but as soon as the snake book was written, we were off on to other projects involving different animals. The snakes had had their day and there were so many other forms of life to study. Continuing our series of volumes, we wrote *Men*

21 Behind the scenes at the London Zoo's Reptile House, with the zoo's director, Leo Harrison Matthews, and a large monitor lizard.

22 With Chi-Chi the Giant Panda in a peaceful mood in her London Zoo enclosure. Later, her temperament changed and she savaged a young keeper.

23–24 The moment of truth in Moscow. *Above*: Chi-Chi approaches me
and allows me to press down on her back with my hand.
Immediately she adopts the sexual invitation posture and the male,
An-An (*below, right*), comes rushing eagerly forward to mate with
her. But she instantly changes her mood and flees from his advances.

and Apes, and then followed that with *Men and Pandas.* There was plenty of material available for the ape book, and I had first-hand information from my studies with Congo and the other London Zoo chimpanzees. But when it came to pandas, there was far less known. Luckily the zoo was the proud owner of Chi-Chi, the only giant panda in the Western world, and I was able to start making a detailed study of her behaviour at Regent's Park. What I discovered was to lead me into one of the strangest episodes of my zoological career – the attempted mating of Chi-Chi with the only other giant panda outside China, the Moscow Zoo's male An-An.

9

No wonder the russians thought I was a spy. Not since the bedding down of a latter-day Czarina had anyone been to Moscow on official sexual business. Yet here was I, jetting my way over a frozen landscape to arrange an international mating between two giant pandas—London Zoo's female Chi-Chi and Moscow Zoo's male An-An. If the K.G.B. thought this was an ornate cover story for something more sinister, who could blame them? The whole project had the air of an extravagant fantasy, obviously concocted by the fevered brain of some over-imaginative intelligence agent, entombed in a concrete cell beneath the corridors of power in Whitehall. But for me, as I sped towards Moscow airport on an icy February day in 1966, it was all too real.

The panda drama had its beginnings back in December 1957, when a team of Chinese animal trappers caught a very young female giant panda in the wilds of Szechuan. She was taken to Peking Zoo, where she was cared for by a young Chinese girl and given the name of Chi-Chi. The name meant 'pretty little girl', but one had to exercise great caution when pronouncing it because, with the wrong tonality, it also meant 'prostitute'. As I discovered later to my cost, this was one criticism that could not be levelled against Chi-Chi. 'Tease', yes; 'prostitute', never.

While Chi-Chi was being cuddled in Chinese arms in Peking, one of the world's great animal dealers, the Austrian Heini Demmer, was assembling a large collection of African wildlife at his headquarters in Nairobi. After several years of difficult negotiations, he had finally managed to persuade the Chinese authorities to do a deal with him – the biggest of his professional life. At the time there was not a single giant panda in the Western world and several American zoo directors were determined to be the first to own and display one. No more than sixteen live specimens had ever been seen outside China, and the exotic creature, like a huge black-and-white teddy bear, remained one of the great prizes of the zoo world. With a little astute bargaining, Demmer had managed to boost the price for one up to an astronomical level. If he could pull off the deal, he would be rich.

The Chinese were badly in need of African stock and when Demmer offered them three giraffes, two rhinos, two hippos and two zebras in exchange for one giant panda, their resistance crumbled. He arrived with his ark in May 1958, and the swap was made. Back in Germany with the delightful Chi-Chi, he prepared for the final trip to the United States. Then disaster struck. John Foster Dulles declared the animal 'Communist Goods' and banned its entry into America. Demmer was dumbfounded. He pleaded and pleaded, but the U.S. Treasury Department confirmed that since America did not officially recognize Communist China, there was an embargo on all trade with that country, even through an Austrian intermediary. Stranded with a panda that had now cost him a fortune, Demmer was forced to take desperate measures. He knew that no European zoo was rich enough to pay the high price he needed, so instead of trying to sell Chi-Chi, he started up a travelling panda-show, hiring her out to different zoos by the week. After Frankfurt and Copenhagen, she came to London, and the crowds flocked to see this new victim of international politics. I presented her in a special programme on British television and she became so popular that the London Zoo began to wonder whether, perhaps, they should give her a permanent home.

Acquiring a single rare animal, from which they could not breed, was completely against the zoo's conservation policy, but in this case the damage had already been done. The London Zoo had previous experience of caring for giant pandas, from before the war, and London was clearly the most suitable home for the now stranded Chi-Chi. Rather than see her touted around to zoo after zoo, they finally agreed to buy her. The problem was the price. In the end, Demmer agreed to lower his figure and, with the help of a gift of money from Granada Television, who saw her as a potential star of my *Zootime* programmes, a bargain was struck. A spectacular enclosure was prepared for her at Regent's Park, complete with an air-conditioned den, and she soon settled in to become London Zoo's major attraction.

Later, when I became curator, and started my 'marriage bureau' project of finding mates for all the single mammals in the zoo, to set up breeding groups, I naturally turned my attention to the problem of the lonely Chi-Chi. I knew that giant pandas were difficult to sex and so the first step was to determine for certain whether she really was a female. Mistakes had been made before in other zoos and I wanted to be sure. The zoo's anatomist, armed with the necessary diagrams of panda private parts, entered her enclosure and, with the help of her keeper, made a close examination. He emerged beaming, with the (misleading) words: 'Congratulations, you are the father of a beautiful bouncing boy!' I was relieved that we had taken the trouble to check, but depressed to realize that the only other panda outside China, An-An at Moscow Zoo, was also a male. That meant Peking was our only hope. Letters went off, but no letters came back. The Chinese were hanging on to the few pandas they had, and Chi-Chi's love-life seemed to be doomed.

At this stage she (as she later turned out to be!) was still too young to care, and luxuriated in her star status. She had her own swimming pool, a mist spray, and blocks of ice to lie on when the weather was too hot. She had a special keeper to play with her daily to prevent her from becoming bored and her own private kitchen, where her meals were meticulously prepared: boiled rice, oranges, bananas, pears, apples, eggs, bread, chicken, grated carrots, vitamins, minerals, and a daily supply of nine pounds of fresh bamboo shoots.

When she arrived she had weighed only 122 pounds, but in a few years she had reached her adult weight of just over 230 pounds. And that was when she started to complain. Her mood changed and she began running around her enclosure depositing scent-marks. She needed a mate. And she was no longer the friendly, lovable companion she used to be. She was found one day sitting on top of a young keeper, tearing his leg to pieces. He was rushed to hospital, while she charged angrily around her territory, her mouth covered in a bloody foam.

Each spring and autumn this mood returned and Chi-Chi refused to eat, spurning the delicious meals that were daily placed before her, until the period of heat had passed once more. The Chinese were approached again and this time there was an official response. Tsui Chan-p'ing, the director of Peking Zoo, wrote a firm but polite reply ending with the words 'We are at present unable to meet your wishes.'

All seemed lost, but then Chi-Chi herself took a hand. She became so agitated during one very strong heat that she seemed to be making herself ill. When she scratched her eye on a piece of bamboo, we decided to take the great risk of moving her to the zoo's hospital, anaesthetizing her and giving her a really thorough examination. During the course of this, her private parts again came under close scrutiny. When she had been examined before by the zoo's anatomist, she had not been fully mature, but now she was, and there was no doubt whatever about her gender: she was female after all. The anatomist had made a mistake. The immature Chi-Chi had fooled him.

Armed with this new information I went to see the zoo's director, Leo Harrison Matthews.

'We have a female panda, the Russians have a male. We simply must try to get them together. The Chinese won't co-operate, so it is our only hope.'

'Then you had better go to Moscow and fix it up.'

'Ah, yes, I suppose so.' I had walked right into that one. East-West relations were rather strained at the time and I did not relish the idea. But there seemed to be no choice. Wheels were put in motion and from Moscow came press reports that the authorities there might perhaps be prepared to consider a panda honeymoon. With the Foreign Secretary's blessing, the London Zoo immediately despatched a cable:

'From press reports we are delighted to hear that you are interested in possible mating of Moscow and London pandas. We are happy to do anything to help this valuable zoological project. London Zoo officials prepared to visit Moscow any time for discussions or we would welcome you as our guests here in London. We await your reply with great interest and hope that this will lead to greater friendship and co-operation between our two zoos.'

That night I was looking pensive. Ramona asked what was wrong.

'What do you think would happen if Chi-Chi killed An-An?' I asked gloomily. 'She's nearly taken the leg of a young keeper – supposing she attacks An-An? What would that do for East–West friendship?'

'Lesser incidents have started wars before now,' she replied encouragingly, 'but perhaps it would just be the salt-mines in Siberia.' I was not amused.

It was with a mixture of great disappointment and mild relief that I learned that the Russians had been misquoted in the press and that they felt there was no point in attempting a mating. Pressmen in Moscow reported that they had been told that the Russians doubted the 'manliness' of their panda, and we all pondered on what this might mean. Later, it emerged that they were of the opinion that both pandas had been too isolated from members of their own species and would not respond appropriately when placed together. It occurred to me that my counterpart at Moscow Zoo was even more worried about the salt-mines than I was – if the pandas hated one another and fought to the death.

The mating project was off, and remained so for another year. Then, early in 1965, An-An changed *his* mood and reports from behind the Iron Curtain indicated that his newly aroused sexuality was giving the Russians second thoughts. Immediately there was a great deal of behind-the-scenes negotiating and this time the prospects looked brighter.

The British press began to lick their lips. They scented a tasty story in the making. A satirical article in the *Observer* suggested that the Russian authorities had originally cast doubt upon their male panda's 'manliness' because they were reluctant to issue him with an exit visa, in case he defected – dashing into the nearest R.S.P.C.A. office and asking for asylum.

'Now, in an astonishing volte-face [wrote Michael Frayn], which suggests that the old guard of the Stalinist heavy-industry men in Soviet zoological circles have suffered a decisive defeat, the spokesman for An-An has said: "Perhaps a long holiday together for the two pandas might be arranged." Friends of the happy couple believe they would choose Ibiza, or possibly Corfu ... Commentators in London point out that any meeting of the pandas would have to be preceded by a meeting at the tapir or wallaby level to prepare the ground.'

I was beginning to get a whiff of what was to come, if the mating attempt went ahead. As the months passed, negotiations rumbled slowly on and it was not until the end of the year that Moscow finally agreed to receive me as an official panda marriage-broker. There was precious little time before Chi-Chi's next period of heat, which was due in early March, and urgent messages began to fly back and forth between the zoo and White-hall, to gain the Foreign Secretary's blessing once more.

As soon as this was done, a top-level meeting was held at the zoo to consider the implications of the project. What had started out as a simple breeding proposal of mine was beginning to take on all the complex subtleties of a delicate political encounter.

'Supposing the mating attempt is successful,' I was asked in earnest tones, 'how many progeny might we expect to see?'

'One or two cubs at the most,' I replied, innocently.

That caused a great deal of consternation. Could I be more specific? Which was more likely, one or two?

'One, at a guess, but we don't have much to go on.'

More consternation. If Chi-Chi became pregnant and produced

a single offspring, would the cub belong to Britain or Russia? This would have to be raised when I visited the Moscow Zoo. I was asked to prepare a detailed memorandum on this point. My suggestion that we might toss a coin for it was rejected as frivolous.

After a lot of thought I came up with four diplomatic solutions: (a) The cub goes to the Moscow Zoo when one year old, in exchange for a second mating. The second cub would then be ours. (b) The first cub stays with us and Moscow takes the offspring of the second mating. (c) The cub stays in London with its mother and is paid for by the London Zoo with other animal stock of equivalent value. (d) The cub goes to the zoo which owns the adult of the opposite sex.

I thought my fourth suggestion was particularly ingenious and indicated a glowing future for me in the diplomatic corps, but it was rejected out of hand. The London Zoo must appear magnanimous and make the grand gesture. Solution (a) was chosen. The first cub would go to Moscow as soon as it was old enough to leave its mother. It was also agreed that we would have to stand all the costs involved, and generally do everything we could to encourage the Russians and clinch the deal. It was all in my hands now and I would have to leave for Moscow immediately.

My 'cub disposal' memorandum was written on January 31st, 1966. On the same day, the Russian news agency, TASS, was putting out its own statement, in a lighter vein:

'The black-and-white An-An, the only giant panda in the U.S.S.R., is gobbling up hard-boiled eggs and birch twigs with particular appetite these days ... He wants Mr Morrison to be impressed by his beauty and strength. Mr Morrison, a representative of the British National Zoo, is coming to Moscow to resume talks on the mating of his bamboo she-bear Chi-Chi with the Moscow An-An ... Meanwhile An-An is feeling very well. He is joyful and has an excellent appetite.'

I was amused that the Russians were treating the matter rather flippantly. What I did not realize was that, in certain quarters, they had grave doubts about the true motive of my visit. There was one very good reason for this, which I had overlooked. The Secretary of the Zoological Society at the time was Solly Zuckerman, a man of intense energy who was not only a full professor at Birmingham University, but was also Chief Scientific Adviser to the Ministry of Defence. I was connected with him solely in my role as a member of the zoo staff, but it seemed clear that the Russians suspected the existence of another, more clandestine link – one that might associate me in some way with his operations at the Ministry of Defence. As a result I was given a more than usually thorough interview at the Russian Consulate in Kensington Palace Gardens, when I went there to obtain my business visa. For some reason that intrigued me, the official I saw there would not begin speaking until he had moved a portable radio next to his telephone receiver, switched it on and turned the volume up loud. The interview was conducted to the strains of the B.B.C. Show Band, and this was to be the first of many odd happenings in the days ahead.

At last I was on my way to Heathrow, heading for Moscow, alone and in the dead of winter. It was a cheerless prospect. The scene that greeted me at the Russian airport did nothing to raise my spirits. From the window of the aeroplane I could see a great expanse of powdered snow blowing across the tarmac like smoke. We were some way from the airport building and when the plane door opened and I stepped out it was like entering a deep freeze, or plunging into icy water. I had been warned it would be cold and I was wearing 'Hamlets' – long black tights that had reduced Ramona to hysterics – a heavy suit and a huge fur-lined overcoat rented from Moss Bros, but nothing could dull the pain of that wall of cold that struck me as I struggled towards the arrivals entrance. With each intake of breath, all the moisture inside my nose froze solid – each hair becoming a tiny, stiff icicle. Then, with each act of breathing out, the whole nasal ice-pack thawed out agonizingly. In, out, in, out – freeze, thaw, freeze, thaw. My eyes ached so much I was convinced they were going to freeze solid too, and splinter into tiny fragments when I rubbed them. How could people live in such a place?

Inside the airport building I noticed that the windows were freezing up on the inside as well as the outside. But at least the welcome was warm. Toya Sokolova from the Ministry of Culture and Igor Petrovitch Sosnovskii, the director of the Moscow Zoo, were there to greet me.

'The hotels are not like London,' said Toya, smiling, 'but be patient, we are nice people.' And she and Igor certainly were.

'You must be crazy!' said Igor, through an interpreter, 'all zoo people are crazy—you have to be crazy to work with animals.' Right at that moment, I knew exactly what he meant.

Official cards were flashed and I was whisked hurriedly through customs and into the centre of Moscow by taxi. There I was deposited in the Hotel National—an old, pre-revolutionary building overlooking the great yellow walls of the Kremlin. My room was vast, with eight chairs, two tables, two beds, a desk, an ornate three-mirrored dressing table, a gigantic wardrobe, a separate entrance hall and a huge bathroom. From my window I could see Red Square, Lenin's Tomb, the gleaming onion-domes of the Kremlin churches, the incredibly ornate St Basil's Cathedral (pure Disneyland, this), and, so help me, the Obelisk of Revolutionaries and Thinkers. Incongruously there was a jazz saxophone wailing up from the floor below.

Left alone to recover from my trip, I wandered down to the hotel bar, a small gloomy room occupied by several rather shady-looking characters. I was beginning to feel like James Bond, and the impression grew stronger when a large, very fat, unshaven man walked straight up to me and, for no apparent reason, said in an American accent:

'What's in there, chief?'

It suddenly occurred to me that I was expected to give some sort of password, and that if I replied: 'The geese are flying tonight', or something of that sort, I would be off on some wild exploit. Instead I muttered that I did not understand him, and he immediately turned on his heel and left.

I went to dinner that first night with Peter Bull from the British Embassy, who told me that my hotel room was bugged and warned me not to do anything silly, as it caused the Embassy so much trouble. I was not at all sure what kind of silliness he had in mind. I had never felt less silly in my life. As far as I was concerned, all I wanted to do was to see An-An, fix the date of the mating attempt, and get home as quickly as possible. But that night I could not resist the temptation to try and locate my 'bug'. I lifted up each of the pictures in turn, squinted behind pieces of furniture, and even peered under the beds, but could find nothing. I should have remembered the radio being moved near the telephone at the Russian Consulate in London – that was where the bug was placed (I learned much later) – inside the telephone mouthpiece.

The next morning it seemed even colder. Looking out of the bedroom window my face froze again, even though the window was tightly closed, double-glazed, and with all inside edges sealed off with sticky tape. When I went to shave I noticed there was something odd about my electric razor. As I took off the plastic cap that protected its shaving-head, all its inside workings spewed out on to the carpet. While I had been at dinner someone had dismantled it (searching for a transmitter?) and had then been unable to reassemble it properly.

Downstairs, the ever-cheerful Toya Sokolova was waiting for me, to take me to the zoo. Inevitably, I mentioned how cold it was.

'Yes, yes, it is 32 degrees below zero – that's centigrade,' she chuckled, 'but not to worry, it is only a cold snap. We'll soon be zooming up to a glorious minus 13 degrees. If it goes above that it's not healthy.'

At the zoo we drank toasts in vodka so strong that it was almost a vapour, viewed a rather miserable-looking An-An, and got down to the details of the mating project. Chi-Chi would have to come to Moscow, rather than An-An making the trip to the West. Agreed. She would have to come very soon. Agreed. All zoo-men understood one another and were friends. Agreed. I brought up the problem of the ownership of the cub. But of course, I was told immediately, it would belong to London;

Russia was only interested in the scientific aspects of the operation. It occurred to me that we had both been given the same instructions – to foster East–West goodwill, but I did not argue. If there was a second panda cub it would be theirs, I said. Agreed.

'My only wish,' said Igor grandly, 'is to visit London to be a godfather at the christening of Chi-Chi's cub!' More vodka, glasses chinking.

'And if the pandas fight?' I ventured.

'We will have water-jets and fireworks standing by.'

That sounded interesting, but I did not risk pursuing it further. After other minor details had been dealt with, I was formally presented with a vast medallion, the Moscow Zoo's Centenary Medal, we drank more vodka and it was all over. I could feel myself winging home to London already. But no. It was necessary to wait a few days so that the results of our talk could be discussed with officials and the whole matter ratified, so that I could return with definite plans. In the meantime, there were entertainments planned for me.

Could this be the point, I wondered, at which the slinky Russian girl agent slides silently into my bed, while hidden cameras whirr behind two-way mirrors … ? But no. Instead it was a visit to the Moscow State Circus to see brown bears on ice-skates playing ice hockey; a visit to the Bolshoi Ballet to see Vassiliev dance *The Firebird*; a visit to the theatre to see a play by an American social-realist in which one of the cast unrealistically drank from a Coca-Cola bottle containing bright *orange* Coke (how isolated can you get?): and many visits to art galleries and museums, to see acres of canvases of 'Tractors at Dawn' and other pastoral Soviet subjects. I had to admit that, although by now I was feeling quite ill with cold, the circus and the ballet were breath-taking. They seemed to belong to another culture altogether. The girls, both in the circus and the ballet, were so young and beautiful, while outside on the streets of Moscow every woman seemed to lumber along like one of the circus bears, bulky and forbidding. The contrast was unbelievable. It was as if there were two distinct species of Russian woman.

All through my Moscow week I had been shepherded everywhere and never left alone for a moment. Then, suddenly, on the
morning of the last day, this changed. I was told that I was free to
go for a walk alone.

'Go anywhere you like, go for a long walk, have a look at the
shops, enjoy yourself ... '

I was puzzled by this switch in mood, but wrapped myself up
as warmly as possible and struck out bravely into the ice and
snow. As I left the hotel, two tall men in long leather overcoats
wearing wide-brimmed, black hats, carefully folded up their
copies of *Pravda* and rose from their seats at the bottom of the
main staircase. As I strode off across Red Square they followed me
at a respectful distance. I was beginning to enjoy this. Hurrying
my pace, I moved off fast in the direction of GUM, the enormous
Moscow department store that looks like a cross between Harrods
and Paddington station. Turning in the doorway, I could no
longer see them. I felt almost lonely without them, as I wandered
through the endless passage-ways of the store, past long files of
people queuing up to buy ballpoint pens, and other such rare
commodities.

Then, in the very centre of GUM I came to an open area with
a small fountain. I was just trying to decipher the signs on a
cigarette machine, when I heard a noise so quaint that it made me
feel I had momentarily strayed into a film farce:

'Psssst!' the noise said. 'Psssst!' I couldn't believe it. It had to
be a joke. Turning round I saw a spotty-faced young man looking
nervously over his shoulder.

'You are English?' he enquired, looking in five new directions
with each word.

'Yes ... '

'Good. Listen. Listen very carefully,' he hissed, coming a little
closer. 'Are you interested in the plans of a secret factory?'

How marvellous, I had always wanted someone to come up to
me in a foreign capital and say: 'Psssst, are you interested in the
plans of a secret factory', and now it was actually happening. I was
just about to say, of course, let's go, when I remembered Peter

Bull's warning: don't do anything silly. This, I told myself, was the moment to avoid the silly bit. No plans for me, I decided. Drawing myself up to my full height and adopting that slightly surprised, brow-raised look employed by Englishmen when they have been mildly offended, I replied in my best Oxford tones:

'Not today, thank you,' which sounded so ridiculous that I almost laughed. This made the young man extremely angry. With a positive kaleidoscope of shifting glances, he sidled in closer still.

'You don't understand,' he hissed, more urgently than ever (glance, glance, glance), 'I am offering to show you the plans of a secret factory. Very important. Very serious. You come with me.'

'No thanks,' I said, more sombrely this time, and started walking as quickly as I could back through GUM towards the exit door. He followed me for a while and then seemed to give up, but I was glad to reach the safety of my hotel again. That afternoon, driving in an Embassy car with Peter Bull to finalize the panda-mating arrangements, I blurted out:

'An extraordinary thing happened to me in GUM today. A young man came up to me and said, "Psssst!" and then ... '

'Let's talk about it later,' said Peter, looking a little strained.

'Why?'

'The car has just been serviced.'

'Oh.' Silence.

Later, near a park, the car pulled up and Peter beckoned me to follow him. We strolled along the frozen paths for a while, until we were miles from any building.

'Now we can talk,' he said. 'Tell me about GUM.'

'You mean, it wasn't safe to talk in the car?'

'No, we haven't had time to de-bug it yet,' he explained patiently. 'Whenever it goes in for servicing it is bugged and then each time we get it back we have to have another search to see where they have put it. It's a sort of East–West treasure-hunt. Quite amusing really. But tell me about the man in GUM.'

I explained, laughing about it as I mimicked the spotty young man's intense seriousness. But Peter was not laughing.

'Thank God you didn't fall for it,' he said. 'If you had gone with him, either out of boredom, curiosity or a misguided sense of patriotism (our three biggest problems with visitors from England), you would have been shown some absolutely useless plans and then the police would have broken in on you and both of you would have been arrested. Once at Lubianka Gaol, you would have been separated. He would have been paid off and taken out a back way and you ... you would have been interrogated and made to sign a confession that you had indeed been caught attempting to spy on the Soviet Union. The trouble is we have just caught two of theirs in London and they want someone for a swap. You would have done nicely. So thank heaven you reacted the way you did.'

'Thanks to you. I'm glad you warned me.'

'Yes, well, there's a lot of it about,' he said, and we walked slowly back towards the bugged Embassy car. What a strange world to live in, I thought. How nice to get back to London. I couldn't wait.

That night there was a farewell party. Everyone was in great spirits and great spirits were in everyone. Toya Sokolova was positively glowing.

'What will you do to me, Toya,' I asked, awash with vaporous vodka, 'if the British panda kills the Russian panda when they meet?' I wanted to see if she came up with the same salt-mine jokes as Ramona, but she didn't. Instead she screwed up her nose and said:

'Then you will have to arrange three free Beatles concerts in Moscow.' And everyone joyously downed another glass of vodka.

The next morning at the hotel shop, before leaving for the airport, I remembered that I had promised Ramona I would buy her a Russian fur hat.

'How will I know the size?' I had enquired in that helpless way males have when asked to purchase female garments.

'I'll tell you my size. It is ... '

'That's no good. They won't have the same system of sizes. It will be a waste of money.'

'Then we'll do this,' she said, putting an old hat of hers on my head. It was about three sizes too small for me and I looked suitably ridiculous. She led me over to a mirror. 'Now, look at that and remember how much too small for you it is. Got it? Right. Now that's how much too small the Russian fur hat must be.'

I had a feeling things were not going to go too easily as I approached the rather haughty lady behind the hat counter. At first she naturally insisted on handing me male hats and I had to buy one to satisfy her. Then I demanded a female hat and she gave me a strange look. Finding an enormous one, she held it out. It was a perfect fit. Useless for Ramona. I rejected it and signalled with my hands for a smaller one. Another strange look, right down her long nose. She searched around and found one slightly smaller. I put it on and stared at myself in the mirror. One or two frowning Russians had stopped to watch this performance. I indicated that it should be still smaller and returned it. The woman behind the counter was now getting visibly angry. She snatched up a tiny female hat and almost threw it at me. I popped it on my head and it stood up on my large domed forehead like an ice-bag. It was perfectly too-small, to exactly the right extent. I beamed at her.

'This one I will take,' I said. I thought I should try to explain that it was for my wife, so I pointed at the hat and swayed my hips, flapping a limp wrist. Sadly, the message did not get across in the way I intended and I scurried out of the hotel, leaving yet another Soviet citizen totally convinced of the decadent decay of the filthy, perverted Western world.

The return flight to London by Aeroflot was a nightmare. The Russian airliner seemed to object to taking off in the icy blizzard that was sweeping the airport and, after a ragged ascent, I noticed that the cabin staff were unusually sombre. I convinced myself that it was their normal in-flight style—none of that phoney bourgeois cheerfulness—until I saw from my window that we had passed twice over the same island. It was a large island with a strange contour—there was no mistaking it—and we had first flown over it from east to west and now we were crossing it from west to east. I mentioned this curious observation to a glum hostess who said nothing, but merely gave a grim shrug. Shortly afterwards we landed in Copenhagen without explanation and were all herded off into a waiting room. As it was supposedly a non-stop flight to London, I enquired again as to what was happening. Nobody seemed to know. After an hour we were herded back on board and headed once more for London, moving, I thought, rather slowly through the air. This time I refused to accept the grim shrug treatment and insisted on some kind of explanation.

'We haff two defwective engince,' she replied reluctantly.

'But ... how many engines are there on this plane?'

'Two,' was the deadpan answer.

'Oh.'

'But that is not our main trooble.'

'No?'

'No. Lundun is haffing theek fog. Is bad for landing.'

They certainly know how to raise your spirits. I gazed around at my fellow-sufferers. They were all Russian males and all dressed in new suits that appeared to be thirty years out of date. They sat stiffly erect as if we were about to make a mass parachute jump. At any moment I expected someone to tap me on the shoulder and shout: 'Now!'

As we began our descent into the dense cloud that purported to be London, five of the Russian males rose from their seats and began conducting community singing, pacing up and down the aisle, beating their arms and bellowing the slow sad tones of a folk song that appeared to be reflecting a period of mourning in the lives of a group of Soviet boatmen. Obediently the entire body of Russian passengers joined in, their deep, sad tones rising above the spluttering of our two defective jet engines, as we juddered down through the dense pea soup of old London town. As we sank lower and lower the song became slower and slower, the necks of the singers stiffer and stiffer.

'Yuuuuu, whoooooo, yaaaaaw, weeeerrrrr ... '

Then, just before we were due to touch down, the fog cleared, and we were able to see the hard tarmac close below us. The wheels thumped the runway as if patting it on the back for being there, then the plane decided to take off again for a few seconds before thumping down a second, a third and a fourth time. Then, at last, we were taxi-ing along the surface and the folk song immediately changed:

'Yaah, Yaah, Waah, Raah, Yaah, Waah ... ' they roared, leaping from their seats and dancing in the aisle, the rhythm speeding up to a wild crescendo as soon as it was clear we were safe. For a scheduled flight, it was certainly different. None of that seat-belt sign and duty-free trolley nonsense.

I staggered somewhat shakily off the plane to find myself waving inanely to film cameras and press photographers. I had quite forgotten about such things, not having seen a newspaper all week, and it came as a shock to realize that I had to start answering questions about the forthcoming panda romance. I was feeling ill from the days of icy cold and dodged the issue by refusing to comment until I had talked to the zoo officials. But I indicated vaguely that things had gone well. This was enough for huge headlines to be plastered all over the morning papers: 'Chi-Chi may be a June Bride'—'Cupid gets the wings of an airliner'—'Chi-Chi to have spring honeymoon' ... and so on. Acres of it. The pandas were no longer merely symbols of East–West friendship, they were now the star-crossed lovers, so lonely, and so far apart, but at last to be united. An-An, An-An, where-fore art thou, An-An?

Reporting to the zoo council the following day, I made a few light-hearted references to the spy-nonsense in Moscow. Solly Zuckerman, I recall, was the only one that did not laugh. The rest thought it was a huge joke, but he knew all too well how easy it was for someone to make a foolish gesture and get caught up in the web. I was grateful that was all behind me. The next trip would be with the giant panda, a keeper and the zoo vet. There would be safety in numbers and there would no longer be any doubt about the reality of the project. Chi-Chi would be there in person to prove it.

As soon as all the details were fixed, I took off for the B.B.C. studios at Bristol, where I had started a new TV series, an adult, one-hour, fortnightly programme called *Life*. As host I tackled any subject of animal or human behaviour that took my fancy. It was rewarding, but exhausting, because it took up each weekend and meant that I was getting no day of recuperation at the end of a busy zoo week. In addition, I was recording batches of my children's programme *Zootime*, for I.T.V., which was still going out weekly, writing a new book, editing another, preparing scientific papers, lecturing constantly, doing book reviews for the *T.L.S.*, taking part in several radio series, running a behaviour research group at the zoo, and painting furiously in my Primrose Hill studio whenever there was a free moment.

In other words, I was heading for disaster. My productivity neurosis was burning me out. There was so much I wanted to do, but I simply did not have the physical stamina to satisfy all the demands I was putting upon myself. The icy blast of Moscow was one stress too many, and one month after my return I collapsed. The official diagnosis was hepatitis, but in truth my body was ready to succumb to any microbe attack that was available. If it had not been hepatitis, it would have been something else – anything to lay me out for long enough to enable me to recover my strength and, hopefully, to think twice about the lunatic way I was pushing myself.

I was flat on my back for nearly five weeks – the only long illness of my adult life – and I made a vital decision. I would cut my work-load in half. Out went *Zootime*, radio shows, lectures, book reviewing, editing, and many of my other activities. I decided to limit my writing activities that year to one single book, and to focus all my energies on to that. The book was to be called *The Naked Ape*, and was to be a zoologist's view of the human animal. I had thought about it for years, but now I was finally going to write it. I took a month's leave from my zoo work in November and completed it in one intense blast of non-stop typing. Having shed nearly all my other worries and preoccupations, I was able to bring a concentration to it that had been lacking in my previous books and, without realizing it, I changed my style. The new book had a condensed crispness about it which made it easy to read.

But that was in the future. Before my 'Month of the Naked Ape', there was the panda romance to resolve. Chi-Chi's spring heat was due in March and she was rushed to Moscow just in time. This was when I was falling ill, so I was left behind. The role of Panda Ponce passed from me to the zoo's vet, Oliver Graham-Jones. He and Sam Morton, Chi-Chi's Head Keeper, were to make the journey without me. I lay in bed scanning the seemingly endless press comments. Interest had become Fleet Street hysteria. They were even composing poems about it now:

> The time has come, the panda said,
> To talk of many things,
> Of love and sex and packing crates
> And aeroplanes with wings.

It was at about this point that I became too ill to read any more, curled myself up, and shut out the whole business. In Moscow, I later discovered, Oliver Graham-Jones was getting plenty of deep breathing down his hotel telephone (why didn't *I* get that, I wondered, feeling rather put out), but none from either An-An or Chi-Chi. The trip, it seemed, had cooled Chi-Chi's heat and after the two animals had circled one another, snarled and started to fight, they were quickly separated until the autumn. Oliver flew home, leaving Chi-Chi to settle in and become fully acclimatized so that her October heat would occur normally and without undue stress.

With a great sense of timing, Chi-Chi began her awaited period of heat on October 1st, the very day on which *Men and Pandas*, the book Ramona and I had written, was published. A message came through from the Moscow Zoo that she had gone off her food and was offering her rump to her keeper, with her back arched and her tail up – the panda invitation for mounting.

I was disturbed to hear that she was directing her advances towards her keeper, rather than to An-An, who was visible in an
adjoining cage. It sounded to me as though I was about to encounter another humanized 'mental hybrid' – a people's panda
rather than a panda's panda. But at least she was sexually active,
and that was nothing to sniff at, unless of course you were a male
panda. So I made a mad dash for the airport, taking with me the
zoo's official photographer, Michael Lyster, and the Whipsnade
vet, Victor Manton, in place of Oliver Graham-Jones who had
since left the zoo.

Feeling well rested after my long convalescence and with
Michael and Victor to keep me company, I was looking forward
to my second assault on the Russian capital much more than my
first. Michael, who had been my assistant at the Granada TV
Unit and had since, like me, moved on to the zoo staff, possessed
a healthily irreverent attitude towards such trivial matters as
international politics, diplomacy and espionage. In his company,
the trip was clearly going to be converted from 'James Bond' to
'Carry On Spying', for which I was more than grateful. The first
incident occurred at the airport, where Victor insisted on declar-
ing his sinister-looking anaesthetic pistol. This fired a large
hypodermic dart and was used to incapacitate a wild animal
without killing it. It was going to be a valuable stand-by if Chi-
Chi and An-An decided to play it rough and had to be separated,
or if one of them was injured and required treatment. Because
the dart it fired was so much bigger than an ordinary bullet, the
gun itself was of most impressive proportions. I felt that it might
be better to say nothing about it. We were going to be whisked
through the airport formalities by our hosts from the Ministry
of Culture, and it seemed unlikely to me that there would be any
rummaging around in veterinary holdalls. But Victor was anxious
about what might happen if his baggage was searched later, at
the hotel, and the gun was found. Surely, he might then be
suspected of foul play? So, when we arrived at the customs
barrier, he was going to declare it. For some reason, instead of
simply lifting it out and laying it impassively on the counter, he

took it out as if about to use it and began waving it about to attract the customs official's attention. There was a moment of frozen horror and I quite expected everyone to flatten themselves on the floor while a hail of lead rained down on us from concealed Soviet marksmen, but Michael somehow managed to turn it into a joke and in a few seconds the Russian officials were laughing and waving us through.

Michael's sense of humour misfired slightly, however, when we were dining later in the vast eating-hall of the Peking Hotel. The enormous, cavernously lifeless room, with its great pillars and its acres of small dining-tables, was almost empty. Not more than five or six of the 250 tables were occupied as we sat down and examined the menu. I made some light-hearted remark about the table being bugged, whereupon Michael leant forward and addressed the table-cloth:

'Testing, one-two-three, testing, one-two-three.'

He was somewhat taken aback when, a few minutes later, a large man in a raincoat entered the dining-hall, weaved his way through the expanse of empty tables and made slowly towards us. Reaching our table, at which there was an unoccupied chair, he sat heavily down next to Michael, opened his copy of *Pravda*, and proceeded to read it intently throughout the rest of our meal. Shortly before we finished, he rose and, without having uttered a word or giving us a single glance, left in the same way he had arrived. After that, Michael was prepared to give a little more credence to the tales I had been telling him of my experiences on my first visit to Moscow, back in February.

At the zoo, it was clear that Chi-Chi was now in a powerful sexual mood and I was anxious to hurry along the mating attempt. Unfortunately Igor Sosnovskii was in Budapest and nothing could be done until he returned. We kicked our heels and filled in the time by going to see an interminable film of *War and Peace* which the Russians for some reason insisted on calling *Peace and War*.

The next day Sosnovskii arrived and the zoo was closed to the public at 1 p.m. With powerful water-hoses and our anaesthetic pistol standing by, we were ready for the first mating attempt of Chi-Chi's autumn heat. In the spring, when An-An had attacked her, she had already lost her sexual mood, but now things were different and we were full of hope. Each animal had been allowed out into their shared paddock the day before, but not at the same time. Each had sniffed the scent of the other and responded strongly. Each was in excellent health. If their mating was ever going to be consummated, this was the moment.

Chi-Chi was let out first, then An-An, and he immediately began to chase her across the paddock. She barked at him and they sparred briefly, but not seriously. Then she lumbered off again and he followed, bleating like a sheep with a sore throat. This curious love-cry seemed wildly out of character for his great, bearlike shape and made him sound almost pathetic in contrast to her yelping and barking ferocity. His approaches now were without any hostility, almost gentle and rather timid. Padding up behind her he eventually tried to mount her, whereupon she spun round and cuffed him with her paw. There was no retaliation, and she plodded off to a safe distance. Frustrated, he moved across to a dip in the ground where bales of straw had been placed and proceeded to tear them to shreds. Then he lay sprawled on his back, while she wandered about in agitation. She was clearly so upset by his attentions that they were separated and allowed to rest.

The next morning the same futile sequence was repeated. We decided to try a different approach. The pair were kept apart for the rest of the day and put together at night. This entailed a rota of night-watches. When it came to my turn, I shared the tiny, steamy room inside the panda compound with Keeper Nemov, who cared for An-An. I spoke only a few words of Russian and he knew no English at all. We nodded and smiled and shrugged a lot and kept taking it in turns to peer through a small glass panel to make sure that we still had two live pandas whose black-and-white fur was unstained by red. Hour after hour nothing happened and for Nemov and myself the strain of being unable to do anything and of being unable to talk to one another was beginning to tell. The lack of communication between us somehow symbolized the lack of communication between the two pandas. In a stupidly fanciful way, I began to feel that if only I could speak to Nemov, that would break down the barrier between the Russian panda and the British one. Which just goes to show what sitting up all night in a humid little keeper's den in Moscow Zoo can do to one's mental processes.

Then I hit on an idea. There was one language Nemov and I did have in common: Latin. Not that either of us was fluent in it, but we both knew the scientific names of our zoo animals, and that was something we could work on. I sat down in front of Nemov and said, very slowly:

'*Ursus arctos*, London,' and then held up four fingers, indicating that we had four brown bears at London Zoo. Nemov understood immediately and his face lit up.

'*Ursus arctos*, Moscow,' he chortled, and held up nine fingers. Score one to Moscow. We were off ...

'*Elephas maximus*, London,' I countered, holding up two fingers.

'*Elephas maximus*, Moscow,' he replied, and also held up two fingers. A draw on that one.

And so it went on, hour after hour, with long pauses while we thought of another suitable Latin name, to see who had most of each of the zoo species in turn. It was an inane form of international exchange, but it formed a curious bond between us that saw us through the long night of panda-watching. Sadly, it had no magical effect on Chi-Chi and An-An. They maintained their stubborn unfriendliness throughout.

Then at dawn, it happened. An-An took Chi-Chi by the scruff of the neck and held her down. Mounting her, he made what was to be his only serious attempt to mate, but she was furious and kept her tail firmly clamped down, thwarting his efforts until she was able to twist round and send him packing with a swift blow to the jaw. Failure again.

This nightmare of frustration, both for us and for the ever-attentive An-An, continued the next night and again and again until we eventually abandoned all hope. There had been eight meetings and no matings. Sixty hours of pandas together, but with no panda togetherness. The final blow for us came when, during one of the last meetings, Chi-Chi approached the bars of the enclosure at the point where I was standing outside. She turned her rump towards me and stood still. Pushing my arm through the bars, I pressed my hand down on her back and she immediately arched her body and raised her tail fully, in the typical mating invitation posture. An-An was only ten feet away and responded immediately. There was the signal he had been waiting for, bleating for, struggling for, hour after patient hour. In an instant he came hurtling towards her, eager for the great moment. She watched him approaching and then, while still arching her back to me, she swiped out at him, roaring angrily. He backed away and she went for him. It was the last straw. It meant that, despite the fact that she was fully in heat and was prepared to offer herself to a human being, she was having nothing to do with this bulky black-and-white clown who was pestering her. There was only one possible interpretation – she was fully humanized. She had grown up with people and, as far as she was concerned, she too was people. She had no interest in this alien species that now confronted her, totally bewildered and utterly frustrated. There was nothing more we could do.

The only possible alternative was artificial insemination, but this the Russians were reluctant to risk, since it would involve anaesthetizing An-An. The only course left was to arrange a visit by An-An to London Zoo, in case a mating attempt on Chi-Chi's home territory might make her more amenable. It was a slender chance, and one that I personally felt was without hope. Chi-Chi was flown home and was soon padding about her old enclosure as if nothing had happened. Two years later, in 1968, An-An set off on his return engagement, but with much the same result, despite a long stay through two of Chi-Chi's heats. Then it was back to Moscow to resume his forlorn, solitary existence.

Four years later, in the summer of 1972, Chi-Chi died, aged fourteen, the zoo's Virgin Queen. A mere twelve weeks later, An-An also succumbed. He was fifteen. Their unsuccessful love-affair had filled thousands of inches in newspaper columns around the world. For the public, Chi-Chi had become the mascot of the World Wildlife conservation movement, and her image was everywhere. But for me she had become the symbol of the tragedy of human tampering with the social life of wild animals. Had she been allowed to grow up with other young pandas, she would almost certainly have bred successfully, like several of the pandas kept together in Peking Zoo.

I had learned this lesson several times over. First with my chimpanzee Congo, who rejected his females both as companions and as mates; then with a whole variety of ex-pets given to the zoo by their harassed owners; then with Guy the gorilla, who also died without issue, despite being given a friendly and amenable female. The answer was plain enough. Wild animals must be allowed to grow up in the company of their own species. They must be given much more natural social settings than had been considered necessary in the past. Zoos around the world would have to change their ideas. They would have to learn from the increasingly penetrating studies of animal ethologists, whose researches into animal behaviour were providing an ever-increasing store of information about the special environmental and social needs of the different species. The antiquated idea of a zoo as a kind of animated museum would have to be replaced with a modern concept of a zoo as a quasi-natural breeding ground where, although more remote from their human visitors, the animals could be seen performing their normal, wild behaviour in self-replenishing social units.

I had gained many insights during my decade at the London Zoo, but now I felt it was time for me to move on. During my zoological career I had studied fish, then birds, then mammals, working my way up to that most complex of all species: the naked ape. Finally, in the autumn of 1966, I had sat down to write my book on the human animal – and in so doing, had tackled the most challenging task of my scientific life. As soon as it was done, I knew that there could be no turning back. I had to go on and take a longer, deeper look, with the eyes of a zoologist, at the species to which I myself belonged. Coming at it from my particular direction, with the insights I had accumulated from my ethological studies of other species, I was convinced that I stood a good chance of seeing many of the all-too-familiar human activities in a new and unfamiliar light. It was not going to be a case of making glib comparisons from one species to another, but rather of having a slightly different approach to the observation of human actions.

Late in 1966, with the first draft of *The Naked Ape* completed, I had no idea how to go about transforming myself into a full-time student of the human animal. I had no wish to join one of the traditional sciences of human behaviour. Psychology, psychiatry, sociology and anthropology were disciplines already deeply entrenched in their own specialist attitudes. My zoological approach would have been out of place there. It was important to keep myself free of them and to develop my own ideas independent of their influences. But how?

As if by magic a golden opportunity fell into my lap. The Institute of Contemporary Arts in London was looking for a new director. They were moving from their modest premises in Dover Street to grand new quarters in The Mall, just down the road from Buckingham Palace, and needed a director who could deal with planners and architects, to supervise the move and then to run the greatly enlarged Institute. Through my work in re-developing the zoo I had gained some experience of replacing old buildings with new ones and had spent many hours in the company of top architects, such as Peter Shepheard, Theo Crosby, Mischa Black, and Hugh Casson. I had learnt enough from them, I felt, to be able to tackle the I.C.A.'s new organizational problems with comparative ease.

I had also followed the fortunes of the Institute since its inception in 1947, when, as a teenager, I had attended its very first exhibition, masterminded by the brilliant art theorist, Herbert Read. It had been his dream to establish a focal-point for presenting the best in all forms of experimental art. As he put it at the time: 'Such is our ideal – not another museum, another bleak exhibition gallery, another classical building in which insulated and classified specimens of a culture are displayed for instruction, but an adult play-centre ... a source of vitality and daring experiment.' That was why, of course, it had been the I.C.A. alone that was prepared to stage my own exhibition of chimpanzee paintings in 1958. No experiment was too daring for them. Over the years the I.C.A. had been the first art centre to exhibit, in turn, each of the latest and, at the time, most outrageous trends in the arts, often incurring scorn or wrath in the process. As each year passed, however, those trends that had originally seemed outlandish, had slowly become accepted and the I.C.A. could justifiably claim to have led the world in its promotion of the avant garde.

It was Herbert Read's phrase 'an adult play-centre' that had stuck in my memory. What better place for me to continue my studies of human behaviour? Once the new, enlarged centre was open, it would become even more important in attracting all the most adventurous and creative brains in the art world, and would be the ideal place for me to witness man's uniquely playful qualities at first hand.

When it was announced that the new I.C.A. director was to be the man who was, at present, the Curator of Mammals at London Zoo, the I.C.A. was once again under fire. Had they gone mad? Many people from inside the art world had wanted the post, so why had they given it to a scientist – a zoologist! To many, it seemed an incredible decision, but Herbert Read, Roland Penrose and the other I.C.A. officials knew of my long-term involvement with the art world, an involvement that had been obscured, in the public mind, by my 'zoo-man' image. They had weathered enough storms in the past not to be worried by this latest reaction. And, according to one newspaper report, Picasso, at least, approved of the appointment, exclaiming: '*Ah! Quelle bonne idée!*' when Roland told him about it, which gave me some encouragement in the face of the other, less friendly, comments. Roland himself also gave vigorous support, countering press queries with the statement that 'Supervising the public exhibition of 300 species of mammals involved precisely the same administrative problems as organizing large exhibitions of paintings. Whether one is dealing with a rhinoceros or a *Guernica* there are essentially the same challenges in terms of transportation, public relations, exhibit presentation, publicity and security.'

When I told the zoo authorities I was going, they reminded me that I was due to give them six months' notice. This was something that I had stupidly overlooked, and resulted in a bizarre situation in which I was still curating my mammals at Regent's Park, while being announced in the I.C.A.'s bulletin as their new Director. For me, it meant rhinos by day and *Guernicas* by night, until, after a few months, the zoo managed to find a suitable replacement. Then, at last, I was off to face my first full-time day in the avant-garde art world of London. The previous evening I had taken a long stroll around the zoological gardens, gazing in turn at each of the mammal enclosures. Large, dark eyes blinked back at me, and I suddenly felt a great sadness. I knew each of the owners of those pairs of eyes so well, knew all their problems and their personalities. It was hard to leave them, and there was a heavy feeling in my chest as I clanked through the exit turnstile for the last time. But my urge to explore new fields had overpowered all my old attachments and my zoo love-affair was finally at an end. Like the exit turnstile, my decision was irreversible.